IDENTITY IN ASIAN LITERATURE

NORDIC INSTITUTE OF ASIAN STUDIES

Studies in Asian Topics

12. ISLAM: STATE AND SOCIETY
    Klaus Ferdinand and Mehdi Mozaffari (Editors)

13. ASIAN TRADE ROUTES
    Karl Reinhold Hællquist (Editor)

14. HUNTING AND FISHING IN A KAMMU VILLAGE
    Damrong Tayanin and Kristina Lindell

15. RENEGOTIATING LOCAL VALUES
    Merete Lie and Ragnhild Lund

16. LEADERSHIP ON JAVA
    Hans Antlöv and Sven Cederroth (Editors)

17. VIETNAM IN A CHANGING WORLD
    Irene Nørlund, Vu Cao Dam and Carolyn Gates (Editors)

18. ASIAN PERCEPTIONS OF NATURE
    Ole Bruun and Arne Kalland (Editors)

19. IMPERIAL POLICY AND SOUTHEAST ASIAN NATIONALISM, 1930–1957
    Hans Antlöv and Stein Tønnesson (Editors)

20. THE VILLAGE CONCEPT IN THE TRANSFORMATION OF RURAL SOUTHEAST ASIA
    Mason C. Hoadley and Christer Gunnarsson (Editors)

21. IDENTITY IN ASIAN LITERATURE
    Lisbeth Littrup (Editor)

IDENTITY IN ASIAN LITERATURE

edited by
Lisbeth Littrup

RoutledgeCurzon
Taylor & Francis Group
LONDON AND NEW YORK

Nordic Institute of Asian Studies
Studies in Asian Topics, No. 21

First published 1996 by Curzon Press Ltd.
St. John's Studios Church Road
Richmond Surrey TW9 2QA
Reprinted 2004
by RoutledgeCurzon,
2 Park Square, Milton Park,
Abingdon, Oxon, OX14 4RN

Transferred to Digital Printing 2004

ISBN 0-7007-0367-5 [Hardback]
ISBN 0-7007-0368-3 [Paperback]

ISSN 0142-6208

All rights reserved

© Nordic Institute of Asian Studies 1996

While copyright as a whole
is vested in the Nordic Institute of Asian Studies,
copyright in the individual papers
belongs to the authors.
No paper may be reproduced in whole or part
without the express permission of
author, publisher or editors.

British Library Catalogue in Publication Data
A CIP catalogue record for this book
is available from the British Library

Contents

Preface   *vii*

Introduction   *Lisbeth Littrup*   1

1. Associative and Dissociative: the 'Self' in Chinese Classical and Modern Literature   *Chen Maiping*   14

2. Confucius' Self-Identity and the Divine   *Pertti Nikkilä*   47

3. Self-Identity and Allegory in the Fiction of Yu Hua   *Anne Wedell-Wedellsborg*   72

4. The Religious and Cultural Identity of Rabindranath Tagore   *Sergei D. Serebriany*   92

5. Ethnicity in Modern Indonesian Literature: the Novels of Abdul Moeis and Pramoedya Anata Toer   *Mason C. Hoadley*   103

6. 'I Felt Like a Car Without a Driver': Achdiat K. Mihardja's Novel Atheis   *Hendrik M. J. Maier*   129

7. From Huaqiao to Minzu: Constructing New Identities in Indonesia's Peranakan-Chinese Literature   *Thomas Rieger*   151

8. Identity in Modern Japanese Literature. The Case of Natsume Sōseki   *Noriko Thunman*   173

9. Framed by Fiction: Malay Literary Characters in the Literatures of Europe and Asia   *Muhammad Haji Salleh*   190

10. 'The Most Important Thing Is What Happens inside Us': Personal Identity in Palestinian Autobiography   *Tetz Rooke*   232

List of Contributors   *255*

Index   *259*

Preface

The articles in this book are based on papers presented at a workshop on 'Identity in Asian Literature', which took place at the Nordic Institute of Asian Studies (NIAS) in Copenhagen in March 1993. The main themes of the workshop were the creation of identity in literature, the nature of this identity and the historical context of this process. It is our hope that the book will promote further interest in the discussion of identity factors as they emerge in literature and that it will be used by scholars of literature as an introduction to Asian literatures and to the research traditions in Asian literature.

The ten contributors have examined how identity presents itself in the literary works of different parts of Asia at different times. Most articles analyse modern literature; two contributors, however, concentrate on identity in traditional Asia, Chen Maiping and Pertti Nikkilä. Naturally, it is not possible to separate the past and the present and all authors in fact integrate cultural and/or historical factors in their analyses.

This book would not have materialized without the generous financial support from the Danish Research Council for the Humanities, for which I owe my heartfelt thanks. Among the many friends I would like to thank Thommy Svensson, Hans Antlöv and all those at NIAS who helped to organize the workshop. My thanks also to Gerald Jackson, Leena Höskuldsson and Jens-Chr. Sørensen, who supported me in the editing process. I am indebted to Professor Vladimir Braginsky, SOAS, for valuable comments on the book. Finally, I thank my husband, Leif Littrup, who facilitated my work by sharing his expertise, both on computers and China, with me.

Lisbeth Littrup

Some Keys to Literary History – Asian and European

Time	East Asia	Southeast Asia	South Asia	West Asia	Europe
2000 BC				Gilgamesh	
1000 BC			Vedic Hymns		
600–400 BC	Analects Shi Jing		Upanishad Mahabharata Ramayana	Torah (canonized)	Iliad Odyssey
AD 300			Kamasutra		
650				Qur'an	
1000	Genji Monogatari			Shah-nameh	
1100				Omar Khayyam	Icelandic Sagas
1200					Dante
1300		Nagarakertagama		Hafez Ibn Khaldun	Chaucer
1400			Candidas		
1500			Babur		Shakespeare
1600	Xi You Ji Jing Ping Mei	Sejarah Melayu			Princesse de Clèves
1700	Hong Lou Meng				Voltaire Goethe
1800					
1900	Sōseki		Tagore		Conrad
1910			Iqbal	Taha Husayn	
1920		Peranakan literature			
1930					
1940			Moeis, Toer Mihardja		
1950	Mishima			N. Mahfouz	
1960					
1970					
1980	Yu Hua			Palestinian autobiography	

Introduction

Lisbeth Littrup

In Asia the first known 'texts' were written[1] on palm leaves or carved in stone and the oldest Chinese writing was made on bones and tortoise shells around 1300 BC. These texts like the Indian Vedic Hymns[2] contained knowledge from one generation to another about the existence of the supernatural as well as instruction of important rituals.

The main religious/philosophical influences in Asia originate from China (Confucianism and Taoism), India (Hinduism and Buddhism) and the Middle East (Islam). Confucianism and Taoism emerged in China around 500 BC; 500 years later Buddhism spread to East Asia, Hinduism (fifth century) and Islam (thir-teenth century) via South India to the Malay archipelago; while Christianity first came later with European traders. The famous epics, the *Mahabharata* and the *Ramayana*, were brought to East and Southeast Asia together with the Indian religions and these epics were told and retold in numerous literary works as well as in theatre plays, in particular in Southeast Asia. Asian theatre, for instance the Chinese theatre, the Japanese *No* theatre and the Malay/Indonesian puppet play, *Wayang Kulit*, conveyed the well-known great stories to listeners and spectators and by doing so recreated and confirmed their common cultural identity.

In historical/mythical texts kings and priests marked important events and reaffirmed their own heroic position in the magical world order. The *Shah-name*, written by the Persian writer

---

1) In the present book 'literature' implies written literature. As such oral storytelling, folk tales and the like are not discussed here.
2) Hindu scriptures from the second millennium BC.

Firdausi around the year 1000, tells the history of the ancient Persia, from the period of the mythical kings to the Arabic invasion around 640. The Malay *Sejarah Melayu* is in the same tradition, written down by Islamic scholars around the year 1600.

Universal beauty, human existence and the presence of God were explored in poetry. In China poetry developed into a lyrical form, closely connected to music, folk songs and dancing, because poetry was often written for social functions like ceremonies. The oldest known Chinese poetry is the *Shi Jing* ('Classic of Poetry') dating from around the time of Confucius. The poems of the *Shijing* describe the problems of common people as well as of the aristocracy. Present-day Malay *pantun* is often used in the same way. Chinese poets also wrote about social and political evils; Tang poet Du Fu described human tragedy and injustice around the year 750 with these words: 'Blue is the smoke of war, white the bones of men'. Poetic form, however, created a refined development of the (written) language and developed a large amount of genres like the famous Japanese *haiku*. Poetry could be considered the most 'individualised' literary form of traditional Asia as it came to represent the single voice of an author, who was often known by name, in contrast to the anonymous scribes of most religious, philosophical and historical/mythical texts.

The bodies of literature analysed in the present book emerged from two major cultural contexts: the Chinese and the Indian. In China, the Emperor, representing Heaven, constituted the central point of reference, delegating his authority down through a society moulded by Confucianism, Taoism and Buddhism throughout the centuries. Pertti Nikkilä examines how Confucius approached the 'self' in his article. Let me also quote De Bary, who says that according to Confucius

> 'Man' defines his 'self' in relation to others and to the Way, which unites them. Thus is constructed the web of reciprocal obligations or moral relations in which man finds himself, defines himself. Apart from these he can have no identity. And yet these relations alone, it is equally important to recognise, do not define a man totally. His interior self exists at the centre of this web and there enjoys its own freedom.[3]

---

3) See Theodore de Bary, *Self and Society in Ming Thought*, Colombia University Press, New York and London, 1970, p. 149 ff.

This Confucian self is basically a social, ethical one. Thus the social and political criticism of Tang poet Du Fu should be understood in this moral, authoritarian context; the poet's work was meant to guide the Emperor to become a more just ruler, not to overthrow him. In Zen-Buddhist Japan the Emperor was not only the centre of authoritarian society but also a God to whom man owed his whole life.

In the Malay, Indonesian, and Indian cultures Hinduism, Buddhism and Islam superseded each other. In these hierarchical, religious societies authority was with the king and human destiny determined by God. The greatest Malay hero in the *Sejarah Melayu*, Hang Tuah, follows his unjust sultan's order to kill his own best, most loyal friend, defending the dynastic world order instead of his own personal interest.[4] And in doing so he carries out his destiny.

Towards Modern Literature

Printing began in China and Japan around 900 and about four hundred years later during the time of the Mongol dynasty the Chinese novel developed. Actually already around year 1000 novels were written both in China and Japan and their authors were also generally known. In Japan women writers produced novels about life at the imperial court; for instance Murasaki Shikibu's *Genji Monogatari* (The Tale of Genji, from 1010) which tells in much psychological detail about the wonderful lover, Prince Genji. In some ways these were similar to the literary works created in France much later, notably Mme de Lafayette's *La Princesse de Cleves* (1678).[5] In China the novels of the sixteenth century could be mentioned; *Xi You Ji* (The Monkey) is about the pilgrimage of the Chinese monk Xuan Zang and his entourage to India in the seventh century, *Xi Yang Ji* (Adventure to Western Ocean) tells the story of a fifteenth century explorer, and *Jin Ping*

---

4) Hang Jebat, Hang Tuah's friend, rebels against the sultan in order to save Hang Tuah from being unjustly killed on the sultan's order. In newly-independent Malaysia in the 1960s literary debates of the true nature of Hang Tuah and the role of his friend Hang Jebat centred round concepts of authoritarian versus democratic, individualistic values.
5) Mme de Lafayette, *La Princesse de Cleves*, Editions Garnier Frères, Paris, 1961.

Mei describes the life of the villain Qing Ximen. The most famous Chinese novel is probably *Hong Lou Meng* (The Dream of the Red Chamber) written in the eighteenth century. It describes the fall of a great merchant family.[6]

In India, Indonesia and Malaysia there existed mythical epic stories, like for instance the Malay *hikayat*, but no written novels to speak of like the Chinese and Japanese. It should be noticed that printing was not introduced in India until the year 1800, in Indonesia and Malaysia first around 1900. The novel emerged in Indonesia soon afterwards. Some of the earliest novels and short stories were written by the so-called *Peranakan*, middle-class Malay Chinese in Southeast Asia; this literature is here analysed by Thomas Rieger. The founding of a printing house, the 'Balai Pustaka', by the Dutch colonial power in 1917 was instrumental in creating the modern Indonesian novel in the 1920s and 30s whereas it was not until after the Second World War, in the 1950s, that novel writing developed in Malaysia. Indonesian and Malay writers were influenced by literary movements in the Middle East, in particular Egypt, where historical-romantic novels emerged at the end of the nineteenth century. In the emerging modern Indian literature of the nineteenth century, the greatest writer was Rabindranath Tagore (1861-1941), discussed in the present book by Sergei D. Serebriany.

In the nineteenth and twentieth centuries the modern European novel has influenced Asian writers with its search for understanding of emerging industrial society and its emphasis on individualism as Noriko Thunman describes in her essay on the Japanese writer Natsume Sōseki. In the same period South and Southeast Asia were colonised and all countries have gone through vast social and economic changes like industrialisation and urbanisation. As a result, Asian countries have started to shift from the agrarian, religious worldviews onto the industrialised and secular ones.

Colonisation has deeply affected Asian societies and minds. The English, French and Dutch languages and cultures were imposed upon the colonies. One of the consequences was that indigenous writers came to know western literature and ideas.

---

6) *Xiyouji* is written by Wu Cheng'en, *Xiyangji* by Luo Maodeng and *Jinpingmei* (the title is composed of graphs of the three female characters) by an anonymous writer. *Hongloumeng* is written by Cao Zhan.

Another consequence was the development of what is often called 'Commonwealth literature':[7] a literature, which was written in English, especially in India, but also in other Asian colonies. Besides promoting literature in the language of the 'mother country', the colonial power did, however, further the development of a literature in the vernacular. This was done by developing the vernacular for educational purposes, but it also had a profound effect on the emergence of indigenous and national self-conscience because the vernacular languages became a means, by which writers could express a new 'modern' identity – an identity in contrast to both the one defined by the colonial powers (indeed the west in general) and that of traditional, authoritarian society. Here Asian writers began to describe and question colonial policies as well as the westernised changes to their societies, as Mason Hoadley and Hendrik Maier discuss in their articles on Indonesian literature.On the whole it is also fair to say that 'identity' in Asian literature before the Second World War tended to centre round individuality and stressed human efforts to liberate themselves from the constraints of old values.

Since the Second World War new, independent states have emerged and Asian 'post-colonial' writers have searched to define an 'identity of their own' or 'national identity', analysing both the colonial past as well as their own cultural past. This is because, as Muhammad Haji Salleh shows in his essay, colonialism left the former colonised people with literary images harmful to their self-respect. His analysis of the post-colonial heritage takes the form of a self being defined by somebody 'other', alien to one's own culture. One thus looks into a mirror that shows the wrong image. Since in colonial days the Asian countries did not have a literature 'of their own' (a literature in the vernacular), this 'faulty' image became even more harmful as it was the only one established and accessible to educated Asian readers.

Also in China, the focus of writers became national and political, as Chen Maiping notes when he says that 'man became political'. Nation-building was on the agenda. Tetz Rooke's article on the genre of Palestinian autobiography, which is part of a long tradition of Arabic émigré literature, also deals with the nation, although it is a nation which for the time being has not been realized as an independent state.

---

7) Or 'Post-colonial literature in English'. Literature from Great Britain is normally not included in these terms.

Identity in Modern Literature

Traditional literature affirmed identity in the sense of the individual being member of a meaningful whole. The meaning of existence was determined in relation to religion or kings and/or both. The individual did not search for identity in the modern sense, where writers in their works mirror a search for factors with which to identify. Traditional writers or philosophers discussed the meaning of the known established identification factors, often God or Heaven like Confucius does; the nature of identity was examined by discussing the nature of God or Heaven, but there was no doubt about the identity itself. Of this follows that there could be no separation between the identification factor and the self – they were one. Traditional 'identity' would differ: in China it would be more moral than mystical, in India it was more epic/mythical than in Southeast Asia. What traditional literature discussed in epics, songs, poetry, religious treaties was how to understand human lives and societies within the established identity framework or cultural framework. Individual voices expressed themselves in poetry and novels as I pointed out above, but these voices were expressions of the same cultural framework.

The contact with the West in all its forms as colonies (India, Indonesia, Malaysia) or exploited when opened up to the western trade (China) or forced into 'modernisation' (Japan) or erased (Palestine) had a profound impact. A strong centre like Europe enforced its economic and social logic onto Asia. The ensuing alteration of the economic organisation from agrarian to one that was increasingly urbanised and industrialised as well as the transformation of the traditional political culture, uprooted old societies and cultural identities. Cultural contacts with the west first touched the Asian upper classes, the educated elites, in the mid-nineteenth century; later in the twentieth century whole societies were changed through educational policies, inspired by the western domination. Secularisation and rationalism now influenced Asian elites and spread with modernisation. In the west this secularisation had developed since the Renaissance and later on the philosophers of the Enlightenment had begun eroding the power of the church and rational thinking placed man, not God, in the centre of the universe.

In modern Asian literature writers began to discuss a growing split between identification factors and self – or as it has often been termed- the social self, where identity is determined by others and the personal self, which indicates the way a person conceives of herself/himself. In China, Japan and India the search for the personal self was shown in many works around 1900. Southeast Asian literature was still young at that time, but there were literary influences from the Middle East, that inspired individualism. The tension between the old traditions and the new ways of life was growing in reality and in the literary mind. In this volume several articles show us how different writers such as Natsume Sōseki, Tagore as well as Chinese ones approached the beginning of the modern identity crisis.

The search for individual identity where 'man becomes measure of man', to borrow Chen Maiping's words, or where the individual man is the main identification factor, was dominant from around 1900. The Asian identity discussion actually followed the western quite closely on the surface, but the significance of the discussion might have been different in the Asian setting as Chen Maiping points to. In the mid-twentieth century, however, identity was no longer to be found within 'the human being itself' but in 'political man'. There was a historical basis for this: revolutions, civil wars and fighting against colonial powers were interrupted by the Second World War, continued afterwards and changed the political Asian landscape completely.

The speed of social, technological and cultural change since the 1950s has created an intensified although still more alienated search for 'identity'. It would seem that the personal self is feeling more separated from important identification factors than ever. This has even affected the language itself, as its function as bearer of cultural codes is eroded by the speedy changes. Post-modernist writers as well as post-structuralist critics have illustrated this process, as Anne Wedell-Wedellsborg shows.

Lately, we have seen a trend towards more national(istic) concerns or identification factors. These factors take the forms of religion, ethnicity, the cultural/literary past and history and they represent a large variety of Asian literary 'identities', which are, however, alike in one important aspect: the need to review the past and the common culture. This trend could be termed neo-traditionalism.

The Essays

Chen Maiping says in his essay 'Associative and Dissociative – The Self in Chinese Classical and Modern Literature' that in China the 'self' is the same as 'man' in classical and modern culture. 'Individualistic' man which Lu Xun, a famous Chinese modern writer, had pledged for in an essay (*On Cultural Extremes*) at the beginning of this century is a modern (western) construction. To Chinese intellectuals, for instance at the time of the May Fourth Movement, 'individualism' was connected with nationalist aspirations. Later the communists rejected individualism and it is not until after the Cultural Revolution and the Tiananmen killings in 1989 that individualism is again treated as an important ideological concept. Traditional culture is often called 'man eating' exactly because of the lack of 'individualism' in the modern (western) sense, just as communism is now seen by many intellectuals in the same way. This leads them to reject both communist ideology and traditional and classical literature. The traditional 'I' is an associative 'I' relating itself to the external world (society, nature and others), whereas the 'I' of modern Chinese writers is dissociative, relating not to the external world but only to themselves. Lately, however, Chinese writers have begun to regret this reliance upon the western modern ideal of individualism as they do need an object for their 'self-identification'.

In his essay 'Confucius' Self-identity and the Divine', Pertti Nikkilä examines especially the role of Heaven in Confucius' self-identity, as described by Confucius himself in the Confucian *Analects*. Pertti Nikkilä concentrates mainly on the 'I' identity of Confucius as it can be extracted from the twenty books of *Lun Yü* or the *Analects*. In his conclusions he points out that identity according to Confucius is created in relation to Heaven, which is something unknown, and also that Confucius perceived his identity as one related to the group of learned; that is why he did not emphasise a two-way communication (prayer/sacrifice) with Heaven, because this form of communication was only performed by royalty.

In 'Self-identity and Allegory in the Fiction of Yu Hua', Anne Wedell-Wedellsborg introduces the concept of allegory and points out that, while western theorists tend to understand and explain modern Chinese literature as oriented towards the public domain,

Chinese writers and critics try to move towards a separation of the private and public domain. In her allegorical reading of Yu Hua's story 'Xianshi yizhong' (A Kind of Reality), she shows the writer's concern with the breakdown of identity as well as of culture. In Yu Hua's story the characters have no self, they merely act as signifiers of an absent self. In her conclusion she suggests that Chinese cultural identity is now closely connected with expressions of the self, and not the other way around.

Societies change and new identities seem to offer themselves. Does one have to choose between them? To Indian writer Rabindranath Tagore, identity is created by the interplay and coexistence of many different identities, as S. D. Serebriany shows in 'The Religious and Cultural Identity of Rabindranath Tagore'. Serebriany analyses Tagore's own analysis of his identity or identities. The essay 'Introducing Oneself', written in 1912, addressed the problem of how the Brahmos should identify themselves vis-à-vis Hindus. Tagore concluded that historically he was a Hindu, this fact was outside his personal choice but he had a very complex identity, which was closely linked to the historical changes in South Asia. So many different layers of identity (Indian, Brahmo, Hindu, Bengali, poet) was a source of ongoing discussion within himself. The interchange between the 'personal self' and the 'social self' seemed to motivate Tagore throughout his life.

Generally, as mentioned, writers in the former colonies have searched for other cultural categories than the western/colonial ones: categories rooted in their own indigenous culture. In 'Ethnicity in Modern Indonesian Literature: The Novels of Abdul Moeis and Pramoedya Ananta Toer', Mason Hoadley examines two Indonesian writers' images of the past. In Hoadley's essay 'ethnicity' is seen as a social metaphor and it is analysed from three perspectives, as a protest, as a contribution to the independence struggle and as an aspect of modern Indonesian society. In their novels at the beginning of the twentieth century they, and in particular Abdul Moeis, depicted the failure of the Dutch Ethical Policy. The authors portray conflicts which emerge in the lives of the literary characters due to this policy, pushing them into an ethnic deadlock. Hoadley analyses in particular Moeis' historical novel *Surapati*, where Moeis has developed a literary character, Surapati, who carries both modern and native values, in a combination which was rarely – if ever – conceived of by the colonial and colonised mind. Mason Hoadley concludes that Moeis tried to create new Indonesian models for modernity in his work and that in the character of Surapati he suggested one.

Moeis offers models of modernity, with which Indonesians can identify. It is a difficult process, however, as Hendrik Maier shows in 'I Felt like a Car without a Driver – Achdiat K. Mihardja's novel *Atheis*'. This novel appeared in 1949 and it has often been read as a national allegory. Maier's analysis is twofold: he presents the complex cultural and political background of the novel at first and then concentrates on the structure of the story and the characters. The protagonists have freed themselves from tradition and religion, but they are tormented by feelings of sin, remorse and despair. They find themselves trapped in a modern(istic) universe, where they cannot identify themselves, but have to be identified by others. Maier interprets the novel as an allegory for the young emerging nation Indonesia, symbolised by the woman Kartini, but also a novel about the struggle between tradition and modernity. One could say that the characters in Moeis' novel are reacting against factors, which they perceive as negative (tradition and religion), but at the same time they are closely linked to them.

In 'From Huaqiao to Minzu: Constructing New Identities in Indonesia's Peranakan-Chinese Literature' Thomas Rieger analyses the role of literature in the identity-formation of the *Peranakan* community at the turn of the century. During the period 1905-1924 the construction of the Chinese nation in Bazaar Malay literature was the dominant trend. In that literature one finds three major topics central to the construction of Peranakan identity as Huaqiao: the pan-Chinese issues, the Indies' Peranakan status of nationality, and the issues of Chinese cultural identity. From 1925 to 1942 there was a reorientation towards an Indies identity brought about by a combination of Peranakan disenchantment with the new Chinese revolutionary government and a more favourable colonial policy towards the Peranakan.

Noriko Thunman shows in 'Identity in Modern Japanese Literature – The Case of Natsume Sōseki (1867-1916)' how the western concept of self influenced a modern Japanese writer. In Sōseki's writings identity seems to be a combination of three major factors: egotism/individualism, oriental nihilism (the disappearance of self), and a critical view of the Meiji society. His individualism was based upon egotism: that a man must find out for himself what is wrong and work for something good. This egotism was in turn based upon Sōseki's trust in man's rationality. Sōseki was also aware of the irrational forces in man and whenever he was tormented, he sought peace in nature. Noriko Thunman says that he was driven towards 'nothingness': a state of no feeling, no conflict, no fear or love. Thunman concludes that his identity was formed by the constant division in him, created by the western idea of self and oriental nihilism.

In 'Framed by Fiction: Malay Literary Characters in the Literature of Europe and Asia', Muhammad Haji Salleh shows how writers in formerly colonised countries reinterpret the colonial images and world order. He examines the literary portrait and identity of Malay characters in some European, Japanese and American works as well as the cultural framework of the writers themselves. He points out that the Malays were seen as 'others' and that they became framed or imprisoned in this image, even by themselves. Some writers from non-colonial powers like Joseph Conrad did however paint Malay characters in a way that did respect them as people or 'the good other' appreciated and left to be different. In his analysis Muhammad Haji Salleh shows how writers from colonial powers actually contributed to the construction of a world-view where Malays were identified as exotic aliens in colonial society.

Creating identity on the basis of how we see ourselves and how we want others to see us; in literature this is the definition even of the genre of autobiography. In 'The Most Important Thing Is What Happens inside Us – Personal Identity in Palestinian Autobiography', Tetz Rooke analyses Palestinian writers who reconstruct not only their own individual identity but also the identity of their country. Basically the autobiography constructs an identity that emerges as a synthesis of inner and outer forces and at the same time as a composite of the past and the present. As the outer force in this case is the lost land, it acquires a specific significance to which all these biographies must relate. Tetz Rooke presents three different categories of autobiography: the didactic, therapeutic and poetic. And he quotes French sociologist Jacques Berque: 'The quest for self (country as self, people as self, history as self) constitutes one of the most prominent sectors of contemporary Arab production'.

Concluding remarks

In traditional literature identity is normally derived from identification with the religious and social hierarchy; there is no concept of an individual or personal 'self'. In the nineteenth and twentieth centuries concepts of identity changed. As industrialisation and secularisation undermined the traditional agrarian society, writers searched for new identities. Around 1900 there was a quest for individual identity. In modernising China and Japan it was a very western concept of individualism. 'Individualism' or the focus upon the self, alien as it was to their culture, seemed to serve as a means by which new understandings of their own changing society and culture could emerge. In the mid-twentieth century the search for identity changed again; 'man' became increasingly social/political as for instance in Chinese literature. The same development can be seen in South and Southeast Asian literature where identity, however, related also to religious and ethnic factors, not only historical/political ones.

The search for identity at the end of the twentieth century is inspired by a feeling of alienation, which is related to psychological and physical exile or both: psychological, as when a colonial power determines the identity of Indonesians or Malays; or when modernisation upsets the balance between old and new; physical as when a major source of identity, the soil, is removed from a people like the Palestinians.

Modern 'individualistic' man, who revolts and asserts himself, is the ideological basis of the twentieth century. This disintegration is expressed in -isms like modernism and postmodernism; -isms which almost seem to represent allergic reactions to the common cultural fabric, language codes and literature included. Today, however, Asian writers have begun to look to tradition, trying to mediate modern and traditional values into a literature of their own. The search for cultural roots is combined with a rejection of colonial and/or western values. This neo-traditionalist trend runs in different directions: in Chinese literature it is cultural, in previously colonised countries it is also nationalistic in nature.

Globalisation of the world might push the individual and/or nationalistic 'I' towards cultural cohesion into a global 'We' and many regional identities. The discussion of 'Asian' identity from this perspective of 'world literature' has begun to unfold. Generally it can be said that literary development in Asia is becoming still more diversified as is the case also in the West.

References

De Bary, Theodore, *Self and Society in Ming Thought*, Columbia University Press, New York and London, 1970.

Gurr, Andrew, *Writers in Exile*, The Harvester Press, Sussex & Humanities Press, New Jersey, 1981.

Herbert, Patricia and Anthony Milner, (eds), *South-east Asia Languages and Literatures. A Select Guide*, Kiscadale Publications,1991.

Lang, David M,. (ed.), *A Guide to Eastern Literatures*. Praeger Publishers, New York, 1971.

Langbaum, Robert, *The Mysteries of Identity*, Oxford University Press, New York, 1977.

Mina, Hanna, *Fragments of Memory, a Story of a Syrian Family*, translated by Olive Kenny and Lorne Kenny, Austin, University of Texas Press,1993

Powell, Irena, *Writers & Society in Modern Japan*, London, 1983.

Pyle, K., *The New Generation in Meji Japan: Problems of Cultural Identity 1885-1895*, Stanford University Press, 1969.

Said, Edward, *After the Last Sky, Palestinian Lives*, with photographs by Jean Mohr, London, Vintage,1993 (1986).

Said, Edward W., *Culture and Imperialism*, Vintage, London, 1994.

1

Associative and Dissociative
The 'Self' in Classical and Modern Chinese Literature

Chen Maiping

The 'Self' in Chinese Literature: from Classical to Modern

Literature is often regarded as a mirror either reflecting the reality of life or reflecting the writer's 'self'. In the latter, the writer expresses his 'self' through his literary work, lets his own image, feeling and emotion be reproduced in the 'mirror'. It is a process of transforming the subjective into the objective, so that the writer can identify himself just as one identifies oneself in a mirror.

In Chinese literature, 'self-expression' through literary writing has a long tradition. A primitive Chinese literary concept shows poetry as a spontaneous expression of human emotions, and even regards this expression of emotion as the genesis of poetry. An etymological study of Chinese characters indicates that the characters *shi* (poetry) and *zhi* (will, intent, wish, or where the heart or mind goes) are in fact cognate. The character *shi* has two component parts: on the right side *zhi* and on the left *yan* (words), so that *shi* means *yan* plus *zhi*, and can be interpreted as words of will, or words of intent, or words of wish, or just words where the heart or mind goes.[1] These three characters form a famous epigram *shi yan zhi* (poetry verbalizes one's will or intent), which first appears in *Shang Shu* (The Book of Documents), a classic book dating back at least to the second century B.C., and which has been referred to again and again by later critics. Even today, Chinese students still learn it in primary school.

---

1) See James J.Y. Liu, *Chinese Theories of Literature*, Chicago, The University of Chicago Press, 1975, pp. 67–8.

In *Shi Jing* (The Book of Songs), the first Chinese anthology of poetry, compiled some time after the sixth century B. C., we can read such lines as 'I made this fine song / To express fully my restless grief' or 'A gentleman made this song / To express his sorrows'.[2] Confucius (551–479 B.C.), who is traditionally regarded as the compiler of the book, made it very clear that one of the functions poetry should have is *yuan* (to complain or to express one's grievance).[3] The famous Chinese historian and writer Sima Qian (135?–93? B.C.) even said that 'the general purport of the three hundred poems of the *Shi Jing* is the indignation expressed by the sages.'[4] From the era of *Shi Jing* until modern times, many Chinese writers and literary critics have emphasized that the object of literary expression should be identified with personal nature, emotion, sensibility.

I do not here intend to mention all the literary works and theories referring to 'self-expression' in Chinese classical literature, as it is impossible to carry out a narrow and detailed investigation within the length of this paper. However, as an example, I would like to mention Li Zhi (1567–1602), a very extraordinary scholar of the Ming dynasty, who in his celebrated essay *Tong xin lun* (On the Childlike Mind) asserted that 'the best literature of the world has always come from the childlike mind.' By this 'childlike mind', he meant an innate pure mind which has not been influenced by the acquired learning of moral doctrines, and also an independent personality free from social and external influence. Li Zhi maintained that whoever retains the 'childlike mind' will be a 'true man'; and that a writer should be such a 'true man' and express his 'childlike mind' in his works, so as to be able to produce great literature.[5] In other words, to Li Zhi, the 'self'

---

2) Bernhard Karlgren, trans. *The Book of Odes*, Stockholm, Östasiatiska Museet, 1950, p. 149 (Ode 199) and p. 156 (Ode 204). Quoted in James J.Y. Liu, *Chinese Theories of Literature*, p. 68.
3) Arthur Waley, trans. *The Analects of Confucius*, London, George Allen & Unwin Ltd, 1964. Book XVII, 9, p. 212.
4) Sima Qian, 'Bao Ren An Shu' (A Replying Letter to Ren An), translation is from Cyril Birch, *Anthology of Chinese Literature, from early times to the fourteenth century*, New York, Grove Press, 1965, p. 101.
5) See Li Zhi, *Fen Shu*, (Burning Books), Beijing, Zhonghua Shu Ju, 1961, p. 98. See also Wm. Theodore de Bary, *Self and Society in Ming Thoughts*, New York, Columbia University Press, 1970, p. 195-6, and James J.Y. Liu, *Chinese Theories of Literature*, pp. 78-9.

expressed in literature should be pure and not soiled by the external world. Li Zhi's theory might be the most radical one referring to 'self-expression' in Chinese classical literature.

Living and writing in a situation where self-consciousness has been considerably developed, many modern Chinese writers are very concerned about 'self-expression' in literature. They have established a closer and more personal relation between their works and their 'selves', and have often more directly presented their 'selves' in their works. A significant change is now taking place: the modern writer believes that he now has a new identity, which has new values. Thus, he adopts a new approach to the 'self' in literature, a new approach different from that of a classical writer. This new approach leads to a new kind of 'self-expression' in literature, to a transformation of content, form, style and language. A deep gap has thus appeared, which divides Chinese literature of 'self-expression' into two pieces of land: classical, and modern. Generally, the difference between the classical and the modern is that, while in the land of the classial, the 'self' often appears as a spirit, invisible but sensible, in the land of the modern, the 'self' is wandering about like a man of flesh and blood. We can see it, feel it and even touch it.

The different approaches to the 'self' are not limited to the scope of literary writing or criticism, but have references to philosophy, religion and the whole cultural context, and are based on different concepts of 'man' in traditional and modern China. Therefore, studying the different concepts of 'man' opens the way for us to see how the 'self' is accordingly expressed in different ways in Chinese classical and modern literature, on different scenes made of the specific literary language chosen by the writers.

What Is Traditional? What Is Modern?

A controversial issue I have to deal with before discussing the different concepts of 'man' is how to define what is traditional and what is modern. The antithesis between the traditional and the modern seems obvious, but the fact is that it is still difficult to draw a clear line between them. One cannot just draw the line according to time, for example, set a certain date, a year when the modern era begins, even if people could agree on such a date. One cannot say: what exists before that date is traditional and what exists afterwards is modern. This is because traditional concepts continue to live and even have a powerful influence in modern times. Many who live in modern times still preserve traditional ideas. On the other hand, modern concepts can also have their roots in the traditional era. It is very likely that some modern concepts are just resurrections of traditional ones. In modern society, the traditional concepts and the modern ones actually often form a jagged, interlocking pattern. This is particularly true in Asian countries which have long cultural traditions.

I shall not argue here about the definitions of the traditional or the modern. I will simply point out one fact: in China, many people have drawn the line according to geography, that means, these people regard 'modern' as 'western', and 'traditional' as 'Chinese'. For them these two pair of words have become synonymous, for example, modernization is regarded as westernization. This definition of the traditional and the modern has become a major discourse that influences Chinese thought even today. As a matter of fact, this definition is also accepted by a number of sinologists and western historians. When they discuss whether modern China begins in the sixteenth century, when western learning was first introduced into China, or in the middle of nineteenth century, when western imperialism invaded the country and the acceleration of foreign activities shattered the Chinese isolation and ushered in a period of revolutionary changes, they are only discussing at what point in Chinese history western influence became significant.[6]

In such a historical context, therefore, if the traditional concept of 'man' is Chinese, then the modern concept of 'man' in China is western; imported from the West. This has been admitted by many Chinese scholars. However, the western concepts of 'man' also vary, and have differences between traditional and modern, and not all of these concepts are welcome in China. So, more precisely speaking, what is imported as 'modern' from the West is only one of the western modern concepts of 'man'; the 'individualistic' concept of 'man'. According to Lukes, individu-

---

6) See Immanuel C.Y. Hsü, *The Rise of Modern China*, Hong Kong, Oxford University Press, 1989, p. 4-5.

alism as a positively evaluated trend is a relatively recent phenomenon even in the West.[7]

The Conception of the Modern Concept of 'Man'

In order to prove that the Chinese modern concept of 'man' is actually western we need to go back in history. The transformation from the traditional concept of 'man' to the modern one took place at the beginning of the century. After China had lost several wars with the western powers and Japan in the second half of the last century, many Chinese intellectuals were inquiring into the reasons why China was weaker than western countries. They not only examined the backwardness of the Chinese science, technology, economic system and political institutions, but also criticised the weakness of Chinese culture in general. In his famous essay *Wenhua pianzhi lun* (On Cultural Extremes) published in 1908, Lu Xun (1881-1936), one of the most famous Chinese modern writers, argued that the western countries' power was based on a culture of 'man'. He explained very clearly in this essay that this 'man' was a *'ge ren '*(individual man). He then criticised Chinese culture because it did not respect 'man' but, on the contrary, respected the 'material' and completely deprived all Chinese of their *'ge xing'* (personality). He asserted that, if China wanted to avoid falling, she should first establish herself as a *'ren guo '*(country of man), and, in order to establish this 'country of man', she should respect 'individual nature' or 'personality', and appoint 'individual man' rather than *'zhong shu '*(collective people).[8]

Since then, Lu Xun's individualistic concept of 'man' has been shared by many Chinese intellectuals. Together with Lu Xun, Chen Duxiu (1879-1942) and Hu Shi (1891-1962) were also enthusiastically promoting 'individualism' in their writings. In 1915, Chen founded the famous monthly periodical *Qingnian zazhi* (The Youth Magazine, later renamed *Xin Qingnian*, The New Youth) in Shanghai, a magazine that became the most important

---

7) Steven Lukes, *Individualism*, New York, Harper and Row, 1973, p. 1. See Donald Munro, ed., *Individualism and Holism, Studies in Confucian and Taoist Values*, Ann Arbor, The University of Michigan, 1985, p 36.
8) Lu Xun, 'Wenhua Pianzhi Lun' (On Cultural Extremes), *Lu Xun Quan Ji* (The Complete Works of Lu Xun), Beijing, Renming Wenxue Chubanshe, 1980, Vol. 1, p. 50.

organ of the May Fourth New Cultural Movement around 1919, and an armoury of thoughts for many modern writers. Lu and Hu were also the backbone of the magazine. In an essay published in the magazine Chen wrote that the fundamental ideological difference between China and the West was that, in their value systems, the Chinese had used the family as the standard to evaluate man whereas the West had used individual man as the standard. The family standard impaired men's capabilities, whereas the individual standard promoted them. He then maintained that 'the only way out for Chinese culture is to replace the family standard with the individual standard.' Chen continues: 'to uphold freedom, right and happiness for the individual man is what all ethics, morality, politics, law and societies yearn for, and what a country prays for.'[9]

Hu Shi studied in America and was John Dewey's student. Back in China he became the major contributor to *Xin Qingnian*. His idea of 'individualism' centred on the growth of the individual's personality and independent judgement. In this aspect, he promoted Ibsen as a model for Chinese intellectuals. In his famous essay *Yibushen zhuyi* (Ibsenism) he maintained that what Chinese intellectuals could learn from Ibsen was the 'independent and free personality which is against the state and society'.[10]

The 'individualism' that these scholars promoted can be defined by the following description: 'each individual person possesses key traits independent of any social relations. Those traits may be interests, abilities, or needs. An account of each person can be given without considering society or any unit larger than the individual. Society is an artificial man construct organized to cater to those traits of individuals, it is simply an aggregate of the many individuals so conceived'.[11]

Since all these intellectuals took an 'individualist' stance when they gave impetus to the May Fourth Movement, the

---

9) Chen Duxiu, 'Dong Xi Fang Minzu Genben Sixiang Zhi Chayi' (The Fundamental Ideological Difference between Eastern Nations and Western Nations), *Qingnian Zazhi*, Vol. 1, No. 4. Refer to Li Zehou, *Zhongguo Sixiang Shigao* (Essays on History of Chinese Thoughts), Beijing, Dongfang Chubanshe, 1987, p. 17.
10) Hu Shi, ed. *Zhongguo Xin Wenxue Daxi, Jianshe Lilun Juan* (Anthology of Chinese New Literature, Vol. of Constructive Theories, xerox copy), Shanghai, Wenyi Chubanshe, 1981, p. 191.
11) Donald Munro, *Individualism and Holism*, p. 16.

movement could, to a certain degree, be regarded as an 'individualist' movement. It has often been compared with the Enlightenment in Europe. To promote human rights, to advocate the liberation of the individual man, and especially the liberation of woman, became fashionable during that period.

The Experience of Modern 'Man' in China: Its Ups and Downs

To conceive 'man' as 'individual man' has after the May Fourth Movement become one of the basic patterns of thought in modern China, and it plays quite an important role in establishing a modern value system and a modern moral standard for Chinese intellectuals. However, the experience of this modern 'man' has not been calm sailing. Sometimes it has been up, sometimes down.

At the time of the May Fourth Movement, 'individualism' drew a lot of attention from Chinese intellectuals, and 'self-expression' was quite popular among literary writers. But this modern concept of 'man' was in fact still very ambiguous and abstract. Those who promoted it were more concerned about how 'man' should be treated by or related to society than about how 'man' became 'man'. In other words, 'individualism' was for them a belief or an ideal, not a scientific theory to study what the essence of man was, or what man's reason, or mind, or will were. Such basic questions about man had occupied western philosophers for centuries and many books had been written in the West, whereas in China, very few intellectuals took to applying modern scientific or psychological methods in order to analyse man, for example by approaching Freud's theory about man, even though Freud's name was already known in China at that time.

This seems odd since the May Fourth Movement emphasizes the promotion of science. However, we shall not wonder if we look at the historical background of promoting 'individualism' in China. Chinese intellectuals' real interest in 'individualism' was not in the study of man itself but in the usage of it to achieve something political, for example to save the country from falling into the enemies' hands. Therefore, although the concept they adopted clearly had a western trademark, it was from the very beginning mingled with nationalist thought. A special inner complex had already been constituted in the minds of many

Chinese 'individualist' intellectuals. The fact that the western powers defeated China and stayed as an oppressive force continued to humiliate Chinese intellectuals and made it difficult for them to carry out an absolute liberal 'individualism' as western individualists often did, for example, as Ibsen did. Ibsen would place individual man above the nation and society, would regard the freedom of man as more important than the freedom of the nation, whereas few Chinese 'individualists' would go to this extreme.

This also explains why the May Fourth Movement could not produce pure philosophers as the Enlightenment did. Furthermore, it explains why most of the Chinese individualists who were active during the May-Fourth Movement soon gave up their original ideal and turned to other theories. For example, Chen Duxiu turned to communism and became the co-founder of the Communist Party of China; Lu Xun joined the Leftist Writers' Union; and Hu Shi became a moderate nationalist. When China was suffering from endless national crises, for example the chaos of the warlords and the invasion of the Japanese in the 1930s and 1940s, the 'individualists' could hardly retain their stance. Since the salvation of the country was regarded as more important, intellectuals would search for new weapons even if it was at the expense of 'individual man'. Although they still treated 'man' as 'individual man', he would then be attached to the nation. 'Individualism' thus very soon came to a premature end. After 1949 when communist ideology achieved full control of the country, 'individualism' found almost no support at all among the people. 'Self-expression' was then suppressed so that it disappeared from Chinese literature.

It was not until the end of the Cultural Revolution in the middle of the 1970s that modern 'man' was recovered and since then has again become the major refrain of the post-Mao era. To call this modern 'man' back, to liberate this 'man' and to rediscover the values of this 'man', all became popular slogans for Chinese intellectuals, especially those from the younger generation. 'Self-expression' became fashionable again. Bei Dao (1949–), a poet representative of the generation, wrote these lines in 1976: 'I am no hero / In an age without heroes / I just want to be a man.'[12]

---

12) Bei Dao, *The August Sleepwalker*, trans. by Bonnie S. McDougall, London, Anvil Press, 1988, p. 62.

To my knowledge, one of the sources of Bei Dao's concept of 'man' is again that of the 'individual man' in early modern poetry. Li Zehou (1937–), a well-known Chinese critic, describes the post-Mao era as a time when 'man' returns to China, and equates it with the era of the May Fourth Movement in that both promote individualism.[13] This recovery of modern man has been connected with the new wave of modernization in the country. So, in Chinese discourse today, the words 'self', 'in-dividualist man', and 'modern man', are often connected.

'Man-Eating': an Accusation of Traditional Culture

In concert with the promotion of 'individualism' and the modern concept of 'man', was a severe attack on the traditional culture and traditional concept of 'man'. Modern intellectuals such as Lu Xun and Chen Duxiu believed that traditional culture does not respect the values of 'individual man'. The most acute attack on traditional culture is again made by Lu Xun. In his first short story 'Kuangren Riji' (The Diary of a Mad Man), which was also published in *Xin Qingnian* in 1918 and regarded as the first work of Chinese modern *baihua xiaoshuo* (oral language fiction), Lu portrayed that, while reading Chinese classical books – mostly the Confucian Classics – the mad man discovered that all the books were just telling him how to 'eat men'. If we understand that, for Lu, 'man' means 'individual man', we know that he obviously used this image to symbolize that classic books represent a culture which strangles Chinese people as 'individual' human beings.

Since then, 'cannibalism' has often been used as a symbol to epitomize traditional culture, particularly the orthodox philosophy of Confucianism. The statement has also become the discourse dominating the development of Chinese thought in this century. It gives many modern Chinese intellectuals an excuse to sublate traditional culture, and, at the same time, it becomes a motive for a series of cultural revolutions or modernization movements. Even the Communist Party accepted this discourse and used it as propaganda to support their revolution. A statement often repeated by the Party is that it has constructed a new society and overturned the 'cannibalistic' old one.

---

13) Li Zehou, *Zhongguo Sixiang Shigao*, p. 239.

Today, 'cannibalism' is still used by many Chinese as a symbol describing traditional culture. Believing that traditional culture strangles the 'individual man' becomes a psychological and aesthetic reason for many young poets to alienate themselves from Chinese classical poetry. Scholars, such as Liu Zaifu, still highly praise Lu Xun for his profound perspective of Chinese traditional culture as 'cannibalistic'. Liu stresses that Lu Xun's profoundness lies in the fact that Lu does not only point to the phenomenon of traditional culture's 'eating of men', but also exposes the phenomenon that 'man eats himself'[14]. By saying that 'man eats himself', Lu Xun, or Liu Zaifu, means that this 'man' would strangle his 'self' for the sake of traditional morality. Having examined the whole Chinese cultural tradition, Liu Zaifu concludes:

> If we say that the Confucian etiquette system dismisses and restrains subjectivity and the self in an external aspect with a pattern of force, Taoism and Zen dismiss and restrain subjectivity and the self in an internal aspect of life by instructing people to subdue their emotion and will. The pressure of the external aspect leads a man to lose his independent personality, and, for an individual, there is no cultural environment or social condition at all that enables him to fulfil his self; the pressure of the internal aspect leads a man to lose subjective consciousness, and, for an individual, there is no capability at all to fulfil his self. This may be the contract between Confucianism and Taoism: that in designing man they are mutually complementary. They take different roads but come to the same end. They have thousands of thoughts but one purpose: to dismiss 'man'.[15]

What is interesting to us is that Liu has repeated Lu Xun's statement in a new social context, that is, after Mao Zedong's Proletarian Cultural Revolution (1966–1976) and the massacre in Beijing in 1989. Liu applies Lun Xun's statement not only to traditional culture, but also to Chinese communist culture, which also denies 'individualism' and the concept of 'man' as an 'individual man'. In fact, it is only because of this connection that

---
14) Liu Zaifu and Lin Gang, *Chuantong He Zhongguoren* (Tradition and Chinese), Hong Kong, Sanlian Shudian, 1988, p. 90. See also Liu Zaifu, *Piao Liu Shouji* (Essays in Exile), Hong Kong, Tiandi Tushugongsi, 1992.
15) Ibid., p. 326.

some Chinese intellectuals regard Chinese communist culture as the continuation or restoration of traditional feudal culture, although these two cultures run counter to each other in many other aspects, while the communist also accuses the traditional culture of 'man eating', and even though the communist concept could also be said to be modern. Apparently, here, 'individualism' has been applied as a standard to decide what is traditional and what is modern. The simple logic here is that communism is traditional since it is against individualism.

Two Different Conceptual Structures

There are some cannibalistic events recorded in Chinese history, but the statement that Chinese traditional culture is a 'man eating' culture is too sweeping and ambiguous. It is a reflection of the appearance of a new concept of 'man' in modern Chinese thought rather than a description of objective historical facts. It is a symbolic way of viewing the situation of 'man' in traditional Chinese society, and this view is based on an obviously modern individualistic perspective, which means that the word 'man' is defined and positively evaluated as an 'individual man'. Looking at 'man' in this way, then, Chinese traditional culture seems less 'individualistic' than western culture, since it is true that Chinese traditional philosophies, no matter whether it is Confucianism, or Taoism, or Buddhism, usually do not give priority to 'individual man'.

However, in my opinion, the statement that Chinese traditional culture eats 'man' can only be relatively correct, not absolutely correct. Otherwise, we cannot understand why classic literature also promotes 'self-expression'. This statement is not unquestionable. Firstly, one can ask: what does Chinese traditional culture mean? Is it composed of only one philosophy or one value system? Since it covers so many different thoughts, are all these thoughts disrespectful of 'individual man' in the same way? Can some thoughts be more 'individualistic' than others? Secondly, as I have indicated above, the statement is made from a modern perspective, and the term 'man' is defined and evaluated as 'individual man'. Therefore, the questions are: can the term 'man' itself be so clear? Can it be interpreted in ways other than 'individual man'? Is the connotation of the term also quite controversial? Is there only one exclusive standard to evaluate it?

If we look at the situation of 'man' in traditional China from another perspective, interpret the term 'man' in a different conceptual structure and evaluate it according to a different value system, we may come to another conclusion. For example, there have been quite a few discussions about 'individualism' in Chinese traditional culture, and many scholars believe that 'individualism' also finds its roots in Chinese traditional philosophies. In other words, whether Chinese traditional culture does or does not absolutely deny 'human values' or 'individualism' all depends on from which perspective we approach the concept of 'man'.

Chad Hansen has cast doubt on claims about individualism in Chinese traditional philosophy. His argument is based on a study of the conceptual structural difference between Chinese traditional philosophy and western philosophy 'in utilizing a contrast between the many (individual) and the one (universal)'. He indicates that 'the contrast which informs most of western philosophy is the one-many contrast', whereas 'philosophical Chinese has a part-whole structure rather than one-many structure'[16]. He then maintains that 'individualism' theoretically focuses on the 'many'. From this point of view, on the one hand, the one-many conceptual structure should not be an interpretative model for a language such as Chinese since the differences stem from a different conceptual structure and different background beliefs. On the other hand, even in the part-whole structure, Chinese philosophers are clustered on the whole side and do not stress particularity. Hansen concludes that 'the conceptual structure (the language) of Chinese philosophy' (is) less individualistic than that of the (English-speaking) West.'[17]

One may argue with Hansen about 'individualism' in Chinese philosophy. He defines 'individualism' first in a western contrast structure and then, according to this western definition, he gives the judgement that Chinese structure is less 'individualistic'. This seems not quite fair since his definition is not an objective standard and he does not stand as a third party. In keeping with what we usually see at a trial, a fair judgement

---

16) Donald Munro, *Individualism and Holism*, p 36.
17) Ibid., p 35.

should be given by a third party, and so a fair judgement on 'individualism' in China should also be given from a non-western standpoint. Anyway, I think that Hansen is closer to the truth when he points out that Chinese traditional philosophy differs from the western philosophy, or at least from western individualism, in its conceptual structure. This statement does explain the basic difference between Chinese traditional philosophy and western individualist philosophy. What is regarded as the 'individual' in the western structuring dichotomy, is treated as the 'part' in the Chinese one. For example, what is treated as one 'coin' for a westerner, will be treated as one side of a 'coin' for a Chinese. As one 'coin', it is 'individual', it can be separated from other 'coins', and it has its own value, whereas one side of a 'coin' is only part of the coin, and cannot be separated from the 'whole', and does not have an independent value.

I would also agree with Hansen when he points out that, in the western dichotomy, the 'particular' side is assimilated as the 'concrete' side, and the 'universal' side as the 'abstract', and that westerners 'tend to trust the one-many contrast as equivalent to the concrete-abstract contrast', whereas 'in the Chinese case, both the parts and the wholes are concrete – the general is also the concrete'.[18] What I would like to add to Hansen's theory is that, as a matter of fact, the difference between Chinese and western philosophy lies not only in the structuring dichotomy, but also in the ontology. Chinese philosophy is basically monist, whereas the western 'individualistic' philosophy is dualistic. In China, not even the Yin-Yang theory is dualistic as some sinologists believe, since Yin and Yang are from one unitary *yuan* (origin), and finds expressions in each single identity, even as male and female aspects of one personality.[19] Chinese philosophy and religion do have a convention of establishing many dichotomies, yet they are derived from one origin.

The two parties in Chinese structuring dichotomies are therefore in a different relationship from the western. In the western, or, the modern, structuring dichotomy, the two parties stand in opposition to each other, such as 'individual' as opposed

---

18) Ibid., p 37.
19) Robert E. Hegel, 'An Exploration of the Chinese Literary Self', in his *Expressions of Self in Chinese Literature*, New York, Columbia University Press, 1985, p. 30.

to 'collective', 'many'– 'one', 'particular'– 'universal', 'self' – 'others', etc. The two sides are regarded as conflicting opposites, and individualism means to champion the side of the 'many', the 'individual' or the 'self'. In Chinese conceptual structuring dichotomy the two parties are organically related to each other, the part is organically related to the whole just like the hand is related to the body. They are not opposing each other but rely on each other. It is also true that, as Hansen indicates, the whole side seems more important than the other side. It is based on this conceptual structure that the traditional philosophies develop their concepts of 'man', and correspondingly promote their 'self-expression' in literature.

Traditional Concepts of 'Man'

In Chinese traditional conceptual dichotomy, 'man' is not defined on one side, but on both sides of the dichotomy. It presents a kind of relationship established between the two sides, rather than any concrete creature on either side. In other words, the whole structure is 'man'. In a monistic perspective, 'man' is organically related to one cosmos and belongs to one organic whole. He does not have an independent existence. Therefore, 'man' can only be identified or defined through such relations with the cosmos or with other objects in the cosmos. This is the common basic idea that traditional Chinese philosophies share and build their concepts of 'man' upon, even though these philosophies have different ways of defining the cosmos or the organic whole. For Confucianism, it is *tian* (Heaven); for Taoism, it is *tao* (the Way), for Chinese Buddhism, it is *kong* (the Void).

Confucianism has been the orthodox philosophy in China ever since the Han dynasty (206 B.C.–220 A.D.). The Confucian concept of 'man' is based on a theory about different relations between people. It emphasizes *ren lun* (human relations), and ethics are called *lun li*, which means a theory of human relations supervising people's behaviour. The kernel of this philosophy is *ren*. Confucius defines this *ren* as 'to love man'.[20] Mencius, the major Confucian philosopher, clearly explains that *ren* equals *ren*

---

20) Arthur Waley, trans. *The Analects of Confucius*, Book XVII, 9, pp. 212.

(man). He says: 'What is *ren*, that is man.'²¹ The Chinese character *ren* here is composed of two *ren*, showing that the connotation of the character is first of all a relation between people. At the same time, this human relation is a good relation, and it is interpreted as 'benevolence, virtue, love, kindness'. *Ren* has been the foundation on which Confucians built the concept of 'man'. Situated in such relations, 'man' will not be treated as an 'individual'. In grammar, a word is neither a singular nor plural form since it covers both, and it often presents a collective concept. A singular person can not be a 'man' when he/she is not related to others. It is only in the relatedness that he/she can be identified and evaluated as 'man'. As Mencius indicates, without being taught about *ren lun* (human relations), people would become almost like the beasts even if they are well fed, warmly clad, and comfortably lodged.²² Therefore, the Confucian concept of 'man' lays particular stress on 'collectivity', *qun*. Confucius says that 'one cannot herd (*qun*) with birds and beasts. If I am not to be a man among other men, then what am I to be?' He obviously emphasizes the association between people.²³ Xun Zi, another important Confucian philosopher, points out that the difference between 'man' and other species is that 'man' can *qun* (be collective).²⁴

Confucianism has therefore defined 'man' in a social context. Every man living in a *qun* has a position in this social relation network, and thus identifies himself according to this position. A man can be identified as father when he has a relation to another male as son, as brother when he has a relation to another as brother, as husband when he has a relation to a woman as wife, etc. Confucians have further prescribed the nature of each relation, for example, between father and son there should be affection, between sovereign and official there should be right-

---

21) Wing-Tsit Chan, *A Source Book in Chinese Philosophy*, Princeton, Princeton University Press, 1973, 7B:16, p. 81. James Legge, trans., *The Four Books*, Hong Kong, International Publication Society, 1954, p. 334. Yang Bojun, *Mengzi Yizhu*, Beijing, Zhonghua Shuju, 1960, p. 329.
22) Wing-Tsit Chan, *A Source Book in Chinese Philosophy*, p. 69. James Legge, *The Four Books*, p. 122. Mencius, 14:16. Yang Bojun, *Menzi Yizhu*, p. 231.
23) Arthur Waley, trans. *The Analects of Confucius*, Book XVIII, 6, p. 220.
24) Xun zi 'Wangzhi' (System of King). Quoted in Ren Jiyu, *Zhonguo Zhexue Shi Jianbian* (Short History of Chinese Philosophy, Beijing, Renmin Wenxue Chubanshe, 1974), p. 191.

eousness, etc. These prescriptions place restrictions on 'man's' behaviour. Later, the *Lixue* (rationalist) school of philosophy of the Song and Ming dynasties, known in the West as Neo-Confucianism, further sanctioned the old Confucian prescriptions with a system of metaphysics, *tianli* (Principle of Heaven). According to Zhu Xi, 'man' should behave according to this *tianli* and dismiss *renyu* (human desires). This doctrine was accepted and practised by the governments of all later dynasties as a moral law for people to follow. It was in this sense that Lu Xun criticized traditional philosophy as 'cannibalistic'.

In fact, Confucian restrictions on 'human' behaviour are not only criticized by modern intellectuals but also denied by Taoists. Taoism is the other major traditional philosophy. In the chapter 'Autumn Floods' of *Zhuang Zi*, it is told that the king of Chu once sent two officials to Zhuang Zi to ask him to administer the realm. Zhuang Zi replied:

> I have heard that there is a sacred tortoise in Chu that has been dead for three thousand years. The king keeps it wrapped in cloth and boxed, and stores it in an ancestral temple. Now would this tortoise rather be dead and have its bones left behind and honoured? Or would it rather be alive and dragging its tail in the mud?
>
> 'It would rather be alive and dragging its tail in the mud,' said the two officials.
>
> Zhuang Zi said, 'Go away! I'll drag my tail in the mud!'[25]

In Zhuang Zi's perspective, although a man can have high social position and enjoy a comfortable life and privileges, he has no life in himself. He is just like a dead tortoise wrapped in cloth and boxed, and stored in an ancestral temple. So, for Zhuang Zi, this social relation is 'man-eating' as well. However, Zhuang Zi is different from modern individualists in that he does not define 'man' in a one-many structure but in a part-whole structure. From this story we know that Zhuang Zi also emphasizes a relation between 'man' and the world, but it is not a relation in a social context but in a natural one, as he describes it: a tail in the 'mud'.

---

25) Burton Watson, *The Complete Works of Chuang Tzu*, New York, Columbia University Press, 1968, pp. 187-8.

'Where the Confucians read the human social order into nature, the Taoists tried to read nature into man.'[26]

For Taoists, everything is diverse parts of *Tao* (the Way), and *Tao* makes all into one. This *Tao* is like Plato's eternal Forms in which the many participate. *Tao* is also unitary, permanent and known by the mind alone. In fact, it cannot be described in words. It is presented in all phenomenal things. 'Man' is one part of *Tao*. This is not an 'individual man', or, a small 'man', but a big 'man'. We understand that, in a part-whole structure, a part itself has no fixed size or shape, and actually the whole part of the whole can also be a part. That is why Lao Zi says: '*Tao* is great, Heaven is great, earth is great, and man is great. There are four Greatnesses in the cosmos and man is one of them.'[27] This great 'man' is everywhere and cannot be identified just as 'individual man'. It is identified with Heaven and earth, and everything born in nature, as Zhuang Zi says: 'Heaven and earth were born at the same time I was, and the ten thousand things are one with me.'[28] It is in this kind of relation that the Taoist concept of 'man' and its value is established.

Another influential traditional philosophy in China is Chinese Buddhism, particularly the School of Zen. Its concept of 'man' is also based on monism. According to this philosophy, the world is nothing but *Sexiang* (Colour Look) of *kong* (the Void). It appears in five elements (*skandha*s): form and matter, sensations, perceptions, emotional states, and consciousness, which are in a constant state of change. Everything in the world, including 'man', is comprised of a transitory aggregate of the elements. 'Man' is nothing but one form of the transitional process at any one moment. It is a result of a previous form and will be a cause for the next. Therefore, 'man' is only a conditioned existence, relatively distinguished by senses for a short time. As a matter of fact, Buddhism believes that 'man' suffers because of these senses, so that a person who understands what 'man' is should ex-

---

26) Donald Munro, *The Concept of Man in Early China*, Stanford, California, Stanford University Press, 1969, p. 121.
27) Lao Zi (Lao Tsu), *Lao Zi Yi Zhu Ji Pingjie* (Interpretation of Lao Zi and Notes and Comments), Beijing, Zhonghua Shuju, 1983, Chapter 25, p. 62. In D.C. Lau's translation, 'man' becomes 'king', see his *Lao Tsu-Tao Te Ching*, London, Penguin Books Press, 1988, p. 82.
28) Burton Watson, *The Complete Works of Chuang Tzu*, p. 43.

tinguish all senses to be one with *kong*. In other words, the philosophy teaches 'man' a method not to be 'man'.

Confucianism, Taoism and Chinese Buddhism are the three major and most influential philosophies in Chinese tradition. My presentation of the different concepts of 'man' in these philosophies is very rough; the actual situation is much more complicated. Even within one philosophy there are different schools of the interpretation of 'man'. These three philosophies have also influenced one another. For example, Wang Yangming (1472–1528), although being a Confucian philosopher, rose to propound the *Xinxue* (School of Mind) as a revolt against *Lixue*. His theory was in fact influenced by Buddhism.

'Self-Identification': Associative and Dissociative

The 'self' is not a *Ding an sich* (thing in itself) but a product of the mind. When a 'man' experiences his existence in the world, consciousness of the 'self' appears in his mind in opposition to the consciousness of the external world. 'Self' for a person simply means his 'I' as a 'man' in his relation to the world. Then, different concepts of 'man' will lead to different approaches to the 'self', and determine how the 'self' is identified, evaluated and reflected in literary writing.

While Chinese writers' approaches to the 'self' vary from age to age and from one to another, they do not skip the patterns of the conceptual structures of 'man' that we have discussed above. Generally, those who hold traditional concepts would identify themselves through establishing an associative relation between their 'self' and the external world (society, nature, and others). I would describe this kind of 'self-identification' as an associative identification. This means that the 'self-identification' involves at least two things: 'I' and an associated object. Without the associated object, the 'self-identification' will not be fulfilled, and the writer can only identify himself as a part of 'man', not the whole.

What I would emphasize here is that these two things, 'I' and the associated object, are in fact not identical. It is in this aspect that traditional 'identification differs from the modern which interprets 'identification' as to be the same as something. It is just like when identifying a man as a husband one needs to associate him with a woman, a wife. If we ask the 'man' a question, 'Who are you?', the answer will be, 'I am associated with X' (narrative), or even 'I am X' (direct metaphor). The subject and the object or the predication will be two different things, but the 'X' here should be something that 'I' is associated with.

This difference between 'I' and 'X' is important, because it means that, when a traditional writer expresses or presents his 'self' in his literary works, he will usually describe 'X', instead of 'I', but through this 'X', we can identify the writer's 'I'. In Chinese lyrical poetry it is particularly rare to directly present 'I', and it is even regarded as a taboo. Poems portray more pictures of landscape than of 'I'. The expression of personal feelings and thoughts are conveyed through the description of nature. Here I would mention one of the three modes of expression in Chinese classical poetry, that is, *xing* (inspire, begin or exalt).The precise meaning of *xing* is still a subject of much controversy. James J. Y. Liu has given this interpretation: 'briefly, *xing* may be explained as the 'associational mode,' in which the poet begins (*xing*) by presenting a natural phenomenon and then expresses the human emotion inspired (*xing*) by or associated with that phenomenon, instead of directly expressing himself.' I would like to accept Liu's interpretation of *xing* because it fits well with the associative 'self-identification' in classical poetry. In narrative classical literature, anyhow, 'I' appears, but it usually appears as a narrator, not the narrated. It is through the narration of other people, 'I' stands out as a man.

Certainly, for 'self-identification' in literature, Confucian writers and Taoist or Buddhist ones will have different objects to associate with. Confucianism emphasizes *ren lun* (human relations), so that a Confucian writer will mostly associate himself with other people. To be concerned with other people is for him the best way to present the 'self'. Du Fu (Tu Fu, 712–770), a famous Tang poet, is the best example of this. His poems often express his own sufferings through vivid descriptions of the people's sufferings of his time.

For a Taoist writer 'I' is a part of nature, or the 'I' and nature are actually one. Only in nature, 'I' would feel free and feel 'itself'. Du Fu's contemporary Li Bai (Li Po, 699–762), another famous Tang poet, is the best example of a Taoist inclination to 'self-identification' in classical poetry. He would have natural things as associated objects for his 'self', instead of other people. In his poem 'On the Mountain: Question and Answer' he says: 'You ask me: / Why do I live / on this green mountain? I smile / No answer / My heart serene / On flowing water / peachblow / quietly going / far away / This is another earth / another sky / No likeness / to that human world below.'[29]

Taoists would even reverse the answer to the question 'who are you?': 'X is I'. According to Taoism, all phenomenal things are diverse parts of *Tao* and can be transformed into each other. This is explained in a story in *Zhuang Zi*, which relates how Zhuang Zi dreams that he is a butterfly, a butterfly happily flitting and fluttering around. The butterfly does not know that he is Zhuang Zi. Suddenly he wakes up and there he becomes Zhuang Zi. At that point, he does not know if he is Zhuang Zi who dreams that he is a butterfly, or a butterfly dreaming that he is Zhuang Zi.[30] We can find many examples of this kind of 'self-identification' through portrayings of natural objects in Chinese classical literature.

For a writer who believes in Chinese Buddhism, the associated object would be the Void, or the Emptiness. The aim of a Buddhist is to achieve selflessness so as to become a bodhisattva, the embodiment of wisdom, whose function is to bring all other living creatures to realize that a man is not to be considered a permanent entity in any regard. In fact, according to Buddhism, the 'self' is a worldly attachment that each person should be liberated and released from. The paradox is that 'self-identification' is thus actually 'anti-self-identification', or rather, it becomes a function of self-denial. A Buddhist-influenced writer should therefore try his best not to leave marks of his 'self' in his literary works. Wang Wei (699–759), another Tang poet, gives us an example of this kind of literary selflessness in his poem 'Empty Hills': 'Empty hills, no one in sight, / only the sound of someone talking; / late sunlight enters the deep wood, / shining over the green moss again.' [31] However, as Robert E. Hegel indicates,

---

29) Translation is from Cyril Birch, *Anthology of Chinese Literature, from early times to the fourteenth century*, p. 225.
30) Burton Watson, *The Complete Works of Chuang Tzu*, p. 49.
31) Translation is from Burton Watson, *Chinese Lyricism: Shih Poetry from the Second to the Twelfth Century*, New York, Columbia University Press, 1971, p. 173.

'Buddhist-influenced writers could celebrate their momentary hopes, fears, and insights in the bittersweet knowledge that such is the only existence that the self can possibly have.'[32]

If the 'self' in traditional literature is often an invisible existence or spirit without a clear image, the modern 'self' often has a distinct image. From the modern writers' symbolic attack on the 'cannibalistic' traditional Chinese culture, we know that for them, 'man' that is also to say, his 'I' is an image. Apparently what has been eaten is not 'man's' body but 'man' in a form of image. The body still exists, but it becomes a walking corpse. The body is not his 'I', or his image of 'I'; the two can be separated. This 'I', in its relation to the body, is very western, just like the 'I' that Descartes describes. 'Although I have a body,' he writes, 'very closely conjoined with me, yet since, on the one hand, I have a clear and distinct idea of myself, in so far as I am a thinking thing and not extended; and, on the other hand, I have a distinct idea of the body in so far as it is an extended, not a thinking thing, it is certain that I (that is the mind or soul, by which I am what I am) am really distinct from my body and can exist without it.'[33]

Nevertheless, Descartes is a pure philosopher, and he tries to define his 'I' as a thinking thing, a thinking thing that everyone can be. It is a definition of 'man' as a species. The modern Chinese writer's 'I', on the other hand, would have much more concrete characteristics. His 'I' will still not only think but also feel, act, have passions and desires. It still has an image or even an appearance, like the souls in Dante's *The Divine Comedy*, either flying in Paradise or being punished in Hell. It is this 'I' modern writers often present in their literary works. Young writers often say now that, by writing, they are looking for the 'self' that they have lost, and they want to take it back.[34]

---

32) Robert E. Hegel, 'An Exploration of the Chinese Literary Self', in his *Expressions of Self in Chinese Literature*, p. 10.
33) René Descartes, 'Objections against the Meditations and Replies', *Great Books of the Western World*, 31. *Descartes Spinoza*, London, Encyclopaedia Britannica, Inc., 1987, p. 120.
34) Zhu Dake, Song Lin and Ke Lequn, 'Sange Shuohua Zhe He Yi Ge Tingzhong, Guanyu Shitan Xianzhuang de Tanhua' (Three Speakers and One Listener, a Conversation about Present Poetry), see Lin Jianfa and Wang Jingtao, ed. *Dangdai Zhongguo Zuojia Mianmian Guan* (Review of All Aspects of Contemporary Writers), Changchun, Shidai Wenyi Chubanshe, 1992, p. 703.

For a modern writer, 'self-identification' is a dissociative procedure, which means the writer tries to extract himself from the external world (society, nature, other people). I have quoted Bei Dao's lines earlier, in which he states that: 'I am no hero / In an age without heroes / I just want to be a man.' It seems that he just wants to be identified as a 'man' and he would not set himself apart from other 'men' by identifying himself as a hero in an age without heroes, but the unspoken message in these lines that is left to the understanding of the reader is that the poet is still different and disassociated from others since his age is commonly con-ceived by the readers as an age in which nobody is a man or is treated as one. So, to be a 'man' is still a heroic action, which separates the author from others.

Just as 'man' is defined as 'individual man' by a modern writer, so is his 'self'. As defined in a western dichotomy, the 'self' stands only on one side of the one-many structure. This 'self' must be independent and exclusive. It is only 'individual man' that can be identified as him, and he alone can possess it. Therefore, he will not involve anybody else in his self-identification. He can apply the first personal pronoun 'I' to this 'individual man', both as a subject and as a predicative word. The answer to the question 'who are you?' will be: 'I am I!' With this answer he shows that he identifies his 'self' without relating himself to others, and that he can fulfil his 'self-identification' by disassociating himself from the external world.

Referring to 'self-presentation' or 'self-identification', we can say that a Confucian writer will show us a picture with a group of people where his 'self' will probably not be, but through this group we come to know the writer's identity; a Taoist writer will show us a picture with a natural background, sometimes we see his 'self' in it, sometimes not, but we can feel it; a Buddhist-influenced writer will show a picture with almost nothing in it, an empty picture, which also proves his 'self'; a modern writer, then, will show us a picture where we see directly the writer's image. In other words, if the traditional writers usually present and express the 'self' through a description of the associated objects, and the 'self' is often absent in their literary works, modern writers, when they wish to achieve 'self-identification' through literary writing, usually present and express the 'self' in a direct way. 'I' in their works often represents the writers themselves, so that these works are like 'self-portraits'. In contrast, we can see that these kinds of 'self portraits' and autobiographical works are not common in traditional literature.

One may argue that 'I' in a literary work should not be directly regarded as the writer's 'self' in reality. Many modern writers also deny that the 'I' in their works is their 'self'. But, sometimes, at least, it is identical with the writer's 'self' in his mind. Among many different interpretations of 'self' in literature, I think that Robert E. Hegel's statement could easily be accepted. He says: 'After all, self in literature is a function of mind reflected in a product of the mind.' So, according to him, 'self' is a product of mind, first created in a writer's mind, then appearing in his literary work. The 'self' in a writer's mind is already different from his 'self' in reality. It may be prettified, and become more lovable, respectable, or miserable. It is actually this 'self' which is often expressed in literature.

'Self-Evaluation': What Is the Measure?

One important aspect which determines how the writers express, present and identify the 'self' is 'self-evaluation'. Modern individualist writers utterly affirm their 'self' and highly evaluate it, so that they always present their 'self' positively in their literary writing. This attitude is based on a western belief, which Charles Taylor describes as: 'they (human beings) are fit objects of respect, that their life and integrity is sacred or enjoys immunity, and is not to be attacked.'[35] For a modern individualist, the 'self' has its own and independent value, and this value is also innate, whereas in traditional Chinese philosophy, the 'self' has a value only when it is related to the whole. As we have discussed earlier, for a modern writer, the 'self' is like one coin, which is concrete and has value itself, and people can keep it, or spend it, or lose it, or get it back. For a traditional writer, the 'self' is just like one side of the coin, which does not have value itself, and only shows a relation to the other side of the coin. One can not get or lose one side of the coin.

The different 'self-evaluations' reflect different measurements. In western classical philosophy, we learn the motto, 'man is the measure of all things'.[36] This may not be the same in Chi-

---

35) Charles Taylor, *Sources of Self, The Making of Modern Identity*, Cambridge, Cambridge University Press, 1989, p. 25.
36) See Georg Wilhelm Friedrich Hegel: *The Philosophy of History*, London, Encyclopaedia Britannica, INC. 1987, p. 280.

nese classical philosophy. *Tao*, for example, would be the measure of all things for a Taoist. 'Man' is usually not the measure but the measured. However, it would be wrong to claim that traditional Chinese philosophies absolutely deny the value of 'man' or the 'self'. On the contrary, it is still highly measured among all the things in the world. As we have indicated before, for the Taoist, 'man' is one of the four Greatnesses in the world, and the 'self' is part of it. On the other hand, although 'man' is not the measure of all things, 'man' is the only creature in the world who can apply the measure of all things. 'Man' can achieve this capability through self-cultivation or by practising philosophy in his life. In fact, the motto that 'man is the measure of all things' may also be applied to Confucianism, at least earlier Confucianism, if we specify that this 'man' is not an 'individual man' but the Confucian concept of 'man', that is, an associated 'man'. This means that a Confucian would in practice evaluate things according to the relations to man. 'As for Goodness,' Confucius says, 'you yourself desire rank and standing, then help others to get rank and standing. You want to turn your own merits to account, then help others to turn theirs to account – in fact, the ability to take one's own feelings as a guide – that is the sort of thing that lies in the direction of Goodness.'[37] In other words, 'self-orientation' is not recommended in Confucianism. On the contrary, it demands that man should learn to limit his 'self': 'he who can himself submit to ritual is Good.'[38] One should evaluate things through an understanding of other people's interest. As Fan Zhongyan, a Song writer, says in his famous 'Yueyang Lou Ji' (Notes on Yueyang City-gate Tower), 'to worry, worry first about what the people are worried over; to be happy, be happy over what the people are happy about.'[39]

Starting from this perspective, Chinese classical writers have established an aesthetic standard in evaluating 'self-expression' in

---

37) Arthur Waley, trans. *The Analects of Confucius*, Book VI, 28, p. 122. D.C. Lau, *The Analects*, London, Penguin Books LTD, 1979), Book VI; p. 85. In Wing-tsit Chan's translation, it goes: 'A man of humanity, wishing to establish his own character, also establishes the character of others, and wishing to be prominent himself, also helps others to be prominent.' see Wing-tsit Chan, Lun Yu 6:28, *A Source Book in Chinese Philosophy*, Princeton, Princeton Univ. 1963, p. 78.
38) *Ibid.*, Book XII, 1, p. 162. D.C. Lau, Book XII, 1, p. 113.
39) Fan Zhongyan, 'Yueyang Luo Ji' (Notes on Yueyang City-Gate Tower), *Gudai Sanwen Jianshang Cidian*, (Readers' Dictionary of Classic Essays), edited by Wang Bing, Beijing, Nongcun Duwu Chubanshe, 1992, p. 554.

literature. To have expressed the 'self' in a literary work does not necessarily mean that this work is good and has an aesthetic value. The writer should establish a good relation between his 'self' and the associated objects, then the work can have a value. Wang Guowei (1877–1927), a Chinese critic, has defined this evaluation as *ge* (estrange, alienate, or disaffect) or *buge* (reconciled, not estranged, or associated), and he thinks that *buge* is an ideal that a writer should be after.[40]

For a modern individualist, the motto 'man is the measure of all things' can be further specified as 'individual man is the measure of all things', or even, 'the Self is the measure of all things.' He also evaluates his 'self'' according to this measure. As Lu Xun advocates in *Wenhua pianzhi lun*: 'the Self should be regarded as the centre, and at the same time as an end.'[41] Chen Duxiu's 'individual standard' was also a 'self-standard'. In other words, they were self-oriented and self-centred. Such a self-aggrandizement is very apparent in May Fourth Movement literature. Lu Xun writes that 'if there are no more torches in the future, I will be the only light.'[42] Hu Shi writes in a poem that 'I laugh at you, Earth, turning around the Sun, you can only make one round day and night; I laugh at you, Moon, turning around the Earth, you cannot always keep full; I laugh at you, all big and small stars, you cannot jump out of you orbits; I laugh at you, radio, you go five hundred thousand Li in one second, but cannot compete with one of my thoughts.'[43] The most famous example is perhaps the poet Guo Moruo's *Nu Shen* (Goddess), a poetry collection which fascinated generations of intellectuals in China. In one poem called 'Tian Gou' (Heavenly Dog), he writes: 'I am a Heavenly Dog!/ I swallow the Moon./ I swallow the Sun./ I swallow all stars./ I am

---

40) See Wang Guo wei, *Renjian Ci Hua* (Worldly Remarks on Ci Poetry), Hong Kong, Shangwu Yinshu Guan, 1961, Remark 36. How to interpret '*ge*' and '*bu ge*' is still an issue of controversy, see Ye Jiaying, *Wang Guowei Jiqi Wenxue Piping* (Wang Guowei and His Literary Criticism), Guangzhou, Guangdong Renmin Chubanshe, 1982, pp. 247-256.
41) Lu Xun, 'Wenhua Pianzhi Lun', *Lu Xun Quan Ji*, p. 53.
42) Lu Xun, 'Re Feng' (Hot Wind), 'Sui Xiang Lu 41' (Random Thoughts 41), *Lu Xun Quan Ji*, p. 223.
43) Hu Shi, 'Yi Nian (One Thought)', *Changshi Ji* (Collection of Experimental Writings). In Cai Yuanpei, ed. *Zhongguo Xin Wenxue Daxi, Wenxue Juan* (Anthology of Chinese New Literature, Vol. of Literature, xerox copy), Shanghai, Wenyi Chubanshe, 1981, Vol. 1, p. 191.

I now./... I peel off my skin,/ I eat my own flesh,/ I drink my own blood, / I swallow my heart and liver,/ I am running on my nerve,/ I am running on my dorsal fin,/ I am running on my brain,/ I am I now! I am going to explode.'[44] In Lu Xun's literary work, we find a mad man afraid of being eaten by traditional culture; in Guo Moruo's we find an 'I' who will swallow the world and his own body as well. The transformation is astonishing. This kind of self-aggrandizement has also left some trace in contemporary poets such as Bei Dao. In his poem 'Answer', for instance, we read: 'I do not believe the sky is blue.'[45] Apparently, he also maintains that he himself would be the measure of the world.

Approaches to the World and the Role of the 'Self'

Another aspect of the writer's approach to his 'self' that we should also take into account is the world that the 'self' inhabits, the world which acts on the self and on which the 'self' in turn reacts. The situation of the world and the approach to the world a writer takes often explains why he approaches the 'self' in that particular way, and even decides what kind of role he will choose for his 'self' to play in his literary writing. Generally, we see a world *for* the 'self' in traditional literature, and a world *against* the 'self' in modern literature.

For a classical writer, the world is what his 'self' should associate with so that he can be identified as a 'man'. No matter whether the world is perilous or comfortable, he considers himself as a part of it. However, as Li Bai indicates in his poem 'On the Mountain', the world is divided into the natural world and the human world, and these two worlds seem to be in conflict with each other. If one world appears hostile, people can choose the other. Li Bai prefers to stay in a natural world, whereas a Confucian writer may choose the opposite. In either case, the world appears as a partner for his 'self-identification'. The sense of harmony with nature, and even of dissolution of the self in nature

---

44) Guo Moruo, 'Tian Gou (A Heavenly Dog)', *Nu Shen* (Godness). In Cai Yuanpei, ed. *Zhongguo Xin Wenxue Daxi, Wenxue Juan* (Anthology of Chinese New Literature), Vol. 1, p. 334.
45) Bei Dao, *The August Sleepwalker*, p. 33.

emerges also in Wang Wei's poetry. Since classical writers have these two alternative approaches, they often apply one of the two according to circumstance. When they cannot fulfil 'self-identification' in social life, they turn to nature for association. That traditional intellectuals often carry both a Confucian and a Taoist approach to the 'self' is an interesting phenomenon already noticed by historians.

Although a modern individualist writer insists that he is independent and self-constituted, he is actually much more concerned about the world. Whereas his self image is always positive, the world to him is always negative and hostile. There is an historical background to this sensibility: the development of 'individualism' in China took place in a cultural context where 'individualism' was not morally favoured. On the other hand, the conception of modern 'man' took place in a bad time when China was suffering many crises. In the beginning it was the downfall of the Chinese empire, followed by the civil war and the war with the Japanese, later it was communist culture and finally commercialization during the economic reforms in the 1980s. Social environment makes the modern writer feel constantly depressed, threatened by being eaten and isolated. Society is a prison, nature is an enemy, the other is hell. So, self-conceit, self-pity, self-love, self-affection, are all very common in modern Chinese literature. The modern writer always assigns himself the role of a tragic hero. Sometimes, he is a hero fighting for freedom and dignity, a challenger of the hostile world. More often, since his 'self' has been eaten or robbed, he is a Dostoevskian 'insulted and injured,' or, as Leo Ou-fan Lee presents him, 'a solitary traveller on a sentimental journey.'[46] Living in an electronic era, he complains that he has become the input of a computer terminal, a word in a dictionary and no more.[47]

As I have discussed before, Confucian philosophy has set up different relations between people. In those prescribed relations, everybody is playing a certain role as in a dramatic performance. What the 'self' plays is in fact an actor. As we understand it, an actor who plays a role is restricted by the nature of the role. He/

---

46) See Leo Ou-fan Lee, 'The Solitary Traveller', in Robert E. Hegel, *Expressions of Self in Chinese Literature*, pp. 282-307.
47) Bei Dao, 'Zou Lang' (Corridor), See *Today Literary Magazine*, Stockholm, No. 1, 1992, p. 98.

she acts out his/her part, and not really his/her own personality as an actor. He/she should even restrain his/her own passions and desires. This kind of associative 'self-identification' has led to a stereotype in classical literature and performing arts, which means that the 'self' is not identified as an 'individual self' but a type of the 'self'. This has also been discerned by Jonathan Chaves in his study of the Ming dynasty's Gongan School of poetry criticism. He observes that, although a Chinese poet may be utterly free to express his 'self' in a Chinese context that sees total identity between the essential self and the Ultimate Reality of the universe, no 'self' differs in the slightest from any other, or even from nature in its totality.[48]

'Self' in the World of Language: Bridge or Wall?

If, as Jonathan Chaves says, 'no literary self is completely like any one person who ever lived,'[49] then, in my opinion, no literary world is completely like the world of the living reality. The relationship between the 'self' and the world in literature is also different from that of reality. In reality, for instance, a modern writer often regards the world as a hostile existence, whereas, in literature, the world he creates is the home of his 'self'. What makes them different is language. In fact, language plays the most important role in 'self-expression' or 'self-identification' in literature.

Let me go back to the sentence 'I am associated with X' or 'I am X', by which I describe the associative 'self-identification' in classical literature. In this sentence the subject and the predicative are two unidentical things, the 'self' and an associated object. One is actually subjective, and the other is objective. When this 'self-expression' is carried out in literary writing, it is the literary language which plays the role as a bridge to relate these two things. This sentence is therefore a symbol to show a literary

---

48) Jonathan Chaves, 'The Expression of Self in the Kung-an School: Non-Romantic Individualism', see Robert E. Hegel, *Expressions of Self in Chinese Literature*, pp. 70-122.
49) Refer to René Wellek and Austin Warren, *Theory of Literature* (3rd ed.; New York, Harcourt, Brace and World, 1956, p. 78. See Robert E. Hegel, *Expressions of Self in Chinese Literature*, p. 3.

world which is combined of both the subjective and the objective. This world, often called the *yijing* (ideal realm) in Chinese aesthetics, is the major characteristic of Chinese classic literature. Wang Guowei has defined it as *jingjie* (lofty realm) and regarded such a literary world as the highest level in literary writing, as well as the best way for 'self-expression'.

This characteristic may explain why Chinese classical writers usually do not create their own images as language symbols to express the 'self', but generally use those objects which already exist in nature or society and have their language symbols ready. Thus, their metaphors or symbols of the 'self' do not become obstacles to the reader's understanding. There is apparently a distance between the subject 'I' and the object 'X', so that the structure of this sentence is also an open framework which permits both the 'self' and the world to enter, and also gives the reader the same possibility. It does not necessarily guide the reader to the writer, but to a world with which the reader's 'self' can also be associated.

If, referring to 'self-expression', the world that classical writers create is a distillation of reality, the world that modern writers create is often an inverted image of it. The sentence 'I am I', by which I describe modern 'self-identification', has an identical subject and predicative. Both are subjective. Therefore, the world the writer creates, is a personal world. Even when the writer uses metaphors to symbolize his 'self', the metaphors are not from the objective world, but created as personal images by the writers. We can see that the sentence 'I am I' is a closed framework, since between the subject and predicative there is not space to permit anybody or anything to enter. Here, the language plays a role as a wall separating the 'I' from the external world. It is a closed door. This means that the writer will create an utterly personal world. As a matter of fact, many modern Chinese writers do announce that when they write, they do not consider the reception by the readers.

Concluding Remarks

In Chinese classical literature there is a tradition of emphasizing 'self-expression'. However, this 'self-expression' usually does not make the writer's 'self' appear in literary works as an 'individual man' with a clear and concrete character and image. Based on a traditional concept of 'man' which identifies 'man' in human relations or in relation to nature and regards the 'self' as only a part of 'man', 'self-expression' in classic literature is therefore fulfilled through an association between the 'self' and the external world (society, nature, or other people). The emphasis on a relation rather than on an 'individual man' leads to an aesthetic trait of classical literature, i.e., the writer's 'self' does not appear directly, but appears as a personal emotion or feeling which finds sustenance in the external world, particularly, in the natural world. This combination of expression of personal emotion or feeling and portrayal of landscape creates a 'lofty realm of beauty', which is regarded as the most ideal 'self-expression'. Literary language functions as a bridge to connect the personal and the external. Narrative literature has thus developed much later as compared with lyric literature.

Gu Cheng, Aug. 1990. "The Rock Which Cannot Be Rooted on Earth"

'Self-expression' in Chinese modern literature has been influenced by western individualism and its expressions in western modern literature. A modern writer's 'self' often directly appears in his literary works as a hero with a concrete image, independent personality and clear character, so that the 'self-expression' often becomes a 'self-portrait'. It is fulfilled in a dis-associative way, which means that the writer always wants to highlight his 'self' by extracting himself from the external world. He tries to create in his literary work a personal realm which conflicts with the external world and protects his 'self' from being lost. Always seeing the society that his 'self' inhabits as a hostile world, the modern writer usually characterizes his 'self' either as a man of self-aggrandizement, or as a man of self-pity, self-love and self-conceit.

Classical writers usually do not have a problem with 'self-identification'. They know clearly their identities, or know how to identify themselves. What concerns them is mostly how to express their 'selves' in a proper way. In contrast, modern writers have been suffering a crisis of identity. They are confused and irritated by the question: 'Who am I?' In China, this is a question left by history as well as being put forward by reality. On the one hand, the writer feels that his 'self' has been eaten or robbed by traditional culture or the communist culture which disrespects him as an 'individual man', and makes him not know who he is. The communist leaders still uphold the totalitarian system at the cost of people's value as 'individual human beings'. On the other hand, the rapid but abnormal development of commercialization makes Chinese intellectuals feel weak in front of money and feel that their value as 'individual human beings' is lost. But, these are only superficial reasons. The basic problem is that 'self-identification' still needs a reliable object, a real disassociation is in fact impossible. However, modern writers will be sceptical about any object, in fear that this object will take their 'selves'. They have adopted a western modern ideal of 'individualism'. In order to be a 'self', to be an 'individual man', they have sublated tradition and even joined in a rebellion against the communist dictatorship. Now, they have found that they may have relied too much on western philosophy and have been controlled by western discourse. They have also experienced the crisis which western individualism has suffered. The aim that one should be unique, single and different seems now a trap and puts them in a helpless and solitary situation. Western culture is after all an alien culture, and its pounding at the Chinese culture leads to a change of the Chinese people's way of living and thinking, and also to a crisis of 'self-identification' in a cultural context. Under these circumstances, some writers have gone back to traditional culture. The so called 'root-searching' literature has already appeared. Again, literary language has provided the writers with a safer and more effective means to fulfil 'self-identification', because the Chinese language becomes the last fortress where Chinese writers can defend their cultural identity and find their home. An unofficial literary magazine *Xiandai Hanshi* (Modern Chinese Poetry), which appeared lately, at the end of the 1980s, can be a good example of this. The poets who launched the magazine stress now both the word 'modern' and the word 'Chinese' in its sense of the language. 'Modern Chinese' is the identity many a Chinese writer seeks today, not only for his literary writing but also for his 'self'.

References

Birch, Cyril, *Anthology of Chinese Literature, from Early Times to the Fourteenth Century*, New York, Grove Press, 1965.

Chan, Wing-tsit, *A Source Book in Chinese Philosophy*, New Jersey, Princeton, Princeton University Press, 1963.

De Bary, Wm. Theodore. *Self and Society in Ming Thought*, New York, Columbia University Press, 1970.

Hegel, Robert E. and Hessney, Richard C. ed. *Expressions of Self in Chinese Literature*, New York, Columbia University Press, 1985.

Lau, D.C., trans. *Lao Tzu, Tao Te Ching*, London: Penguin Books, 1963.

Lin Jianfa & Wang Jingtao, *Zhongguo Dangdai Zuojia Mianmian Guan* (Review of All Aspects of Contemporary Writers), Changchun, Shidai Wenyi Chubanshe, 1992.

Liu, James J.Y. *Chinese Theories of Literature*, Chicago, The University of Chicago Press, 1975.

Liu Zaifu, and Lin Gang, *Chuantong He Zhongguo Ren* (Tradition and Chinese), Hong Kong, Sanlian Shudian, 1990.

Munro, Donald. ed. *Individualism and Holism: Studies in Confucian and Taoist Values*, Ann Arbor, Center for Chinese Studies, the University of Michigan, 1985.

—— *The Concept of Man in Early China*, Stanford, California, Stanford University Press, 1969.

Taylor, Charles, *Sources of The Self, the Making of the Modern Identity*, Cambridge, Cambridge University Press, 1989.

Waley, Arthur, trans. *The Analects of Confucius*, London, George Allen & Unwin Ltd, 1964.

Watson, Burton, trans. *The Complete Works of Chuang Tzu*, New York, Columbia University Press, 1968.

Ye, Jiaying, *Wang Guowei Jiqi Wenxue Piping* (Wang Guowei and His Literary Criticism), Guangzhou, Guangdong Renmin Chubanshe, 1982.

Confucius' Self-Identity and the Divine

Pertti Nikkilä

Often Confucius has been described as having been intellectually between secularism or agnosticism and divinity. This article tries to clarify what the role of Heaven in Confucius' self-identity was. Before going into this matter, after considering the term 'identity', I shall introduce the Confucian *Analects* and see how Confucius' self-identity is placed in the source. Then I shall describe some of the main factors of his self-identity, and more profoundly the function of Heaven in it.

The Term 'Identity'

Erikson says about identity:

> When we want to establish a person's identity, we ask what his name is and what station he occupies in his community. Personal identity means more; it includes a subjective sense of continuous existence and a coherent memory. Psychological identity has even more elusive characteristics, at once subjective and objective, individual and social.
>
> A subjective sense of identity is a sense of sameness and continuity as an individual – but with a special quality probably best described by William James. A man's character, he wrote in a letter, is discernible in the mental or moral attitude in which, when it came upon him, he felt himself most deeply and intensely active and alive. At such moments here is a voice inside which speaks and says: 'This is the real me!' Such experience always includes an element of active tension, of

holding my own, as it were, and trusting outward things to perform their part so as to take it a full harmony, but without any guaranty that they will. Thus may a mature person come to the astonished or exuberant awareness of his identity.[1]

Düsing says that the concept identity has been generally used in the research of literature together, with or, instead of the concepts 'person', 'personality', or 'individuality'. He refers to the findings of Erikson, that the concept identity has two aspects, a psychological aspect and a social one. Düsing adds another conception of the dimensions of identity: 'I' and 'me'. 'I' is the subjectivity which acts spontaneously and 'me' is the self as an object. 'Me' is the picture which is made by other people about me as a bearer of my role.[2]

The *Analects* reflect Confucius' identity as 'I', in Confucius' own statements about himself and also as 'me' in other people's statements about Confucius. The *Analects* also contain general principles stated by Confucius. Some of these principles clarify Confucius' statements about himself.

The present article concentrates on Confucius' identity as an 'I' identity, the 'real me' as it is revealed by the source. The concept 'Confucius' self-identity' is used about this identity.

The literature lists several types of specific identities of a person, like one's bodily identity, sexual identity, cultural identity, social identity, sub-cultural identity, national identity, religious identity,[3]

---

1) Erik H. Erikson, 'A Way of Looking at Things' in Stephen Schlein, (ed.), *Selected Papers from 1930–1980*, New York, 1987, p. 675.
2) See Wolfgang Düsing, 'Aspekte der Identitätsdarstellung', pp. 18, 19, Erwin Roth, 'Selbst und Identität', pp. 57-65, Walter Schultz, 'Identität Selbstezug, Selbstfindung', pp. 83-101, in *Studium Generale der Johannes-Gutenberg-Universität, Mainz*, Mainzer Universitätsgespräche Wintersemester 1982/83. Also Ida Schädelin-Gmür, *Identität, Ein Begriff und seine pädagogische Bedeutung*, Diss., Zürich, 1988, p. 77.
3) See Dieter Claessens, 'Verunsicherung und Identität', *Studium Generale der Johannes Gutenberg-Universität, Mainz*, Mainzer Universitätsgespräche Wintersemester 1982/83, pp. 7-13; Hanne Bang, 'Religious Identity over Two Generations Roman Catholic Immigrant and Convert Families in Sweden' in *Studies in Comparative and International Education*, 18, Stockholm, 1990:8, 9; Schädelin-Gmür, op.cit., p. 77, Lothar Krappmann, *Soziologische Dimension der Identität Strukturelle Bedingungen für die Teilnahme an Interaktionsprozessen*, Stuttgart, 1988, pp. 207-211; Derek Parfit, 'Personal Identity' in *The Philosophical Review*, vol. 80, 1971:3-27; G.L.Doore, 'Mackie on Personal Identity' in Mind, vol. 91, 1982:593-598; James E. Broyles, 'Wittgenstein on Personal Identity: Some Second Thoughts' in *Philosophical Investigations*, vol. 9, 1985:56-65; David Cockburn, 'The Idea of a Person as He is in Himself' in *Philosophical Investigation*, vol. 11, 1988:13-27; Donald L. M. Baxter, 'Identity in the Loose and Popular Sense' in *Mind, A Quarterly Review of Philosophy*, vol. 97, 1988: 575-582, and Roland Puccetti, 'Multiple Identity' in *The Personalist*, vol. 54, 1973:203-215.

identity in God.[4] The term has also a remarkable philosophical and theological importance. As such, the term is by no means a simple one, as Hare says: 'Puzzles about personal identity are extremely vexed and complex.'[5]

The Organization of the Confucian *Analects* and Confucius' Self-Identity

The earliest, most important and most reliable source of early Confucianism is the *Analects* of Confucius (551–479 B.C.). Fung summarizes the biography of Confucius recorded in Shih Chi: 'Confucius was poor in his youth, but entered the government of Lu and by the time he was fifty had reached high official rank. As a result of political intrigue, however, he was soon forced to resign his post and go into exile. For the next thirteen years he travelled from one state to another, always hoping to find an opportunity to realize his ideal of political and social reform. Nowhere, however, did he succeed, and finally he returned to Lu as an old man, where he died three years later in 479 B.C.'[6]

The name of the *Analects*, Lun Yü, 論語 was given to the work by the compilers and it means a collection of sayings or selected sayings.[7] The earliest quotation from *Lun Yü* is in *Li ki*, which

---

4) Jürgen Moltmann, 'Die Menschliche Identität und der Tod', in *Studium Generale der Johannes Gutenberg-Universität, Mainz*, Mainzer Universitätsgespräche Wintersemester 1982/83:55.
5) R. M. Hare, *Moral Thinking its Levels, Method and Point*, Oxford, 1991, p. 96. See also the works: Werner Beierwaltes, *Identität und Differenz*, Frankfurt am Main, 1980; Paul Ludwig Landsberg, *Selbstauffassung und Selbstgestaltung*, Hamburg, 1987; Jürgen Schnelle, *Das 'Selbst-Berüchsichtigung non-egoisher Theorien des Bewusstseins*, Bielefeld, 1985.
6) Shih Chi or Historical Records was the first dynastic history of China, completed about 86 B. C. Yu-lan Fung (Feng), *A Short History of Chinese Philosophy*, New York, (1931) 1966, p. 38; Szuma Chien, *Records of the Historian*, (translated by Hsien-yi and Gladys Yang), Hongkong, 1975, pp. 1-27; Chavannes, *Les Mémoires Historiques de Se-ma Ts'ien*, Traduits et Annotés, vol. 5, Paris, 1905, pp. 283-445; Tang I-chieh, 湯一介, K'ung Tsu, 孔子, *K'ung Tzu yen chiu lun wen chi*, 孔子研究 論文集, Peking, 1987, pp.67-71; Wu Teh Yao, *Confucius, The Man*, Singapore, 1989, pp. 1-6,. See also Pertti Nikkilä, *Early Confucianism and Inherited Thought in the Light of Some Key Terms of the Confucian Analects, I. The Terms in Shu Ching and Shih Ching*, Helsinki, 1982, pp. 73-75; Most of the following text follows Pertti Nikkilä, *Early Confucianism and Inherited Thought in the Light of Some Key Terms of the Confucian Analects, II. The Terms in the Confucian Analects*, Helsinki, 1992, pp. 8-13, 20-31, 164 shortened and with some modifications.
7) Yang Pe-chün 楊伯峻 *Lun Yü i chu*, 論語譯注, Shanghai, 1965, pp. 1-2, and Arthur Waley, *The Analects of Confucius, Translated and annotated by Arthur Waley*, London, 1964, p. 21.

was compiled in the first century B.C. Thus we know that a work called *Lun Yü* existed before the Han dynasty (206 B.C.– A.D. 220). D.C. Lau notes that the earliest source of information about the *Lun Yü* is the chapter on bibliography in the *Han Shu*, History of the Han Dynasty, by Pan Ku, finished toward the end of the first century A.D.[8]

Giles says about *Lun Yü* that it is 'a work in twenty short chapters or books, retailing the views of Confucius on a variety of subjects, and expressed so far as possible in the very words of the Master. It tells us nearly all we really know about the Sage, and may possibly have been put together within a hundred years of his death.'[9] It was compiled by Confucius' disciples and partly also by their students. The final compilation of the work was undertaken at the end of Ch'un Ch'iu or at the beginning of the Warring States period.[10]

Lau says:

> In the first part of the Western Han it was the practice for a scholar to specialize in only one of the three versions of the Lun Yü. It was not until Chang Yü that this was changed... He used his own discretion in the choice of what readings to follow. The result was an eclectic version which came to be known as the Chang hou lun (Marquis Chang's Lun Yü). In the reign of Ch'u Yüan (48–44 B.C.) Chang Yü, because of his expert knowledge of the Lun yü, was appointed tutor to the heir apparent who in 32 B.C. became Emperor Ch'eng. As a result, Chang Yü became prime minister in 25 B.C. Because of the high Imperial esteem he enjoyed, marquis Chang's ver-

---

8) D. C. Lau, *Confucius, The Analects, Translated with an Introduction by D. C. Lau*, Suffolk, 1979, p. 220; William Watson, *Early Civilization in China*, London, 1966, p. 9. Using quotations from Mencius as evidence, Wang claims that the Confucian *Analects* were already in existence during the time of Mencius (371–288 B.C.). Wang Tieh, 王鐵, 'Shih Lun *Lun Yü* ti chieh chi yü pan pen p'ien ch'ien chu wen t'i' 試論<<論語>>的結集與版本變遷問藝in *Studies on Confucius, Quarterly*, no. 3, 1989, p. 60.
9) Herbert A. Giles, *A History of Chinese Literature*, New York, s.a., orig. 1923, p. 32.
10) Yang Pe-chün 楊伯峻, *Lun Yü i chu*, 論語譯注, pp. 3-4. Yang draws his conclusion concerning the date of compilation of the work or the basis of the terminology used in the *Analects*. The usage of the term as a second person pronoun in AN. 17:7 refers to the beginning of the Warring States period. James Legge, 'Confucian *Analects*' in *The Chinese Classics*, vol. 1, Taipei, 1969:321.

sion in the Lun Yü became so popular that it eclipsed all other versions... The present version of the Lun yü that we have was edited by Ho Yen (190-249 A.D.). This is based, in the main, on the versions of Chang Yü and Cheng Hsüan and is, therefore, eclectic.[11]

It has been suggested that Books 16 to 20 are of a later date than the rest of the work. These last five Books have certain common characteristics which distinguish them from the rest of the work. Nevertheless, they still contain some of the genuine Confucian tradition of Confucius' disciples and of Confucius himself. But Books 10 to 20 have been regarded as less genuine than Books 1 to 9. Dawson says: 'It looks as if Books 3-9 (out of a total of twenty books) may form the oldest stratum, but even they may contain later insertions; and although they have a clearer ring of authenticity, it is impossible to vouch for the genuineness of any of the sayings included in them.'[12]

Lau finds some principle of organization in most of Books 1-15: Books 1 and 2 are exceptions. Book 3 is completely devoted to music. Book 4 has several parts which deal with various topics. Book 5 is concerned with people, like parts of Book 6 (1-21). The rest of Book 6 is mixed. Book 7 is entirely about Confucius; either Confucius' sayings about himself or what other people had to say

---

11) Lau, *Confucius, The Analects*, p. 221.
12) The usage of the name K'ung Tzu is not uniform within the Books 16 to 20. In other Books Confucius has been referred to as Tzu 子 and if he is speaking with a high official he is referred to as K'ung Tzu 孔子. During the Warring States period Fu Tzu 夫子 was used when addressing a person spoken to. This has been used in AN 17:3, 17:7, 19:17. The last five Books have in addition numbered sets and apocryphal stories and references to historical personages. Lau suggests that this concern with historical personages, often without relevance to Confucius, shows that some historical texts similar to the *Book of History* must have been used as a textbook by some of Confucius' disciples, if not by Confucius himself. Lau concludes that these features link parts of the last five Books to one another and shows that they probably shared a common origin and that some of these features signify a late date. Lau, op.cit., pp. 222-227. It is noteworthy that in Lau's work he does not deny the tradition of referring to the historical personages as being a genuine Confucian tradition of Confucius' disciples or even Confucius himself recorded in this earlier part of the *Analects*. See also Ch'ien Mu 錢穆, 'Pen Lun Yü lun K'ung hsüeh,' 本論語論孔學 in *New Asia College Academic Annual*, vol. 1, no. 2. (Hsin Ya hsüeh pao 新亞學報), (1977) 1958:12, 13, Waley, *The Analects of Confucius*, pp. 11, 2;, Legge, 'Confucian *Analects*', p. 16, and Raymond Dawson, 'Confucius' in *Founders of Faith*, Oxford, 1986, p. 101.

about him. Book 8 consists of several topics. Book 9:1-19 are about Confucius, the next three or four chapters are about Yen Yüan and the rest are mixed. Book 10 is about the daily life of Confucius. Book 11 is devoted to Confucius. 22 chapters out of 24 in book 12 are questions put to Confucius. Book 13:1-17 concerns government. Chapters 18-28 deal with how one should conduct oneself and with the Gentleman *chün tzu* 君子 but 13:20 and 28 deal with the Gentlemen, *shi* 士. Book 14 has a central theme: how to be a man. Book 15 has the same theme, except in the first five and last five chapters. Lau discusses the saying of the disciples and concludes:

> We can roughly divide the Lun yü into three strata. The first stratum consists of the books well ordered and in which no sayings of disciples are included. The next consists of Book I (and possibly Book II) and Book VII. Although these books show a lack of internal organization of the chapters and contain sayings of disciples, they, yet, do not use 'K'ung Tzu' for Confucius. Lastly, there is the stratum consisting of Book X and the last five chapters. These are all interlinked through several features and are likely to be much later in date than the bulk of the work.[13]

The theme of identity reveals itself in the organization of the *Analects* in the following way:

- The chapters of Book 1 have two characteristics in common: all chapters, except 4 and 10, state ethical principles on a general level.
- Book 2 includes the moral rules, ethical laws and principles which are to be used in governing on a general level. In this respect the book continues the theme of general rules started in book one.
- Book 3 consistently handles rites, music, archery, dance, temple, and sacrifice. Only chapters 5, 14, and 20 are exceptions to these themes.

---

13) Lau, *Confucius, The analects*, pp. 227-233. Waley, *The Analects of Confucius*, p. 21, suggests: 'I should hazard the guess that the books III-IX represent the oldest stratum. Books X and XX (first part) certainly have no intrinsic connection with the rest.' See also Max Hamburger, 'Aristotle and Confucius, A Study in Comparative Philosophy' in *The Journal of the Royal Institute of Philosophy*, vol. 31, no. 119, London, 1956:338.

- Book 4 treats general ethical principles, laws and definitions except chapters 6, 14 and 15.
- The pattern of organization from Book 4 to 5 moves from general rules to special cases. Book 5 does not discuss general ethical principles or rules but the chapters are related to named persons, except in the two last chapters. The theme of this book is Confucius' appraisals of other persons. Chapters 12 and 13 are exception; the two last chapters do not mention a person by name.
- In Book 6 chapters 1 – 14 and 26 concern named persons, the other chapters do not. The Book continues the theme of the previous book but deviates from it towards the end. In Books 5 and 6, the specific characteristic appears because certain persons are mentioned by name.
- In Book 7 the specific characteristic is brought to a summit: to Confucius himself. Confucius is described in this Book by himself or by other persons, except in chapters 6, 35, 36.

What is said above shows that the object of the organization of the Books from 4 to 7 is the formation of Confucius' self-identity. The presentation of this identity is prepared by the general ethical principles in Book 4 and the appraisals of different people in Books 5 and 6. This shows that in this part of the *Analects* Confucius' self-identity is regarded as an important topic.

- Book 8, chapters 3 to 7 are part of the Tseng-tradition. The remaining chapters are discussions of statements by Confucius. Confucius appears as a distant teacher of ideals, whereas Tseng appears to be closer. The statements about him are more personal, longer, and more familiar.
- The essential patterns of Book 9 are the systematic descriptions of Confucius in chapters 1 to 20, the more general principles discussed at the end of the book, and the theme of continuity or stability from chapter 16 to chapter 28. This book continues the presentation of Confucius' self-identity told by himself or by other people. On the basis of this topic it belongs together with Book 7. It is possible that Book 8 has been placed between Books 7 and 9 when compiling the *Analects*.
- Book 10 is concerned with the behaviour of a Gentleman in different practical situations. It has been generally understood that the gentleman refers to Confucius.

What is said above, shows that Confucius' self-identity is an important topic in the organization of the more reliable parts of the *Analects*.

Some Main Factors of Confucius' Self-Identity

The Books 7, and 9 reveal different factors of Confucius' self-identity. Below are listed the types and a quotation from the *Analects* is given to illustrate the different types of the identity. The types of identity as 'me' in which other people describe Confucius are left out.

- Intellectual identity: 'I transmit but do not innovate.' AN. 7:1. (7:2.) 'Grant me a few more years so that I may study at the age of fifty and I shall be free from major errors.' AN. 7:17. (Other related statements: AN. 7:28, 3, 9:8,19.)
- Ethical and intellectual identity together: 'It is these things that cause me concern: failure to cultivate virtue, failure to go more deeply into what I have learned, inability, when I am told what is right, to move to where it is, and inability to reform myself when I have defects.' AN. 7:3. (AN.7:6,34, 9:25)
- Traditional dimension of his identity: 'How I have gone downhill! It has been such a long time since I dreamt of the Duke of Chou.' AN.7:5. (AN.7:20.)
- Confucius' identity as teacher: 'I have never denied instruction to anyone who, of his own accord, has given me so much as a bundle of dried meat as a present.' AN. 7:7. 'When I have pointed out one corner of a square to anyone and he does not come back with the other three, I will not point it out to him a second time.' AN. 7:8. (AN. 9:20-24)
- Confucius' identity as an official: 'The Master said to Yen Yüan "Only you and I have the ability to go forward when employed and to stay out of sight when set aside."'AN. 7:11. (AN. 9:7,15,16.)
- Confucius' sentimental identity: 'The governor of She asked Tsu-lu about Confucius. Tzu-lu did not answer. The Master said: "Why did you not simply say something to this effect: he is the sort of man who forgets to eat when he tries to solve

a problem that has been driving him to distraction, who is so full of joy that he forgets his worries and who does not notice the onset of old age?"' AN. 7:19.

- Heaven and Confucius' self-identity: 'Heaven is author of the virtue that is in me. What can Huan T'ui do to me?' AN. 7:23. (AN. 9:5,12.)
- Religious identity: 'The Master was seriously ill. Tsu-lu asked permission to offer a prayer. The Master said, "Was such a thing ever done?" Tsu-lu said, "Yes, it was. The prayer offered was as follows: pray thus to the gods above and below." The Master said, "In that case, I have long been offering my prayers."' (AN. 7:35.)
- Social identity: 'My friends, do you think I am secretive? There is nothing which I hide from you. There is nothing I do which I do not share with you, my friends.' AN. 7:24. (AN. 7:26,29)
- Ethical identity: 'Is benevolence really far away? No sooner do I desire it than it is here.' AN. 7:30. (AN.7:33, 9:6.)
- The outer behavioural dimension of his self-identity: Confucius' attitude towards rites. (AN. 9:3.)

These types of Confucius' self-identity are only examples in the two books 7 and 9. Most of the types are represented by more than one passage of the *Analects*. The relevant passages of the rest of the *Analects* could be taken into account. This would provide a more profound picture of the matter. However, already the present classification shows the diversity of identity in the *Analects*. In the following, one type of his identity is discussed; that of Heaven and Confucius' self-identity.

Confucius' Self-Identity and Heaven

There are 16 references to Heaven in the *Analects*, two of 'Son of Heaven' 天予, one of 'Way of Heaven' 天道, four of 'The Mandate of Heaven' 天命, altogether 23 cases. The 16 references to Heaven fall into several categories of which the largest describes the mutual relationships between Confucius and Heaven. These relationships include the positive and negative attitudes of Heaven towards Confucius and secondly his communication with Heaven.

All the positive actions of Heaven spoken about in the *Analects* also concern Confucius himself. Confucius' self-reflective statements are here dealt with first. In Books 7 and 9, which mostly concern his personal characteristics, Confucius says that 'Heaven is the author of the virtue 德 that is in me. What can Huan T'ui do to me.' This shows that the origin of *Te* 德 is Heaven. The foundation of *Te*-virtue is not in Confucius himself, but is in Heaven. This leads to the effect of *Te* as a protective force against the minister of war in Sung, who according to tradition wanted to kill Confucius.[14] Here Confucius shows heroism which diminished the value of survival in his mind.[15] The virtue of *Te* is not something to be acquired by man's own effort only, it is given by Heaven. In Confucius' teaching this does not need to apply to all the virtues, since only *Te* is said to originate from Heaven.

The culture of Wen Wang, inherited by Confucius, also has a protective function. Confucius understood that Heaven does not intend to destroy this culture. By destroying him, the culture would have been destroyed as well, so Confucius had nothing to fear. Through this personalization of culture in his self-identity he had confidence in the power of Heaven to preserve him. Tu Wei-ming explains this:

> Confucius' insistence that he loved the ancients and that he was a transmitter rather than a maker symbolizes his conscious attempt to provide a transcendental anchorage for human civilization. To Confucius, what had already been created, notably the 'ritual and music' of the human community, was not merely of humans, it was also sanctioned and sponsored by the Mandate of Heaven. Confucius' strong conviction that Heaven will not allow 'this culture' (Ssu-wen) to perish must therefore be taken to mean that his sense of mission, far from being a conservative desire to return to the past, was inspired by his critical self-awareness that 'Heaven

---

14) AN. 7:23, Lau, *Confucius, The Analects*, p. 89. AN. 7:22; Waley, *The Analects of Confucius*, p. 127. See also Chan Wing-tsit, Chinese Philosophy and Religion in Arnold Toynbee, (ed.), *Half of the World*, London, 1973, p. 114, and Benjamin Schwartz, *The World of Thought in Ancient China*, Cambridge and London, 1985, p. 125.
15) David Wiggins, 'Needs, Values, Truth, Essays in the Philosophy of Value' in *Aristotelain Society Series* Volume 5, Oxford, 1991: 306.

knows me!' The idea of 'this culture' is thus laden with cosmological significance.[16]

So both Te and culture according to Confucius have a transcendental foundation, and work as a protective shield against any invaders.

Confucius did not regard it as of the utmost importance to be well-known, understood, or employed. Not being recognized on earth is compensated for being known by Heaven.[17] According to this, the ultimate self-identity of Confucius is based on Heaven. His identity does not collapse as long as he is known by Heaven. At the same time Confucius confesses that he regards it as more important to be successful before Heaven than in the human society.

It can be seen that Confucius believes he is known by Heaven when he writes: 下學而上達 'In my studies I start from below and get through to what is up above.' This is understood to be a corrective which causes heavenly positive action to compensate for the lack of not being known.[18] Studies are an accumulative, continuous process to 'get to what is up above', an ongoing and developing process through which Confucius strengthens his transcendentally based self-identity.

In the Analects T'ien ming 天命 (Decree of Heaven) appears in three passages. Confucius said about himself: 'At fifteen I set my heart on learning; at thirty I took my stand; at forty I came to be

---

16) Tu, Wei-ming, 'The Way, Learning and Politics in Classical Confucian Humanism' in *The Institute of East Asian Philosophies, Occasional Paper and Monograph Series*, No. 2, Hong Kong, 1989, pp. 2-3. AN. 9:5, Lau, *Confucius, The Analects*, p. 96; Waley, *The Analects of Confucius*, p. 139. According to Yang Bojun 楊伯峻, *Lun Yü i chu*, 論語譯注, p. 94, Confucius' idea was: 'After Chou Wen Wang had died wasn't all the culture inherited in myself? If Heaven wants to destroy the culture then I shall not have chance to learn this culture. If Heaven does not want to destroy this culture, what can the people of K'uang do to me?' See also Ch'eng Shu-te 程樹德, Lun Yü chi shih, 論語集釋, p. 501; and Kalle Korhonen, *Kungfutsen Suuri Oppi*, Johdatus kongfutselaiseen elämänkatsomukseen, Helsinki, 1921, p. 41; Philip J. Ivanhoe, 'A Question of Faith, A New Interpretation of Mencius 2B.13' in *Early China* 13:161, 165.
17) 知 'to know' in the sense 'to be employed': 'No ruler recognizes my merits and employs me'. AN. 14:37, p. 189. 'To understand', AN. 14:35; Lau, *Confucius, The Analects*, p. 129.
18) AN. 14:35, Lau, *Confucius, The Analects*, p. 129. Waley translates this as 'But the studies of jen here below are felt on high.' What is referred to here is 'The self-training consisting in the study of antiquity.' Waley, *The Analects of Confucius*, p. 189. 下學 refers to learning the affairs of men and 上 refers to knowing the Heavenly mandate. Holy man (= Confucius), Heaven and earth, these three things form his Te. Ch'eng Shu-te, op.cit., p. 887.

free from doubts; at fifty I understood the Decree of Heaven 五十而知天命; at sixty my ear was atuned; at seventy I followed my heart's desire without overstepping the line.' Liu explains the passage in a Neo-Confucian manner, wanting to polish the Confucian identity from the transcendental dimensions: 'Confucius' originality lies in his belief that there is no need to depart from human ways in order to know the Mandate of Heaven. Confucius put the emphasis entirely on man himself.' Ching explains:

> This is the description of a man who consciously cultivated an interior life, who trained his mind to apprehend the truth and his heart to grasp the will of Heaven, until his instincts were also transformed, and who learned to appreciate the things of the spirit. Still, the mention of Heaven is discreet. Confucius' words do not vibrate with a passionate longing for union with Heaven, or God, as do the words of many Western mystics.

Schwartz offers the explanation that Confucius may mean that he has a clear understanding of what it is that is not in his control as well as of what is his true sphere of autonomous action.[19]

---

19) AN. 2:4; Lau, *Confucius, The Analects*, p. 63; Legge, 'Confucian *Analects*', p. 146. Waley, *The Analects of Confucius*, p. 88, translates 'At fifty, I knew what were the biddings of Heaven.' According to Chu Hsi 命 is the prevalence of heavenly Tao 天道, it is the natural reason of all things and affairs. Chu Hsi 朱熹, Szu shu chi chu, Sung Chu Hsi chi chu, 四書集註，宋朱熹集註, Taipei, 1952, p. 7. This explanation is followed by other interpreters too: see Toshio Shigezawa, 'Development of Rationalism in Ancient China' in *Philosophical Studies of Japan*, vol. 3, (1961) 1962:97. Chen supposes that Confucius studied the Book of Changes at fifty. He refers to AN. 7:17, where Confucius says, according to the Ku version 'If some years were added to my life, and I could study the *Book of Changes* after fifty, then I might come to be without great faults'. Chen adds that Confucius 'could well see that the *Book of Changes* would give him knowledge of Heaven and destiny.' Chen Li-fu, *The Confucian Way, A New and Systematic Study of ' The Four Books"*, London and New York, 1987, p. 67. Liu refers also to AN. 15:28, 11:11, pp. 199, 155. Liu Shu-hsien, 'The Problem of Orthodoxy' in Wing-tsit Chan, (ed.), *Chu Hsi's Philosophy, Chu Hsi and Neo-confucianism*, Honolulu, 1986, p. 445. The view of the present author (that the often quoted passage AN. 11:11 is of a doubtful origin, because it does not follow the general theme of the book, which is Confucian appraisals of different people or groups of people) does not support the Neo-Confucian views. See also AN. 20:3, p. 233; Wang Ming-sun 王明孫, 'Lun Yü pi chieh shih t'an, 論語筆解試探 [Trying to Investigate the Explanations of Confucian *Analects*] in *Journal of Confucius and Mencius Society*, no. 52, Sept, 1986:203, Chen Richard Min-jui, *Confucius' Concept of Man*, University Microfilms, Princeton, 1974, pp. 91-93; Julia Ching, 'What is Confucian Spirituality' in Irene Eber, (ed.), *Confucianism. The Dynamics of Tradition*, New York, 1986, p. 66; and Schwartz, *The World of Thought in Ancient China*, p. 126.

This personal self-appraisal by Confucius shows clearly that his self-identity has obvious transcendental dimensions[20], but also that he has himself developed as a moral agent towards greater autonomy and freedom. As an autonomous, free, ethical agent, he was able to follow naturally his hearts' desire without failure in his moral behaviour. This is his harmonious and well-balanced ethical self-identity. In this way he separated morals, at least to some extent in principle, from the ready-made list of moral rules or from the given moral codes, and also introduced intellectuality into morality.

The theme of knowing the Decree of Heaven is continued in the *Analects* by the following general principles of Confucius: a Gentleman 君子 is in awe of the Decree of Heaven and 'The small man 小人, being ignorant of the Decree of Heaven, does not stand in awe of it.' Knowing the *T'ien Ming* and standing in awe of it are closely related with each other.[21] Here the knowledge leads to an awe-inspiring attitude towards *T'ien Ming*. This has a vestige of the conception about God which is *tremendum et fascinosum*, fascinating to be known and tremendous to be standing in awe of.

To know fate refers to an 'attempt to learn the predetermined course of events in advance so as to enable man to gain success and avoid failure.' This is 'a necessary quality of a superior man'.[22] The predetermined course of events is expressed by the sentence: 'Life and death are a matter of Destiny; wealth and honour depend on Heaven', and in the idea that the four seasons run their course and the hundred creatures, each after its kind, are thereby born. Here it is understood that things run by command of Heaven.[23]

---

20) Moltmann, 'Die Menschliche Identität und der Tod', pp. 43-45.
21) AN. 16:8, Lau, *Confucius, The Analects*, p. 140. Ch'eng Shu-te 程樹, *Lun Yü chi shih*, 論語集釋, p. 65.
22) C.K. Yang, 'Some Characteristics of Chinese Bureaucratic Behavior' in David S. Nivison and Arthur F. Wright (eds), *Confucianism in Action*, Stanford 1959, repr. 1969:274.
23) AN. 12:5; Lau, op.cit., p. 113; 14:38, pp. 189, 190; 17:19, p. 214; 20:3, p. 233.

This has also been interpreted to show some determinism, although it is not made clear here whether it is question of blind natural forces or of a personal God.[24] Fung says:

> Confucius thought a person's birth and death, whether he was rich or poor, eminent or humble, a success or a failure all were decided by heaven. But one could still do one's best to do the things one thought had to be done, no matter whether the result would be success or failure. Confucius thought that even with something in which you knew you did not have a chance of success, as long as you thought it needed to be done, you should still work at it with your best (effort). People of that time said that Confucius was 'one who knows the impracticable nature of the times and yet is willing to act in them.'[25]

This explanation by Fung reveals that Confucius was by no means a fatalist relaxing all efforts and believing that one cannot do anything, since Heaven anyway will determine everything. On the contrary, Confucius was active, and Heaven had given him the

---

24) Herrlee G. Creel, *Confucius the Man and the Myth*, London, 1951 quotes on page 132 AN. 12:5 'Death and life are as decreed, wealth and rank depend upon Heaven; the gentleman is serious and does not fail in his duties, he behaves courteously to others and accords with li.' Creel interprets this to mean: ' Life and death are matters about which one can do relatively little; he does his best, but when death comes after all one must simply resign himself and say "It is fate"'. Shih interprets this passage: 'Here ming is a synonym of T'ien in the sense: ming or T'ien determine death and life, as well as riches and honours; they are not dependent upon man. Again we note in Confucius a certain determinism. But whether it is the result of blind natural forces or the decision of a personal God remains unclear.' Based on AN: 14:37, p. 189, Shih concludes that this passage shows that Confucius implicitly recognized a relationship between the ordinances of Heaven (ming) and the personal God (T'ien) whom he acknowledged to be the one supreme God. It is said in the passage mentioned, AN. 14:47: '... perhaps after all I am known; not here, but in Heaven.' Joseph S.I. Shih, 'The Place of Confucius in the History of Chinese Religion', *Gregorianum*, vol. 53, 1970:499-502. See also Wang Gung-hsing, *The Chinese Mind*, New York, 1946, pp. 27, 28.
25) AN. 12:5; Lau, *Confucius, The Analects*, p. 113, Fung, *A Short History of Chinese Philosophy*, p. 88. AN. 14:41, p. 190; Legge, 'Confucian *Analects*', p. 290. According to T'ang the 'Ming' of Confucius means 'Heavenly ordinance'. Confucius travelled throughout the world and confronted with the fact, that his Tao was not to be realized in the world. He also understood that, whether or not the Tao was realized, he had to accept whatever happened willingly. T'ang, Chün-I, 'The Tien Ming (Heavenly Ordinance) in Pre-Ch'in China' in *Philosophy East and West*, vols. 11 and 12, 1959, 1962:212-217.

heavenly mission, which is the way *tian ming* has been understood in connection with Confucius too. This mission was an important element of Confucius' self-identity.

Hattori suggests that for Confucius, virtue depends on the grace of Heaven. From time immemorial, there have been saints, who received the grace of Heaven. They all represented Heaven and ruled people on account of Heaven. The people were also educated by them. The Way had not been practised for a long time and therefore during many hundreds of years the people did not enjoy a quiet life. Heaven finds and charges a suitable man to make the way clear and to bring peace for the sake of human life. According to Hattori, Confucius was a man who received such a mission from Heaven. Confucius himself believed that he was provided with the virtue enabling him to be charged with this mission. Thus, the phrase 'to know the decree of Heaven' is nothing other than the profound belief of Confucius that a mission to clear the Doctrine and to practise the Way was bestowed by Heaven. To carry out this mission Confucius needed a rank, and so he became a provincial officer. After the situation in Lu became such that he could not continue any longer, he sought a new post in order to carry out his mission. In this he failed. However, he thought that he ought to make the Way known after his death. At fifty Confucius became confident of his mission from Heaven. This confidence in his mission as an integral element of his self-identity was the origin of his power and of his zeal.[26]

To possess or to get the mandate by traditional means would have meant to be a king or at least a helper or a minister of a king, but Confucius did not say that he had received the mandate. His mission was to help the king and the authorities to obtain the ethical qualification which was necessary for them in order to keep the mandate of a ruler. In this way he knew the mandate, but not in a sense that he had it himself, like the rulers. Confucius' self-identity was not that of a king. It was the self-identity of a king's helper. In this way he 'participated' in the mandate of the

---

26) Explaining AN., 9:5 Hattori says that 'Cause of truth' is wen 文 and means the same as Tao 道. King Wen died and the Way lodged in Confucius. He received the Way because Heaven did not like to let this way perish. U. Hattori, 'Confucius Conviction of his Heavenly Mission' in *Harvard Journal of Asiatic Studies*, vol. 1, no. 1, 1936:105-108.

rulers. This means that Confucius had a special mutual relationship with Heaven.[27]

Although Confucius had not got the mandate from Heaven, like kings, his emphasis on his personal relation to it may reflect his group identity as a member of the *shi*-class. The importance of *shi*, scholars, was rising, and Confucius, in accordance with this historical development, tried to find justification for his position in his doctrine about *ming*. Between this, and his favourite doctrine about 'rectification of names' there may be some tension.[28] However, this looks quite natural, since if a new class is rising, it necessarily implies new 'names'. If the rising class has any power, there must be corresponding diminution of the former power of the old ruling class, and consequently at least some kind of modification to the old 'names', or old definitions of rights and duties of those in power, is necessary.

Confucius feels the unfavourable attitude of Heaven personally. He submits to his fate not to be known or to be employed. He neither complains against Heaven nor blames man. He turns his fate to a positive notion of being known by Heaven. Given the background of Zou thought, it must have been a real disappointment for Confucius not to be employed as a virtuous person, with virtue given by Heaven.[29] However, here Confucius does not show submission to the inexplicable Heaven, but tries to find a positive solution to the problem and he tries to see some hope in immersing himself in studies. In showing this attitude he is behaving differently from the sad deploring attitude commonly expressed in *Shih*. Here Confucius follows neither *Shih* nor *Shu*

---

27) Chiu suggests that the saying 'At fifty, I knew the Mandate of Heaven' indicates Confucius' 'belief in that the Mandate of Heaven was given to him'. Later he says that Confucius claimed that he had personally received that mandate as well. Chiu continues ' But Confucius himself did not regard himself as a king as such; instead, he understood his own mission as that of transmission and preservation of ancient culture and tradition'. Referring to AN. 9:5, he says 'At this point we acquire a new awareness of T'ien, that of being the 'guardian' of culture, with the mandate of T'ien as being the transmission of culture; and Confucius, as an educator, took that as his personal mission'. Milton M. Chiu, *The Tao of Chinese Religion*, New York, London, 1984, p. 110.
28) According to this doctrine the prince is prince, the father is father etc, that is, each man in his relations is what the name of his relation would require. AN. 13:3, pp. 171, 172, AN. 12:11, p. 166.'Let the prince be prince, the minister a minister, the father a father and a son a son'.
29) AN. 14:37, 89; AN. 14:35, Lau, *Confucius, The Analects*, p. 129. AN. 7:22, p. 127; AN. 7:23. See also p. 96.

Jing (*Book of Documents*). The solution for this problem of his self-identity is his own: to pursue his studies, which have a heavenly character aiming at being known by Heaven.

When Zi Lu disliked Confucius visiting the wicked concubine of Duke Ling of Wei, he replied: 'If I have done anything improper, may Heaven reject me, may Heaven reject me.'[30] Here Confucius recognizes that wrong action would evoke the anger of Heaven and he submits himself to this fact.

---

30) AN. 6:26, Legge, 'Confucian *Analects'*, p. 193; AN. 6:28, Lau, *Confucius, The Analects*, p. 85. AN. 6:26 is 子見南子，子路不説，夫子失之，曰，子所否者，天厭之，天厭之.'之' here could be an empty word or a pronoun denoting the improper things, or I = Confucius. Waley translates 之 as 'it'. Waley, *The Analects of Confucius*, pp. 121, 241. His translation: ' Whatsoever I have done amiss, may Heaven avert it, may Heaven avert it', implies, that Confucius probably did something wrong. Chu Hsi 朱熹, *Szu shu chi chu, Sung Chu Hsi chi*, 四書集註，宋朱熹集註, p. 40, interprets 厭 as 'dislike, detest, reject'. There is also an interpretation to explain 厭 as a phonetic loan meaning 'to press, to oppress'. Ch'eng Shu-te, 程樹德, p. 365 and Liu Pao-nan, 劉寳楠 Liu Kung-mien, 劉恭冕. *Lun Yü cheng i*, 論語正義, Taipei, 1973, p. 132. The meanings 'to be disliked by Heaven' or 'being suppressed to death by Heaven' are not very far from each other. The translation ' Whatever I have done amiss. may Heaven like or suppress it' does not have the proper sense '厭' requires here a person as an object. The most probable translation is 'If I have done anything improper, may Heaven reject me, may Heaven reject me'. This implies that Confucius did nothing wrong. The passage has some further explanation: Confucius tried to say that he visited that lady, and if the reason for seeing her was not to get peace to the world, may Heaven dislike him. According to this explanation Confucius had a good motive for visiting the wicked lady. Because of this motive he did right. Another explanation says that Confucius' idea was to say that if Heaven does not dislike her, must he dislike her? What he does not do, is the same as what Heaven does not do. A third explanation says that because many people did not like the fact that Confucius saw Nan-tzu, this means that Heaven did not like Confucius seeing her. However, Nan-tzu represents the society of the time. Confucius asks whether Heaven wished to reject the society. Another explanation says that the wicked lady employed good men, like Confucius. The view that the disciples of Confucius put forward was that they did not want to help wicked people. See Ch'eng op.cit., pp. 365-369 and Chiu Koon-hoi, 'The Religious Elements in the Teaching of Confucius' in *Chinese Social and Political Science Review*, vol. 12, 1928:46. Confucius himself acted according to this last idea, see Nikkilä, 1982, *Early Confucianism and Inherited Thought in the Light of Some Key Terms of the Confucian Analects*, I., pp. 74, 75. Apparently Nan-tzu did not employ Confucius, the visit might not have lasted long, and it is not known what was discussed during the visit, so there may be no tension between Confucius' actions and this passage. Clearly there is no question here of Confucius having deeply violated his moral principles and tradition, nor of his having caused great harm, and so he is not condemning himself now. See John Kekes, *Moral Tradition and Individuality*, Princeton, 1989, p. 21.

Confucius experienced the disfavour of Heaven when he lost his favourite young disciple Yen Yüan. He said: 'Alas, Heaven has bereft me. Heaven has bereft me.'[31] Obviously it would have been more in conformity with justice if such a person could have lived longer, especially as he was fond of learning. Similarly Confucius had to admit that a good person could become ill.[32] Confucius here does not ponder the reasons for this type of heavenly act; his attitude here resembles that of the people in *Shih Ching* when they met with heavenly disfavour. If he had followed the general attitude in *Shu Ching*, he would probably have speculated as to why Heaven committed this action. His religious self-identity here follows the traditional attitude of submission to the will of Heaven.

One's guilt against Heaven will prohibit one's prayers: 'When you have offended against Heaven, there is nowhere you can turn to in your prayers.' Confucius does not explain what it means to offend against Heaven, 罪於天. Presumably this has an ethical connotation resembling the virtuous prayer mentioned in Shu,[33] and means that any wrong action causes Heaven not to receive prayers. The passage implies logically that if one has not offended against Heaven one can pray. Confucius does not reject prayer with this sentence.

Expiation has been mentioned in connection with Confucius' illness, but it was directed towards the sky spirits above and the earth spirits below. Heaven is not mentioned in this context. Confucius said: 'My expiation 禱 began long ago.' On another occasion, when he was ill and thought he would soon die, Confucius said: 'In pretending to have retainers when I have none, whom do I deceive? Do I deceive Heaven?' Waley suggests that this shows that Confucius was confident that his disciples

---

31) AN. 11:8, p. 154. See also AN. 11:6-12; Legge, 'Confucian *Analects*', pp. 239-241.
32) AN. 6:2, p. 115, (AN. 11:6, p. 154) AN. 6:8, p. 117.
33) AN. 3:13, Lau, *Confucius, The Analects*, p. 69. Chu Hsi explains Heaven as reason or principle. Chu Hsi 朱熹, *Szu shu chi chu, Sung Chu Hsi chi* 四書集註, 宋朱熹集, p. 16. Ch'eng has an explanation that offending against Heaven would mean to act against reason. 理 cannot be Heaven, but it can be from Heaven. Ch'eng Shu-te 程樹德, *Lun Yü chi shih*, 論語集釋, p. 158. Nikkilä, 1982, *Early Confucianism and Inherited Thought in the Light of Some Key Terms of the Confucian Analects*, I., pp. 101, 102, 110, 111. See also Howard D. Smith, *Confucius*, London, 1973, p. 51.

could give him a decent burial even if he was buried without public honours.[34] These passages show that Confucius most probably prayed, even if this is by no means a proper two-way communication with Heaven, but this 'prayer' does reflect Confucius' relation to Heaven and the fact that Confucius takes Heaven seriously. If Confucius had possessed a mandate of a king, he would have had a two-way communication with Heaven.

When considering the possibility of communication from Heaven to man, Confucius says that Heaven does not speak, yet the four seasons run their course thereby, (by command of Heaven), the hundred creatures, each after its kind, are born thereby.[35]

Confucius' attitude towards prayer links up to monotheism, on the one hand, and to polytheism on the other. It is a monotheistic idea that there is no one other than Heaven to pray to. But it is a polytheistic idea that there are several kinds of spirits towards which the expiation rites can be directed. Confucius displayed a certain ignorance concerning these, but admitted that his expiation began long ago.[36] One can try to invent an artificial harmonization for this contradiction between monotheism and polytheism, for example, that Heaven was a supreme monotheistic god, whereas there were many kinds of spirits under this

---

34) AN. 7:34, pp. 130, 131. Dubs explains this: 'When our master was ill, (Jung Yu) Dz-lu asked permission to have prayers said (for him to the spirits and ordinary gods). Our master replied, "Is there such a thing (in ancient authorities?" (Jung Yu) Dz-lu answered, "There is. In the *Dirges* it says: 'We pray to the ordinary gods above and to the earthly deities beneath'". Our master replied, " To me (K'ung) Ch'iu prayer is not an occasional matter".'
Dubs offers this interpretation: 'Here Confucius implies that if his ordinary life had not secured for him protection against death from whatever spiritual powers there are (here of course referring to Heaven), any ceremonies performed in the haste of an emergency would give no aid. So, in a highly superstitious age, Confucius gave no offence to those who believed in ordinary gods and spirits, yet maintained his inward faith in one God.' Dubs connects this with Confucius not answering questions about the gods. In Lau's interpretation Confucius was more positive to the idea of prayer, as he translates the sentence as ' In that case, I have long been offering my prayers.' Lau, *Confucius, The Analects* , p. 91. See also Homer H. Dubs, 'The Archaic Royal Jou Religion' in *T'oung Pao*, vol. 46, 1958: 249-251; AN. 9:11, p. 141; Waley, *The Analects of Confucius*, p. 141.
35) AN. 17:19, p. 214.
36) AN. 7:34, pp. 130, 131.

Heaven and that the spirits could be affected and that they had a certain power over Confucius' life.

These passages show that Confucius stresses the communication with Heaven very little. However, this communication is not entirely absent from the *Analects*. To a great extent Confucius ignores the traditional thoughts about sacrifice and prayer directed to Heaven, (*Shi Ching*), and does not emphasize the two way communication with Heaven clearly expressed in *Shu Ching*. One explanation for this is apparently that the communication was performed by the royal persons; Confucius spoke about his personal attitude towards Heaven, but could not say too much about prayer and sacrifice, because he was not a king. He limited his identity to the group of the learned.

Conclusion

Confucius' self-identity is an important topic in the organization of the more reliable parts of the *Analects*.

It was important for Confucius' self-identity that he is recognized by Heaven. His studies are a tool to strengthen his transcendental-based sense of identity.

Confucius had a calling from Heaven, an active mission to introduce his doctrines to those in power. This mission was an important element of Confucius' self-identity. Confucius was fully conscious of this mandate and this knowledge led to an awe-inspiring attitude towards it. Confucius, however, had not received the heavenly mandate in the same way as the kings. His relationship towards the mandate was to know it as a task given to him by Heaven.

When he experienced disappointments because his doctrines were not accepted by the rulers, Confucius neither deplored inexplicable Heaven, nor started to consider whether his personal virtue had any fault in it. He only wanted to pursue his studies with the aim of being recognized by Heaven.

When he encountered the disfavour of Heaven, Confucius did not start to ponder the reasons for such actions by Heaven. He simply submitted himself to Heaven's will.

In Confucius' mind prayer is a delicate matter. The relationship towards Heaven has to be ethically spotless, otherwise prayer is impossible.

Confucius believed that there is Heaven, which is the ultimate basis of things in the natural world, and which also maintains the whole of this world. This same Heaven is also the ultimate basis of Confucius himself and for what he is doing. However, Confucius did not define this Heaven more clearly. It was a knowledge of Heaven's existence and influence, a strong feeling of personal dependency from Heaven, but it was not a philosophical or theological system of thought about Heaven and about the essence of Heaven.

To a great extent Confucius was silent about Heaven, but this silence did not mean denial; it meant approval.

Additional research could illuminate further the other factors of Confucius' self-identity. A comparison between his 'I'-identity and 'Me'-identity could be made as well. The general ethical principles in Books 1 to 4 could be compared with these identities

References

Primary Sources

'A Concordance to the Analects of Confucius in *Lun Yü yin te*, 論語引得' in *Harward-Yenching Institute Sinological Index Series, Supplement*, no. 16, Taipei, (reprint) 1972.

Lau D.C., *Confucius, The Analects,* Translated with an Introduction by D.C. Lau, Suffolk, 1979.

Legge, James, 'Confucian Analects' in *The Chinese Classics*, vol. 1., Taipei, (reprint) 1969.

Lun Yü, 論語 *The Analects of Confucius,* (AN).

Waley, Arthur, *The Analects of Confucius,* Translated and annotated by Arthur Waley, London, 1964.

Secondary sources

Bang, Hanne, 'Religious Identity over Two Generations Roman Catholic Immigrant and Convert Families in Sweden' in *Studies in Comparative and International Education,* 18, Stockholm, 1990.

Baxter, Donald L. M.,'Identity in the Loose and Popular Sense, Mind' in *A Quarterly Review of Philosophy*, Vol. 97, 1988.

Beierwaltes, Werner, 'Identität und Differenz' in *Philosophische Abhandlungen* Band 49, Frankfurt am Main, 1980.

Broyles, James E., 'Wittgenstein on Personal Identity: Some Second Thoughts' in *Philosophical Investigations*, Vol. 9, 1985.

Chan, Wing-tsit, 'Chinese Philosophy and Religion' in Arnold Toynbee, (ed.), *Half of the World*, London, 1973.

Chavannes, Edouard, *Les Mémoires Historiques de Se-ma Ts'ien, Traduits et Annotés*, vol. 5, Paris, 1905.

Chen, Li Fu, *The Confucian Way, A New and Systematic Study of 'The Four Books'*, London and New York, 1987.

Chen, Richard Min-jui, *Confucius' Concept of Man*, University Microfilms, Princeton, 1974.

Ch'eng Shu-te, 程樹德, Lun Yü chi shih, 論語集釋, Taipei, 1974.

Ch'ien Mu, 錢穆,'Pen Lun Yü lun K'ung hsüeh, 本論語論孔學' in *New Asia College Academic Annual*, vol. 1. no. 2. (Hsin Ya hsüeh pao, 新亞 學報), 1977, 1958.

Ching, Julia, 'What Is Confucian Spirituality' in Irene Eber, (ed.), *Confucianism, The Dynamics of Tradition*, New York, 1986.

Chiu, Koon-hoi,'The Religious Elements in the Teaching of Confucius' in *Chinese Social and Political Science Review*, vol. 12, 1928.

Chiu, Milton M.,*The Tao of Chinese Religion*, New York, London, 1984.

Chu Hsi 朱熹, *Szu shu chi chu Sung Chu Hsi chi*, 四書集註，宋朱熹集, Taipei, 1952.

Claessens Dieter,'Verunsicherung und Identität', *Studium Generale der Johannes Gutenberg-Universität, Mainz*, Mainzer Universitätsgespräche Wintersemester 1982/83, 1983.

Cockburn, David, 'The Idea of a Person as He Is in Himself' in *Philosophical Investigation*, Vol.11, 1988.

Creel, Herrlee G., *Confucius the Man and the Myth*, London, 1951.

Dawson, Raymond, 'Confucius' in *Founders of Faith*, Oxford, 1986.

Doore, G. L. 'Mackie on Personal Identity' in *Mind*, Vol. 91, 1982.

Dubs, Homer H., 'The Archaic Royal Jou Religion' in *T'oung Pao*, vol. 46, 1958.

Düsing, Wolfgang, 'Aspekte der Identitätsdarstellung', *Studium Generale der Johannes Gutenberg-Universität, Mainz,* Mainzer Universitätsgespräche Wintersemester 1982/83., 1983.

Erikson, Erik H., 'A Way of Looking at things' in Stephen Schlein, (ed.), *Selected Papers from 1930 to 1980*, New York, 1987.

Fung (Feng) Yu-lan, *A Short History of Chinese Philosophy*, New York, 1931, 1966.

Giles, Herbert A., *A History of Chinese Literature*, New York, s.a., orig. 1923.

Hamburger, Max, 'Aristotle and Confucius, A Study in Comparative Philosophy' in *The Journal of the Royal Institute of Philosophy*, vol, 31, no 119, London, 1956.

Hare, R.M., *Moral Thinking its Levels, Method and Point*, Oxford, 1989.

———, *Essays in Ethical Theory*, Oxford, 1991

Hattori, U., 'Confucius' Conviction of his Heavenly Mission' in *Harvard Journal of Asiatic Studies*, vol.1, no. 1, 1936.

Kekes, John, *Moral Tradition and Individuality*, Princeton, 1989.

Ivanhoe, Philip J., 'A Question of Faith, A New Interpretation of Mencius 2B.13' in *Early China* 13, 1988.

Korhonen, Kalle, *Kungfutsen Suuri Oppi, Johdatus kongfutse-laiseen elämänkatsomukseen*, Helsinki, 1921.

Krappmann, Lothar, *Soziologische Dimension der Identität Strukturelle Bedingungen für die Teilnahme an Interaktionsprozessen*, Stuttgart, 1988.

Landsberg, Paul Ludwig, *Selbsauffassung und Selbsgestaltung*, Diss. Hamburg, 1987.

Liu Pao-nan, *Liu Kung-mien* 劉寶楠 劉恭冕 1973. Lun Yü cheng i, 論語正義, Taipei, 1973.

Liu Shu-hsien, 'The Problem of Orthodoxy' in Wing-tsit Chan, (ed.), *Chu Hsi's Philosophy, Chu Hsi and Neo-Confucianism*, Honolulu, 1986.

Moltmann, Jürgen, 'Die Menschliche Identität und der Tod', *Studium Generale der Johannes Gutenberg-Universität, Mainz*, Mainzer Universitätsgespräche Wintersemester 1982/83., 1983.

Nikkilä, Pertti, *Early Confucianism and Inherited Thought in the Light of Some Key Terms of the Confucian Analects, I. The Terms in Shu Ching and Shih Ching*, Helsinki, 1982.

——, *Early Confucianism and Inherited Thought in the Light of Some Key Terms of the Confucian Analects, II. The Terms in the Confucian Analects*, Helsinki, 1992.

Parfit, Derek ,'Personal Identity' in *The Philosophical Review*, Vol. 80, 1971.

Puccetti, Roland, 'Multiple Identity' in *The Personalist*, vol. 54, 1973.

Roth, Erwin, 'Selbst und Identität', *Studium Generale der Johannes Gutenberg-Universität, Mainz*, Mainzer Universitätsgespräche Wintersemester 1982/83., 1983.

Schnelle, Jürgen, *Das 'Selbstbewusstseinsproblem' im historischen und systematischen Kontext der Erkenntnistheorie unter besonderer Berücksichtigung non-egologisher Teorien des Bewusstseins*, Bielefeld, 1985.

Schwartz, Benjamin, *The World of Thought in Ancient China*, Cambridge and London, 1985.

Schultz, Walter, 'Identität, Selbsterzug, Selbstfindung', *Studium Generale der Johannes Gutenberg-Universität, Mainz*, Mainzer Universitätsgespräche Wintersemester 1982/83, 1983.

Schädelin-Gmür, Ida, *Identität, Ein Begriff und seine pädagogische Bedeutung*, Diss. Zürich, 1988.

Shigezawa, Toshio, 'Development of Rationalism in Ancient China' in *Philosophical Studies of Japan*, vol. 3, 1961, 1962.

Shih, Joseph S.I., 'The Place of Confucius in the History of Chinese Religion' in *Gregorianum*, vol. 53, 1970.

Smith, Howard D., *Confucius*, London, 1973.

Szuma Chien, *Records of the Historian*, translated by Yang Hsien-yi and Gladys Yang, Hong Kong, 1975.

T'ang, Chün-i, 'The T'ien Ming (Heavenly Ordinance) in Pre-Ch'in China' in *Philosophy East and West*, vols. 11 and 12, 1959, 1962.

T'ang I'chieh, 湯一介, *Kung Tzu* 孔子, *K'ung Tzu yen chiu lun wen chi*, 孔子研究 論文集, Peking, 1987.

Tu, Wei-ming, 'The Way, Learning and Politics in Classical Confucian Humanism' in *The Institute of East Asian Philosophies, Occasional Paper and Monograph Series*, no. 2, Hong Kong, 1989.

Wang, Gung-hsing, *The Chinese Mind*, New York, 1946.

Wang Ming-sun 王明孫, 'Lun Yü pi chiai shih t'an, 論語筆解試探, [Trying to Investigate the Explanations of Confucian Analects'] in *Journal of Confucius and Mencius Society*, no. 52, 1986.

Wang T'ieh, 王鐵, 'Shi lun *Lun Yü* ti chieh chi yü pan pen p'ien ch'ien chu wen t'i, 論《論語》的結集與版本變 遷諸問 in *Studies on Confucius, Quarterly*, no. 3, Sept 25, 1989.

Watson, William, *Early Civilization in China*, London, 1966.

Wiggins, David, 'Needs, Values, Truth, Essays in the Philosophy of Value' in *Arisotelian Society Series* Volume 6, Oxford, 1991.

Wu, Teh Yao, *Confucius, The Man*, Singapore, 1989.

Yang, C.K., 'Some Characteristics of Chinese Bureaucratic Behavior' in David S. Nivison and Arthur F. Wright, (eds), *Confucianism in Action*, Stanford 1959, repr., 1969.

Yang Pe-chün,楊伯峻, *Lun Yü yi zhu*, 論語譯注, Shanghai, 1965.

Self-Identity and Allegory in the Fiction of Yu Hua

Anne Wedell-Wedellsborg

When I met the young Chinese writer Yu Hua in Beijing in 1990, I asked him what he was reading at the moment. Somewhat to my surprise he answered 'Walter Benjamin's essays on Baudelaire' and told me they made a great impression on him. A central concept in Benjamin's discussion of the French poet is allegory, and I was reminded of Yu Hua's words when I recently came across the much debated article by Fredric Jameson (1986) on self and allegory in third-world literature.[1]

Now, the idea of applying the concept of allegory to Chinese literature is anything but new, and with regard to modern literature closely related to the 'obsession with China' syndrome. But despite the renewed focus on this syndrome in recent discourse on modern Chinese literature, little attention has been paid to the radical changes in the concept of allegory as perceived in western literary theory starting from Benjamin, towards a much more ambiguous and heterogeneous notion. In the 1980s, questions of individual and national identity came to be the underlying theme in most Chinese literature, at the same time as this literature, heavily influenced from the west, became much more technically sophisticated and complex. In this context it seems to me that precisely the modernist notion of allegory could be an appropriate tool for dealing with the vague sense of some undefined allegorical tenor which is often evoked from the reading of recent Chinese 'avant-garde' literature. This article will therefore pro-

---

1) Fredric Jameson, 'Third-World Literature in the Era of Multinational Capitalism' *Social Text*, 15, Fall 1986.

pose a reading of one of Yu Hua's most famous texts from that perspective. But first let us take a look at the concept of allegory itself.

Modern Allegory

Allegorical readings of Chinese literature, both inside and outside China are numerous, ranging from rigorous scholarly efforts, such as Andrew H. Plaks' reading of allegory in *Xi You Ji* and *Hong Lou Meng*,[2] to crudely politicized interpretations. Plaks (1977) defines allegory as 'a mode of composition in which extended structural patterns of a narrative text are intended to refer, in their overall configurations, to correspondingly complex patterns of intelligibility on some level not directly presented'. (165) He insists that 'meaning' in allegory presupposes actual authorial intention (the difficulties in establishing this notwithstanding). The question of allegorical meaning 'must ultimately depend upon the elusive yet decisive issue of authorial intent'. (171) Plaks thus assigns to allegory an objective validity which, as we shall see, is opposite to Benjamin's notion.

The distinction between allegorical composition and allegorical reading inherent in Plaks' definition is often glossed over in allegorical interpretations where it would have been useful. But for the concept of allegory I shall be employing with regard to Yu Hua, such distinction is no longer relevant since we are not dealing with allegory in the traditional sense.

Fredric Jameson's much discussed theory from 1986 of third-world literature on self as always simultaneously being national allegory, called attention to the question of allegory and Chinese literature from a new angle: 'The story of the private individual destiny is always an allegory of the embattled situation of the public third world-culture and society.' (69) Jameson's prime demonstration of his theory of allegory is a reading of three stories by Lu Xun, 'Diary of a Madman', 'The True Story of Ah Q' and 'Medicine', i.e stories written more than 70 years ago, that have all been subjected to allegorical reading by scores of critics before,

---

2) Andrew H.Plaks, 'Allegory in Hsi-yu Chi and Hung-lou Meng' in Andrew H. Plaks (ed.), *Chinese Narrative. Critical and Theoretical Essays*, Princeton University Press, 1977.

western as well as Chinese. His argument is based on a conceptual polarity between allegory (pointing to larger issues of the public and political domain) and self. He also points to the radical split in the West between the spheres of private and public, where, he says, political commitment is recontained and subjectivized.(71) Whereas this opinion may be debated, no one would question that in China the opposite has been the case – the private and poetic has been overly politicized.

Still, it is ironic that at the same time as Chinese writers and critics have been trying to change the discursive parameters away from the fusion between the political/nationalistic and the private/aesthetic towards a separation of the private and public domain, western theorists try to explain all Chinese literature as essentially oriented towards the public domain.

It is probably in this context we should see Zhang Longxi's recent critique of Jameson as somehow repeating the political allegorical reading controlled by the Chinese Communist Party (CCP) which has been dominant in China until recently, and not sufficiently stressing the ambiguity and self-reflecting side of Lu Xun, neglecting his wish to 'mould a sense of the independent and responsible individual against the effacement of the self in a repressive moral and political totality'[3] (76) What Zhang does here is, in effect, to set up a contradiction between the conception of Lu Xun as an individualist loner and the possibility of interpreting some of his texts as containing allegorical allusions to a problematique of wider national relevance. However, the fact that the CCP and other readers in China have read Lu Xun as traditional one-to-one allegories, should not prevent a more sophisticated reading of his and other modern Chinese stories as complex texts weaving together the problematics of self-identity with a heterogeneous modern notion of allegory. And surely it would be as wrong to reject the allegorical tenor of the three stories as to deny their aspects of self-probing and existential doubt.

Leaving aside the validity of Jameson's theory and the dubious implications in his designation of modern Chinese literature as simply belonging to a broad general category of

---

3) Zhang Longxi, 'Out of the Cultural Ghetto: Theory, Politics, and the Study of Chinese Literature' in *Modern China* vol. 19, no.1 January 1993.

third-world literature, his article is valuable for calling attention to the ambiguity and complexity inherent in the modern usage of the concept of allegory. He explains the difference between the traditional concept of allegory as a set of figures to be read against a one-to-one table of equivalencies, and the modern one in which 'the equivalencies are in constant change and transformation at each perpetual present in the text'. (73) He also notes the complexity and possibilities in its use with regard to Lu Xun, 'its capacity to generate a range of distinct meanings or messages simultaneously as the allegorical tenor and vehicle change places.' (74) The attraction of allegory today, he says, lies in its profoundly discontinuous spirit, as being a matter of breaks and heterogeneities, of the 'multiple polysemia of the dream rather than the homogeneous representation of the symbol'.(73)

The modern concept of allegory here expounded is quite a long way from the original concept closely associated with religious texts, primarily biblical exegesis. In the second half of the eighteenth century allegory was eclipsed by the prominence of the symbol as a designation of figural speech and came to be viewed by many, notably Goethe and Coleridge, as its antithesis. During the nineteenth century the symbol predominated and was conceived of as an expression of the unity between the representative and semantic function of language.[4] Hans Georg Gadamer has explained this as the consequence of an aesthetics which refused to distinguish between experience and the representation of this experience. Everything was united in the poetic language of genius.[5] However, by the twentieth century allegory was given a radically new interpretation in the work of Walter Benjamin.[6] Based on his studies of the baroque German Trauerspiel (1924)[7], and developed in his analysis of Charles Baudelaire he came to see the allegorical mode as dynamic and dialectical and now as

---

4) See Paul de Man: *Blindness and Insight. Essays in the Rhetoric of Contemporary Criticism* Second edition, Revised. London. Methuen 1983, p. 189.
5) Ibid., p. 188.
6) Walter Benjamin's theory of allegory was introduced in China by Zhang Xudong in 'Yuyan piping' in *Wenxue Pinglun*, 1988,4. Recently, Xue Yi has employed this modern concept of allegory in an analysis of works by Han Shaogong, Wang Anyi, Liu Heng and others. See 'Yuyan de dansheng' in *Shanghai Wenxue*, 1993,2.
7) Walter Benjamin, *The Origin of German Tragic Drama*, London 1977.

closely linked to the experience of modernity.[8] In these modern allegories the original divine relation between things and their proper meanings – their names – has been sundered.[9] Since there is no longer a common established world-view or a unified frame of reference against which to interpret allegory, it can only have subjective validity. The allegorical relationship is characterised by 'obscurities in the connection between meaning and sign' – it is a broken and arbitrary language in which 'any person, any thing, any relationship can mean anything else'.[10] In contrast to the self-contained totality of the symbolic mode, allegory does point to something outside the text. But that which it points to is no longer fixed and commonly recognized. That itself is just another 'signifier', without absolute meaning in itself.

Paul de Man is among those later literary theorists who have taken up the note of Benjamin and reflected on the modern function of allegory. To de Man allegory suggests the disjunction between the way in which the world appears in reality and the way it appears in language. 'The relationship between the allegorical sign and its meaning is not decreed by dogma.... Instead we have a relationship between signs in which the reference to their respective meanings has become of secondary importance. But this relationship between signs necessarily contains a constitutive temporal element. It remains necessary if there is to be allegory that the allegorical sign refers to another sign that precedes it.'[11] (207) In this way allegory comes to designate primarily a distance in relation to its origin, and it establishes its language in the void of this temporal difference.

The modern notion of allegory is thus related to the often noted 'gap between sign and meaning' said to be a dominant concern of modernism. But as a figural speech originating out of the traditional allegorical forms, it still retains the extratextual reference, the link to the larger social or cultural conflict. At the same time as being itself, it is also something else, but this some-

---

8) Walter Benjamin, *Charles Baudelaire: a Lyric Poet in the Era of High Capitalism*. London 1973.
9) Richard Wolin, *Walter Benjamin. An Aesthetic of Redemption*, Columbia University Press, New York 1982, p.70.
10) Michael W. Jennings, *Dialectical Images. Walter Benjamin's Theory of Literary Criticism*, Cornell University Press, 1987, p. 108.
11) Paul de Man, *Blindness and Insight*, p. 207.

thing else is now intangible or even conspicuous by its very absence. As Umberto Eco has written in reference to Kafka: 'Trial, castle, waiting, metamorphosis, torture etc. should not be understood in their immediate literal meaning. But, in contrast to allegorical constructions of the middle ages, their connotative meanings are not unambiguous, they are nor guaranteed by any encyclopedia, and they do not rest on any world order.'[12]

So in this article I suggest that the allegorical mode is indeed present in contemporary Chinese literature, even in writers who do not seem to use it consciously as the overall structuring framework of the text. Whereas works such as Liu Suola's 'Xunzhao gewang', Ah Cheng's 'King' stories and Han Shaogong's 'Bababa' seem to invite allegorical interpretation that imply concerns with the fate of the nation and national culture, also in the more traditional sense, other fictional works from the 1980s specifically challenge the very ambiguity of the modern notion of allegory. In the following I shall concentrate on the fiction of Yu Hua (born 1960), one of the distinctive contributors to the rise of experimental fiction from the mid 1980s on. As I shall show, his stories take on specific relevance when read as allegorical representations in the modernist sense of the predicament of the individual self in contemporary Chinese culture.

One Kind of Reality

Yu Hua is a prolific writer. He started publishing in 1984 and by the late 1980s he was considered among the most promising avant-garde or post-new-wave writers, regarded by many critics as perhaps the best exponent of a kind of Chinese meta-fictional or postmodernist writing.[13] He has continued to write in the 1990s and within the last two years he has published at least two novellas and one long novel, in which he seems to have changed

---

12) Umberto Eco, *Opera Aperta: Forma e indeterminazione nelle poetiche contemporanee*, Milan, Bompiani, 1962, p. 32. (Transl. A. W.-W.)
13) See for example Wang Ning, 'Hou xiandaizhuyi yu Zhongguo wenxue' in *Dangdai Dianying*,1990, 6, Y.H.Zhao, 'The Rise of Metafiction in China' in *Bulletin of Oriental and African Studies* vol. LV, 1, 1992, and also 'Yu Hua: Fiction as Subversion' in *World Literature Today* Summer 1991 by Y.H.Zhao.

his style towards a more traditional 'psychologized' narrative[14] Like much of the literature written in the late 1980s, Yu Hua's fiction of that period deeply problematizes and reflects the predicament of identity-loss and cultural breakdown.[15] But in contrast to the composite fragmenting selves created by contemporaries such as Can Xue or Liu Suola, Yu Hua's surgical knife cuts the connection between sign and meaning by presenting his characters as nothing but signifiers for an absent self.[16]

Yu Hua, photographed in 1994.

In several of his stories the narration, or part of it, is carried on through the subjectivist perceptions of an insane person. In

---

14) See 'Huhan yu xi yu' (Shouts and Fine Rain), in *Shouhuo*, 1991, 6 (changpian xiaoshuo) and 'Huozhe' (Living) in *Shouhuo*, 1992, 6 (zhongpian xiaoshuo).
15) Anne Wedell-Wedellsborg, 'The Changing Concept of Self as Reflected in Chinese Literature of the 1980s' in Viviane Alleton and Alexeï Volkov (eds), *Notions et perceptions du changement en Chine*, Paris 1994.
16) For a discussion of Yu Hua's work and Chinese critics' evaluation of it in the context of the relationship between modernity and nationalism see Wendy Larson, 'Literary Modernism and Nationalism in Post-Mao China' in Wendy Larson and Anne Wedell-Wedellsborg (eds), *Inside Out. Modernism and Postmodernism in Chinese Literary Culture*, Aarhus University Press, 1993.

'Yijiubaliu nian' (1986) it is a middle-school teacher who disappeared without a trace during the Cultural Revolution, and who in the story suddenly turns up as a beggar in the small town where he used to live. His wife has remarried and his daughter taken a new name. The school teacher has turned mad and become obsessed with his old hobby – methods of punishment and torture in ancient China ranging from cutting off the nose and castration to being torn apart by five horses, all of which he manages in the course of the story, to inflict upon himself in a mixture of reality and fantasy. He also imagines himself torturing people in the street. The text cuts between the madman and his former family, who do not recognize him, but who are strangely affected by his presence. At the end of the story when the madman has died, they feel an unexplained relief. In the final section, however, another madman is approaching the town....

In this story, the selves of both the madman and his daughter – both of whom are depicted from the inside, though in the third person – are 'flat' signifiers, their thoughts nothing but surface registration of phenomena, in the case of the madman meticulously detailed descriptions of bodily mutilation. The frequent repetition of the verb 'kandao' (to see) detached from any kind of reflective reactions on the part of the subject, is a constant reminder of this. As I shall show below, this stylistic device is even more conspicuous in another text by Yu Hua.

The title '1986' of course recalls George Orwell and the torture and dehumanization of a totalitarian society. But on a different level it can be read as an allegory of Yu Hua's view of what we may call 'the self of Chinese history'. The mad school teacher (the choice of profession with its deep connotations to Confucian culture is hardly a coincidence) represents the suppressed, dark, violent, destructive forces, which are refused recognition in daily-life consciousness. And since they are never faced, except as surface phenomena, they are bound to return again and again. The madman's sado-masochism – a result of the torture and persecution inflicted upon him and now the sole constituent element of his identity – is then symbolic of the evil of Chinese history which in a vicious circle repeats itself, the Cultural Revolution being merely its latest expression. The elimination of individual identity in this and other stories by Yu Hua may therefore be read as a new kind of investigation into the negative aspects of 'national essence' in which the self is seen as having suffered defeat.

Yu Hua's most consistent demonstration of human alienation and absence or eradication of a 'self' is his long story 'Xianshi yizhong' (One kind of reality) from 1988.[17] According to Zeng Zhennan it is to some extent based on real events which took place in a small town in south China.[18] The dramatic plot of death and revenge between two brothers could indeed be the stuff of high tragedy: the four-year-old son of one of the brothers happens to kill his baby cousin. The baby's father then kills the four-year old, whose father in turn kills his brother – in a very special manner. He is caught by the police and executed in a scene reminiscent of the execution of Ah Q. In the meantime their senile old mother with whom they live also dies without anybody noticing. The lives of the two brothers, their wives and children, take place in an emotional void, day in and day out according to a dull routine, eating meals, going to work etc. Despite the dramatic events fuelling the narrative dynamics, at no point are any of the characters shown to feel the emotions one would normally associate with such horrible events. On the contrary, throughout the story expressions of emotion, such as smiling, crying and laughing, are explicitly shown to be separated from the inner motivations we would expect. This is most magnificently demonstrated in the scene where one brother kills the other by tying him to a tree, smearing his feet with stew, and letting a little dog lick them, till he simply dies from laughter. The lack of emotion and moral reflection on the part of the characters is substituted by their attention to surface detail – ants crawling in the blood, a leaf swaying in the wind – or to physical phenomena: the old woman feeling her bones break like chopsticks, moss growing inside and her stomach rotting. They all seem to live in total alienation, having lost touch with reality, their actions generated by some pre-existing pattern, which simply is there, reducing these people to robots.

---

17) See Yu Hua, *Shiba sui chu men yuan xing*, Zuojia chubanshe, Beijing, 1989, pp.200–258. I have also had access to a forthcoming translation of the story by Helen Wang to be published in an anthology of Chinese avant-garde fiction edited by Zhao Yiheng. The translations in this paper follow Helen Wang.

18) See 'Xianshi yizhong ji qita' in *Beijing Wenxue*, 1988,2.

Of course the Chinese reader may see the driving force in the story as the underlying traditional idea of the necessity of having male descendants. But this is never actually consciously part of considerations inside the characters, and not explicitly mentioned until the very end of the story, when we learn that the testicles of the executed were transplanted on to a young man, who nine months later became the father of a son.

The individual selves of the persons in the story are completely without an inner core, or even a self which is split or fragmented. They are nothing but physical surface (or substance), motivated by, in Yu Hua's eyes, some deep structure emanating from the darkness and violence of Chinese history or culture. Seen in this light, the final scene where the executed brother's body is being dissected and taken totally apart, from skin to intestines and skeleton, leaving nothing, is deeply ironic. Even the totality of a physical self is denied. All that remains is the perpetual reproduction of compulsory structures, as symbolized by his transplanted testicles.

Zhao Yiheng has called the story 'a scathing satire on the Chinese myth of family'.[19] And there is certainly an unmitigated subversive irony in this presentation of the traditional identity forming structure – the family of several generations living together (here in its reduced modern version where women go to work) – as bound together by nothing but shared meals and indifference. An indifference whose other side turns out to be eye-for-eye-tooth-for-tooth aggression. Lacking authority to guide and suppress, aggressive violence erupts and becomes the external signifier of – nothing! not even hatred or anger.[20]

On the level of its overall structure we could read this story as a modernist allegory on the 'self' of the Chinese family. Just as for example the character Kurtz in Joseph Conrad's 'The Heart of Darkness' can be seen as a representative western self, who has disintegrated into the random lusts that his persona had previously denied, so Yu Hua's family has disintegrated into the negative, inhuman constitutive determinants that were previously controlled and repressed by the Confucian persona.

---

19) See 'Yu Hua: Fiction as Subversion' p. 418.
20) To some this may recall theories of Lucian Pye of the repression of aggression as a fundamental feature of Chinese identity formation. Lucian Pye, *The Spirit of Chinese Politics*, Cambridge Massachusetts, 1968.

In the context of this paper we might also say that the story is an allegorical representation of the larger cultural problem: the emptying of old moral norms without anything to replace them. The motivational structures are there but largely unexplained, even in terms of repressed agression, thus creating a vacuum in the text where morality and reflection should have been. This vacuum is very often 'filled up' by visual attention to surface. This visual attention is nearly always that of the characters, not of the implied author. The reader is made to follow the gazes of the persons as they move from one surface to another, often calling forth other surfaces in a metonymical chain of associations.

The constant and monotonous repetition of the verb 'kandao', to see, to look at, to watch, stresses the visual character of the text, and becomes emblematic of the externality of the self's relation to reality. He or she sees, registers, but doesn't connect, understand, feel, reflect or search for meaning. And when the verb 'gandao', to feel, is used it is almost exclusively referring to physical sensations, or to some vague indistinct impression:

> (The old lady said) 'It's like there is moss growing in my guts'. The two brothers began to think of the moss that worms climb over, that grows on the sides of wells, and on the corners of broken down walls, with its glistening greenness.....(199)

And a few paragraphs later:

> (Pipi) was too small, so he had to strain his neck to see the windowpane, and the rain outside that was beating on the glass, twisting and turning like worms as it slid downwards.

> Breakfast was over. Shangang watched as his wife wiped the table. Shanfeng watched as his wife went into the bedroom with the baby in her arms, leaving the door open, then came straight out again and into the kitchen. Shanfeng looked round at his sister-in-law's hand as she wiped the table. On the back of her hand were the veins that sometimes stood out and sometimes didn't. Shanfeng watched for a while then looked up and over towards the crisscrossing drops of water on the window, and said to his brother: 'It feels like it's been raining a hundred years'.(200)

Here the image of moving worms serves to metonymically link the bodily dissolution of the old woman to the rain and to the wormlike veins on the hand of the sister-in-law. At the opening of the story we were told that 'as it had been raining for over a week now, the two brothers felt that fine days were as far away as their childhood days' indicating the absence of any reflective memory, and perhaps a subconscious sense of disintegration. The identical 'thoughts' of the two also point to the lack of individual personality. But the worm-image does not really 'stand for' anything, neither does the picture of the shiny green well which pops up again in Shangang's mind when he sees his son kicked to death. If it has any function it is to signify a hole, an absence of something – of feelings perhaps or recognition of reality.[21]

The gaze is important in this story not only as signifying externality, but also to show the lack of human contact. Despite the profusion of gazes, very rarely do two pairs of eyes meet, and when they do it is mostly creating unease or implying a threat. In view of the importance attached in western psychological theory (Freud and Lacan) to the 'being seen' for identity formation, the western reader can hardly avoid associating the averted gazes and oblique glances with a state of incomplete identity-formation.

But even more significant is the way the gaze or the visual movement is employed to highlight the gap between object/event and the perception of it. In Yu Hua`s texts this gap exists as a virtual time-lag, which sometimes is never caught up with. For example when the mother of the baby first killed finds her son lying dead, she first notices the blood which seems unreal, looks at the glistening sky and goes inside. Here her eyes start to search the room, swaying from the wardrobe, then sliding from the glasstop on the round table, on to the sofa and from there to the rest of the room and finally to the cradle. Only through the visual impression of the empty cradle does she come to think of the child lying outside. (207)

The time-lag separating action – consciousness – action is a recurring feature in the story. The glance or gaze focused not on the 'thing' itself or the face itself, but beside it – on the door rather than the room, on the 'seal print' of the wound on the pillow or on

---

21) The well-image could also indicate an ironic allegorical reference to Mengzi's famous argument in favour of the inborn goodness of man: whoever sees a child about to fall into a well is bound to feel alarm and distress.

the ants crawling rather than on the blood itself, on the blood rather than the wound, and on the wound rather than on the body – becomes emblematic of the subject's feeble and distorted relation to reality. Or one might even say that the averted, unseeing gaze becomes an allegory of the self lost in the abyss between sign and meaning.

But the function of this narrative device can, by extension, be transposed to a higher level. If we regard the text as a projection of the narrator's gaze, then he too, throughout the text, could be said to focus 'beside' the full real human being, showing only an external shell. Until finally, in the dissection scene, he redirects his gaze and – with pitch-black nihilist irony – tells us in every detail what is inside.

The narrative structure is characterized by a number of repetitions. Repetitions of verbs, the most conspicuous being as noted 'kandao', and of descriptive verb/adjectives, such as 'shan', glistening (again a word associative of surface, repellent of penetrative gazes) the glistening of blood, bodies and of sunlight enhancing the impression of oppressive monotony, the blazing sun recalling *L'étranger* (Camus), a classic of human alienation. But also repetitions of images and situations. Hillis Miller in *Fiction and Repetition* (1982) distinguishes between two forms of repetition, one of them closely related to Benjamin's concept of allegory.[22] The first type is that in which the repetition is 'grounded' and, like the mimetic copy, establishing its validity by its truth of correspondence to what it copies. The second type of repetition however, like the modern allegory, is 'ungrounded', based on differences, arising out of the interplay between opaquely similar things. In the gap of the difference between two similar things a third thing which Benjamin calls 'Bild' image, is created. 'The image is the meaning generated by the echoing of two dissimilar things in the second form of repetition'. (9)

In 'Xianshi yizhong' the inner bodily dissolution, so vividly visualized in the old grandmother's imagination as 'a pile of higgledly piggledly bits of broken bone crushing together any old way. Her foot bones might be pushing out her stomach, and her arm bones could be sticking into her overgrown moss guts,' (205)

---

22) Hillis Miller, *Fiction and Repetition. Seven English Novels*, Blackwell, Oxford, 1982.

is repeated in the final scene where Shangang's body is being taken apart. In the tension between these two descriptions, between the imagined and the real disintegration, arises an allegorical image of a self reduced to physicality. The licking of the baby's blood by first Pipi's mother and then Pipi, both of them on all four relishing the blood, already signifies their animalistic nature (not to mention the cannibalistic) but the third repetition of licking, this time by the dog employed as an innocent tool for killing, ironically stresses the lack of distinction, further underscored by the baby's mother's desire to 'bite to death' Pipi.(218)

The image of wild grass is repeated several times, along with that of the well, as a mental picture blocking or rather substituting thought or feelings at critical points in the text. In the scene of the execution it is repeated again, this time however in a different way. As Shangang approaches the execution ground he sees the concrete green stretch of grass and also 'the crowd of people standing like wild grass'. And just a few lines later he feels the actual wild grass tickling inside his trouser legs and discovers 'the crowds on all sides like tall grass'.(246) The crowd of spectators, by metonymical displacement, have become the wild grass. And as Shangang realizes for a moment where he is, he also remembers that he himself used to be among the spectators rushing to the front row every time a criminal was executed. So he too is the crowd, the grass. This final and different repetition of the grass-image casts a new light on its previous occurrences, and we come to see it as a metaphor of the lack of subjectivity.

This scene and its implications for the problematics of subjectivity evokes in the reader another famous literary execution: the execution of Lu Xun's Ah Q, doubtless the most analysed scene in modern Chinese literature. Like Ah Q, Shangang turns his gaze towards the crowd, but where Ah Q sees the 'dull yet penetrating eyes' of the crowd 'more terrible even than the wolf',[23] Shangang's unfocused glance 'floated on past the hair of a short person, and on past the ears of a tall one'. Lu Xun's shift in narrative focus from criminal/victim to crowd noticed by Anderson, Huang, and others, and the narrator's 'intervention' (Anderson) on behalf of Ah Q – the cry for help, have no parallel

---

23) *Selected Stories of Lu Hsun*, Foreign Languages Press, Peking, 1978, third printing, p.111.

here.[24] On the contrary, Shangang is mercilessly exposed in his pathetic lack of self-consciousness and dull incomprehension as to the reality of the situation. He even believes he will be taken to hospital and saved when his ear is blown off by the first shot. Ah Q at least for a moment had the subjective intention of giving the crowd a good performance and acting out the role of criminal. Shangang, by contrast, does actually give a good show, but quite unintentionally, making the crowds laugh by his ridiculous behaviour: wanting to urinate and, his hands tied up, having to ask the guard to take out his penis. The guard tells him to piss in his trousers, but nothing comes out. And later when after the first shot he keeps asking whether he is dead or alive. (The first episode is actually a kind of reversed repetition of a previous one in which, before he was caught by the police, he also wasn't able to urinate, forgot to put his penis back into his trousers and was laughed at by the people in the street.) So this time the crowds had not 'followed him for nothing'. (Cf. Ah Q). For Ah Q the empty role was still there to enter, had he been able to. For Shangang not even the role is available as substitute for individuality.

So in this story the original divine relation between things and their proper meaning has indeed been sundered, just as the last killing, the execution, in Shangang's mind is separated from its intended 'meaning' and completely dissociated from anything he has done.

This discrepancy or gap not only works on the epistemological level, but is reflected in the specific tension on the level of textuality created by the peculiar combination of the highly subjectivist point of view and the detached, cold, objective eye of the narrator. This narrative technique serves effectively to highlight the conspicuous absence of a voice or consciousness to condemn, moralize or at least get shocked. This is further underscored by the contrast between the clear, straight, almost relentlessly unhesitating voice of the narrator and the incomprehension and blurred perceptions of the characters.

---

24) Marston Anderson, *The Limits of Realism. Chinese Fiction in the Revolutionary Period*, University of California Press, 1990, pp.80–85, and Martin Weizong Huang, 'The Inescapable Predicament. The Narrator and His Discourse' in 'The True Story of Ah Q' in *Modern China* vol.16 no.4 October 1990, pp. 441–2.

As neither implied author, nor narrator, nor any of the characters seem to react 'normally' to events, this reaction is left entirely to the reader. Yet, as I read the story, the emotional repulsion one is left with after the execution scene, which might well have been the last, is curiously sabotaged by the final dissection scene which functions as an absurdly ironic 'overkill'. Here no gazes are averted but directed straight at the process of bodily mutilation. Narrator and characters alike watch unperturbed, and the reader is forced to join in, as Shangang's body is being 'scattered' (Ah Q again) through an act of extreme visual violence – taking an individual physically apart – which is not violence, just some people doing their job.

But we might be allowed to speculate a little further: in view of the predominance of averted gazes throughout the text, we might perhaps by analogy interpret this last gaze as also 'averted', signifying that there is something absent that we do not see in this story, something beyond mere physicality and violence – be it a deeper reason for what happened, or even a genuinely feeling and reflecting human being.

Several Chinese critics have also interpreted this story as having allegorical connotations though they do not always use the term *yuyan*. For example Zhang Yiwu and Zeng Zhennan whose different readings indicate the range within which an allegorical resonance can be perceived.

Zhang Yiwu sees the break and disruption between language and meaning as the most important thing in the text.[25] 'Behind the orderly world of language raves the disorderly world of actuality and meaning'. (43) Thus Yu Hua's text deconstructs itself, as language destroys and dissolves meaning, and meaning also destroys and dissolves language. This shows man's desire to break the confines of the imposed order/language. In Yu Hua's work violence is subversive as a way of mocking and opposing the rule of language, and it becomes an 'omen'/'sign' of the fate and inescapable predicament (*wunai*) of mankind. Zhang Yiwu interprets Yu Hua's fiction as allegories of a sort (though he does not use the word) for modern man's inability to 'grasp himself' submerged as he is in the dual oppressive forces of linguistic order and violence. This, he argues, implies a criticism of traditional western and May Fourth humanism and its view of 'man'

---

25) See Zhang, "Ren' de weiji' *Dushu* 1988,12.

as the powerful centre of the world. (46) Zhang Yiwu, who is to be counted among 'avant-garde' critics, here posits himself in a role characteristic of the ambivalence inherent in much literary criticism in the late 1980s: on the one hand, his analysis of Yu Hua's texts is obviously inspired by readings of 'objectivist' post-structuralist and deconstructionist theories imported from the West; on the other hand he places his reading within an openly prescriptive framework of what is needed for China in its present historical situation.

Zeng Zhennan, somewhat more aligned with the establishment, proposes a more traditional allegorical reading of 'Xianshi yizhong'.[26] To him the allegorical resonance is not to be found on the level of textuality in the allegorical implications of the tension between language and violence, but rather in the way the plot functions as a kind of moralizing fable, exposing man's creaturely side. This, Zeng says, is how senseless aggression works, and the story might as well be about wars between social classes or nations.(72)

China and the Self

The two Chinese readings of Yu Hua referred to above illustrate how differently it is possible to derive allegorical meaning from the same story. To most people Yu Hua's story would hardly qualify as allegory in the purely traditional sense that can be objectively and consensually interpreted. But read as a modernist subjective allegory, as a matter of 'the multiple polysemia of the dream', it does, in its own way, point to the distance which has invaded language. On the surface level the story certainly deals with the private individual destiny, and as I read it, it is a story deeply concerned with the problematique of self-identity, even if this self-identity is brought to the fore precisely because of its absence. Following Fredric Jameson that alone should make it an allegory of Chinese culture and society.

It could well be argued that Yu Hua's story is as much about the lack of a social identity as of a private. It is an allegorical tale with clear references to Chinese social norms, yet its main concern

---

26) See Zeng Zhennan, 'Xianshi yizhong ji qita'.

is nevertheless with the (absent) self. The question of identity and what happens when you lose it is strongly connected with the issue of the devaluation of traditional structures. But this problem of Chinese culture and society is here seen through the predicament of the self, rather than the other way around. I would therefore propose to turn Jameson's argument upside down and suggest a change of priorities. So, instead of saying: even when it is about the self it is also about China, it would be more appropriate to say: even when it is about China it is primarily about the self (i.e. for the literature of the 1980s on, if such vast generalizations have any meaning at all). The impression gained from reading not only stories by Yu Hua, but also by many other writers such as those mentioned earlier (Liu Suola, Ah Cheng, Han Shaogong) is that the image of a collectively perceived entity of China, as previously insisted on in official communist party rhetoric and reflected in socialist realism, has collapsed. Cultural identity has become inextricably linked to the self, it is only through the filter of the confused, disrupted or even absent self that Chinese culture can be perceived.[27]

References

Anderson, Marston, *The Limits of Realism. Chinese Fiction in the Revolutionary Period*, University of California Press, Berkeley, 1990.

Benjamin, Walter, *The Origin of German Tragic Drama*, (transl. John Osborne), New Left Books, London 1977.

Benjamin, Walter, *Charles Baudelaire: a Lyric Poet in the Era of High Capitalism*. (transl. Harry Zohn), New Left Books, London, 1973.

de Man, Paul, *Blindness and Insight. Essays in the Rhetoric of Contemporary Criticism* (Second edition, revised), London, Methuen, 1983.

Eco, Umberto, *Opera Aperta: Forma e indeterminazione nelle poetiche contemporanee* Milan, Bompiani, 1962.

---

27) See also Wendy Larson, 'Literary Modernism and Nationalism in Post-Mao China'.

Huang, Martin Weizong, 'The Inescapable Predicament. The Narrator and His Discourse in The True Story of Ah Q' in *Modern China*, vol.16, no.4 October, 1990.

Jameson, Fredric, 'Third-World Literature in the Era of Multinational Capitalism' *Social Text*, 15, Fall 1986.

Jennings, Michael W., *Dialectical Images. Walter Benjamin's Theory of Literary Criticism*, Cornell University Press, 1987.

Larson, Wendy: 'Literary Modernism and Nationalism in Post-Mao China' in Wendy Larson and Anne Wedell-Wedellsborg, (eds), *Inside Out. Modernism and Postmodernism in Chinese Literary Culture*, Aarhus University Press, 1993.

Miller, Hillis, *Fiction and Repetition. Seven English Novels*, Blackwell, Oxford 1982.

Plaks, Andrew H., 'Allegory in Hsi-yu Chi and Hung-lou Meng' in Andrew H. Plaks, (ed.), *Chinese Narrative. Critical and Theoretical Essays*, Princeton University Press, 1977.

Pye, Lucian, *The Spirit of Chinese Politics*, Cambridge, Massachusetts, 1968.

Selected Stories of Lu Hsun, Foreign Languages Press, Peking, 1978, third printing.

Wang Ning, 'Hou xiandaizhuyi yu Zhongguo wenxue', *Dangdai Dianying*, 1990,6.

Wedell-Wedellsborg, Anne, 'The Changing Concept of Self as Reflected in Chinese Literature of the 1980s' in Viviane Alleton et Alexeï Volkov (eds), *Notions et perceptions du changement en Chine*, College de France, Paris 1994.

Wolin, Richard, *Walter Benjamin. An Aesthetic of Redemption*, Columbia University Press, New York, 1982.

Xue Yi, 'Yuyan de dansheng', *Shanghai Wenxue*, 1993, 2.

Y.H. Zhao, 'Yu Hua: Fiction as Subversion' in *World Literature Today*, Summer 1991.

Y.H. Zhao, 'The Rise of Metafiction in China' in *Bulletin of Oriental and African Studies* vol. LV, 1, 1992.

Yu Hua, 'Huozhe', (Living), *Shouhuo*,1992, 6.

Yu Hua, *Shiba sui chu men yuan xing*, Zuojia chubanshe, Beijing, 1989.

Yu Hua, 'Huhan yu xi yu', (Shouts and Fine Rain), *Shouhuo*, 1991,6.

Zeng Zhennan, 'Xianshi yizhong ji qita', *Beijing Wenxue*,1988,2.

Zhang Xudong, 'Yuyan piping', *Wenxue Pinglun*, 1988,4.

Zhang Longxi, 'Out of the Cultural Ghetto: Theory, Politics, and the Study of Chinese Literature' in *Modern China* vol. 19, no. 1 January, 1993.

Zhang Yiwu, '"Ren" de weiji', *Dushu* 1988,12.

The Religious and Cultural Identity of Rabindranath Tagore
Some stray preliminary remarks on a vast theme

Sergei D. Serebriany

Rabindranath Tagore (1861–1941) is (or at least was) one of the twentieth-century world celebrities. But being famous, especially world famous, does not necessarily mean being really known and understood. In Tagore's case, his fame outside India (at times turning virtually into a cult) was very often based on wrong (or at best incomplete) ideas about his personality and cultural background, on wrong apprehensions of his identity, so to say.

Speaking about Tagore and 'identity', I may be permitted to distinguish between 'identity for oneself' (what the person himself thinks he is) and 'identity for others' (what other people think the person in question is).[1] In Tagore's case (as probably is the case with many a person), what others thought about him very often strongly influenced on what he thought about himself, and, with time, he often had to discard such 'induced' elements of his identity.[2]

---

1) Cf. the analysis of the 'identity' concept in the introduction by Lisbeth Littrup.
2) Western conceptions and misconceptions about Tagore are reviewed in the book by Alex Aronson, *Rabindranath through Western Eyes*, Allahabad, Kitabistan, 1943. The dynamic interaction between Tagore's ideas about himself, India, Asia, and the world at large, on the one hand, and various receptions of the poet's ideas in Japan, China, and India on the other, is traced and analysed by Stephen N. Hay in his book *Asian Ideas of East and West, Tagore and His Critics in Japan, China, and India*, Cambridge, Mass., Harvard University Press, 1970.

Indeed, for a historian, Tagore's identity, in both its aspects, is a very complex and variable entity, which kept changing both during his life time and later, together with the historical changes in South Asia. For most outsiders, Tagore was and is an 'Indian', a definition of his identity with which he certainly agreed. Next, he must be described and actually described himself as a 'Bengali' (just like, say, Hans Christian Andersen may be described as both a European and a Dane). In 1947, when the South Asian subcontinent was partitioned into India and Pakistan, Tagore's identity was also, as it were, partitioned. In India (since 1950, the Republic of India) Tagore remained a great figure of all-Indian significance, which was emphasized by choosing a song by Tagore ('Jana-gaṇa-mana...') for the national anthem. In predominantly Muslim East Bengal, which became East Pakistan, Tagore became a great problem, almost coextensive with the problem of the cultural identity of East Bengal's Bengali Muslims: were they Muslims in the first place who happened to speak the Bengali language or were they Bengalis in the first place who happened to profess Islam? In 1971–72, with the formation of Bangladesh, an answer to this question was given, and yet another song of Tagore's ('Our golden Bengal') was made the national anthem of a newly independent state in South Asia.

It means that Tagore's legacy transcends the differences between Bengali Hindus and Bengali Muslims, though it may be presumed that for Bengalis with different identities Tagore's own identity should look different. For all Bengalis, in any case, Tagore is and will remain one of the creators of their language. This is his abiding identity in terms of linguistic, literary and cultural history.

As for Tagore himself (i.e. as a specific human being, rather than a historic figure), descending to the third level of description (after an 'Indian' and a 'Bengali'),[3] we may call him a 'Hindu' inasmuch as he was neither a Muslim, nor a Buddhist, nor a Christian, nor a member of any other world religion. As I will show shortly, Tagore, as late as 1912 (but probably not always in later years), accepted such an identification, though, it is true, he might have given to the very word 'Hindu' an interpretation

---

3) To be less controversial, I should probably write: 'coming up to another dimension of description'. It may be argued that 'being a Hindu' is a more comprehensive kind of identity than 'being a Bengali' or even 'being an Indian'.

which most other Hindus would not accept. For that matter, there is hardly a definition of 'a Hindu' that would be acceptable to all those who call themselves Hindus.

Moving further, we may choose either Tagore's caste identity or his 'sectarian' identity (which two types of identity often overlap in India). By caste, Tagore was a Brahman, but, again, one of a very special kind. His ancestors disgraced themselves in the eyes of orthodox Hindus by too close contact with Muslim rulers of Bengal and were given the derogatory name of 'Pirali Brahmans'. Their status (identity) within the Hindu society was rather ambiguous: for orthodox Brahmans they were a kind of outcaste, but for lower castes they remained Brahmans, addressed as 'Thakur' ('Lord'), whence the Anglicized form 'Tagore' which became the family name. From his Pirali ancestors Tagore inherited a complex consciousness (and an actual status) of being both elitist and outcaste, simultaneously rooted in tradition and unorthodox.

By the end of the seventeenth century one of Tagore's great-grandfathers settled near the place where later Calcutta developed and started profitable transactions with Europeans. As Tagore himself once put it: 'My... ancestors came floating to Calcutta upon the earliest tide of the fluctuating fortune of the East India Company. The unconventional code of life for our family has been a confluence of three cultures, the Hindu, Mohammedan and British'.[4] Thus cultural synthesis was also part of the poet's family traditions.

Rabindranath's grandfather, 'Prince' Dwarkanath Tagore (1794-1846), one of the richest men in Calcutta, was a friend of another unorthodox Brahman, Rammohan Ray (1772-1833), who founded by the end of his life the Brahmo-samaj (literally: 'The society of the worshippers of the Brahman'). Started actually as a kind of society for free religious discussions, the Brahmo-samaj later developed into a very influential socio-religious movement which attracted many members of the new Bengali 'intelligentsia'.[5] And it was Rabindranath's father, Debendranath Tagore (1817-1905), who for many years headed and guided the

---

4) R. Tagore, *The Religion of Man*, London etc., Unwin Paperbacks, 1988, p. 105.
5) See e.g.: D. Kopf, *The Brahmo Samaj and the Shaping of the Modern Indian Mind*, Princeton, Princeton University Press, 1979.

Brahmo-samaj. In a nutshell, the Brahmo-samaj was an attempt at a religious synthesis between Hindu, Muslim and Christian traditions, though both Rammohan Ray and Debendranath Tagore claimed that they just restored Hinduism in its pristine purity. Orthodox Hindus considered the 'Brahmos' as apostates, and for the 'Brahmos' themselves their relations with Hindus were always a problem, which could be solved in different ways.

In 1912 Tagore wrote an essay in Bengali under the title 'Atma-parichay'. The eminent Bengali man of letters Buddhadev Bose translated this title as 'Introducing Oneself',[6] but we may as well translate it as 'Identifying Oneself' or '[The Problem of our] own Identity'. Tagore addresses the problem of how the Brahmos should identify themselves vis-a-vis Hindus. Are the Brahmos Hindus or something altogether different (as some of them claim)? The essay contains a lot of ingenious (if not always fully convincing) arguments, all of which cannot be analysed here. But the central point is that the Brahmos are Hindus, because being a Hindu means, according to Tagore, just belonging to a particular cultural tradition from which one cannot possibly tear oneself away. To quote Tagore (in B.Bose's translation):

> There is no denying that I am historically a Hindu, that is a fact which is outside the area of my personal choice.[7]
>
> Can I cease to be a Hindu just because most Hindus deny me that name and I too deny it to myself?... The creed we have chosen [i.e. the creed of the Brahmo-samaj - S.D.S.] is universal and yet it belongs to Hinduism, for our mind is Hindu and we could not have arrived at this universality but by thinking it out in our Hindu way... Deep within our beings has entered all we have received as Hindus; it is a part of our flesh and blood and woven into the pattern of our sensibilities.[8]

Tagore was quite aware of the fact that many, if not most Hindus had different ideas about the Brahmos and about what it meant to be a Hindu. But Tagore claimed to know better than orthodox Hindus themselves what they, Hindus, really were, because 'it is

---

6) R. Tagore, 'Introducing Oneself', *Quest. A Quarterly of Inquiry, Criticism and Ideas*, Calcutta, May 1961: 9-17.
7) Ibid., p. 11.
8) Ibid., p. 17.

common knowledge that what one knows oneself to be is not invariably true'.[9] Surely, this kind of argument could be turned against Tagore himself.

The special kind of emphasis in this essay must have been conditioned by the special kind of audience (the Brahmos) to which it was addressed. Elsewhere Tagore talked and wrote, it seems, more about India and Indians in general (or about Bengal and Bengalis in general) than about Hinduism and Hindus. The relations and conflicts between the Brahmos and the Hindus were only one among so many problematic oppositions and contrasts in India. The generation of Tagore had to face the task of defining not only the identities of this or that social group, but the identity of India as a whole.

Now we may take for granted the existence of India (the Republic of India) as one state ('nation') among others. But when Tagore came into this world, it was all too fresh in everybody's memory that what was called India had been just recently 'collected' by the British power from many pieces (most of which, though, had been also at one time or another parts of the Mughal empire, 'collected' by other foreigners, the Mughals). In 1888, Sir John Strachey, one of those who ruled India, wrote:

> This is the first and most essential thing to learn about India – that there is not and never was an India, or even any country of India, possessing, according to European ideas, any sort of unity, physical, political, social or religious... That men of the Punjab, Bengal, the North-Western Provinces, and Madras, should ever feel they belong to one great nation, is impossible.[10]

And yet, in 1947, only six years after Tagore's death, there appeared independent India and Pakistan. Tagore was one of those who contributed substantially to what A.T. Embree calls 'India's search for national identity', though what was actually 'found' in 1947 and later did not exactly coincided with what Tagore had 'sought'.

---

9) Ibid., p. 16.
10) Sir John Strachey, *India*, London, Kegan Paul, 1888, pp. 5-8. Quoted from A. T. Embree, *India's Search for National Identity*, Delhi, Chanakya Publications, 1980, p. 17.

Sisirkumar Ghose, an eminent Bengali scholar, in his book on Tagore, recently published in the series 'Makers of Indian Literature', makes the following statement: 'Not just one of the makers of modern Indian literature, Rabindranath Tagore was also a maker of the modern Indian mind and civilization'.[11] We may take it as an exaggeration of a fellow-Bengali, but there is, no doubt, some truth in this claim.

Tagore was first and foremost a poet, and he stressed this himself many times both in his poems and in his prose writings. It would be misleading to call him a philosopher (inasmuch as this word implies systematic and consistent thinking). Nevertheless it fell to Tagore's lot to articulate the ideas (not always perhaps exclusively his own) which were both to explain to his fellow Indians their country's past (as well as the present) and suggest her ways to the future. In other words, the ideal of post-British, post-colonial India, her ideal future identity, so to say, had to be worked out. Meeting this challenge, Tagore articulated rather an elaborate philosophy of Indian history and culture, expressed in a number of essays and poems, as well as in his most famous novel *Gora*, published in 1910. According to Tagore, India was de-stined to be a meeting ground of various cultures, and her task, indeed her genius, was to evolve out of them a harmonious whole, which would be a nucleus of the future all-world (global) cultural synthesis. On the political plane, Tagore hoped that India (now we must say South Asia) would not follow the western way of developing separate egotistic 'national' states and would pass straight from being a 'non-nation' to what may be called a 'post-national' stage. To implement these ideas, Tagore founded, in 1918, a university called 'Vishva-bharati', which name may be translated as 'universally Indian' or 'Indian as universal'.

As I have already shown, Tagore, as late as 1912, did not mind being identified as a Hindu. But in the same essay he gave the word 'Hindu' such an interpretation which is rather like that ideal type of an 'Indian' which appears in Tagore's other writings. And he himself may be described as a kind of anticipation of that ideal future Indian. Or, to put it another way, Tagore's ideal of India (the ideal identity of India that he suggested to his contemporaries) correlated with what he himself aspired to be,

---

11) S. Ghose, *Rabindranath Tagore*, New Delhi, Sahitya Akademi, 1986, p. 114.

with his own ideal identity. The German author H. Keyserling wrote in 1931:

> Rabindranath... is the great model of the full-grown oecumenic Indian of centuries to come. In this he should mean much the same to India as Goethe has meant and means to Germany.[12]

But it would be wrong to suppose that Tagore was constantly preoccupied with the issues of India's political or even cultural identity. From his youth till his last days he was rather egocentric (which may be considered normal for a poet) and often admitted this himself, sometimes as a matter of fact, sometimes with a kind of remorse. He was always much more concerned with the problems of his own personal identity, and not so much in terms of history (cultural or otherwise), but in terms of eternity, in absolute terms, so to say. This may be described as the issue of Tagore's religious identity.

He himself wrote not a little about his religious views and his religious evolution. The lectures delivered in Oxford in 1930 and later published as a book titled *The Religion of Man* are usually taken as the latest and most detailed (though not the best) exposition of his religious views in English. It is indeed not an easy book to read through, but some passages are striking and revealing. The main theme, that is elaborated in various ways through the book, is the individual nature of the poet's religion (though based mostly on the *Upanishads*, again in his individual interpretation). Here are some key quotations.

> Man's history 'is the history of his strenuous answers in various forms to the question... "What am I?"... But Man has taken centuries to discuss the question of his own true nature and has not yet come to a conclusion'.[13]

> ... My life... has always realized its religion through a process of growth and not by the help of inheritance or importation.[14]

> ...It is evident that my religion is a poet's religion, and neither that of an orthodox man of piety nor that of a theologian. Its

---

12) *The Golden Book of Tagore*, ed. by Ramananda Chatterjee, Calcutta, 1931, p. 127.
13) R. Tagore, *The Religion of Man*, p. 38.
14) Ibid., p. 56.

touch comes to me through the same unseen and trackless channel as does the inspiration of my songs.[15]

I have already made the confession that my religion is a poet's religion. All that I feel about it is from vision and not from knowledge. Frankly, I acknowledge that I cannot satisfactorily answer any questions about evil, or about what happens after death.[16]

I have my conviction that in religion, and also in the arts, that which is common to a group is not important. Indeed, very often it is a contagion of mutual imitation. After a long struggle with the feeling that I was using a mask to hide the living face of truth, I gave up my connections with our church [i.e. with the Brahmo-samaj - S.D.S.].[17]

Let me assert my faith by saying that this world, consisting of what we call animate and inanimate things, has found its culmination in man, its best expression.[18]

We can never go beyond Man in all that we know and feel...',[19] but 'any limited view of man would... be an incomplete view. He could not reach his finality as a mere Citizen or Patriot, for neither City nor Country, nor the bubble called the World, could contain his eternal soul'.[20]

And here is what Sisirkumar Ghose has to say about *The Religion of Man*:

> Perhaps exposition was not Tagore's strong point. His poems are a more intimate guide to his thought than the prose defence... Much of *The Religion of Man* is rationalization, in an idiom not his own, and made worse by an obvious playing to the gallery. The shorter Bengali version, *Manusher Dharma*, reads so much better. *The Religion of Man* sounds like a nightingale bent on sermonizing.[21]

---

15) Ibid., p. 58.
16) Ibid., p. 67.
17) Ibid., p. 68.
18) Ibid., p. 64.
19) Ibid., p. 72.
20) Ibid., p. 122.
21) S. Ghose, *Rabindranath Tagore*, p. 88.

To give a balance, here is one of Tagore's very last poems, written on the 27th of July, 1941, shortly before the poet's death. The theme is familiar: the problem of man's identity in the universe.

> The first day's Sun
> asked
> at the new manifestation of being –
> Who are you?
> No answer came.
> Year after year went by,
> the last Sun of the day
> the last question utters
> on the western seashore,
> in the silent evening –
> Who are you?
>   He gets no answer.[22]

A Postscript

The (rather agnostic) views of Tagore on the problem of man's ontological identity can only be adequately appreciated, if we take into account the great differences between the concepts of man that the West has inherited from the Judeo-Christian tradition and the concepts of man in traditional (pre- and non-Muslim) Weltanschauungen of South Asia, first of all in traditional Hinduism. For some reasons (which in themselves should be an interesting issue for research) these differences have not so far attracted much attention of scholars. Here suffice it to quote Wilhelm Halbfass, one of those few scholars who did write about these problems:

> ... Among those central themes of Western thought, which seem to be conspicuously absent in Indian, specifically Hindu thought, man appears as one of the most conspicuous ones. There is no tradition of explicit and thematic thought about man as man in India, no tradition of trying to define his essence and to distinguish it from other forms of life. There is

---

22) Amiya Chakravarty's English rendering. Quoted from K. Kripalani, *Rabindranath Tagore. A Biography*, New York, Grove Press, 1962, pp. 394-95.

nothing com-parable to the Western fascination with man as 'rational animal'...; there is no emphasis on the unity of the human species, no notion of a uniquely human dignity, no proclamation of human rights or of human sovereignty over nature. There is, in general, nothing comparable to that tradition in the West which has its roots in ancient Greek as well as Biblical sources and leads through the Renaissance and Enlightenment periods to the growing anthropocentrism of modern Western thought. There is no suggestion in any of the religious traditions of India that *only* man is endowed with an immortal soul or an irreducible personal and spiritual identity.

...Traditional Indian thought seems to be preoccupied with the *atman*, that 'self' and immortal principle *in* man which it also finds in animals and other forms of life; *manusya*, man as a particular species of living beings, man as *homo sapiens*, seems to be insignificant compared to this self *in* man and other beings.[23]

This passage is a telling commentary on Tagore's *Religion of Man*. Among other things, it gives an idea about what kind of changes, under the impact of western thought, had to take place (and is still going on) in Indian thinking about man, self and similar matters, what kinds of 'cultural distances' were (and still are) there for Indian thinkers to overcome.

References

Aronson, Alex, *Rabindranath through Western Eyes*, Allahabad, Kitabistan, 1943.

Chatterjee, Ramananda (ed.), *The Golden Book of Tagore*, Calcutta 1931.

Embree, A.T., *India's Search for National Identity*, Delhi, Chanakya Publications, 1980.

Ghose, S., *Rabindranath Tagore*, New Delhi, Sahitya Akademi, 1986.

---

23) W. Halbfass, *Tradition and Reflection. Explorations in Indian Thought*, Albany, SUNY Press, 1991, pp. 266-67. (Chapt. 8: Man and Self in Traditional Indian Thought).

Halbfass, W., *Tradition and Reflection. Explorations in Indian Thought*, Albany, SUNY Press, 1991.

Hay, Stephen N., *Asian Ideas of East and West. Tagore and His Critics in Japan, China and India*, Cambridge, Mass., Harvard University Press, 1970.

Kopf, D., *The Brahmo Samaj and the Shaping of the Modern Indian Mind*, Princeton, Princeton University Press, 1979.

Kripalani, K., *Rabindranath Tagore. A Biography*, New York, Grove Press, 1962.

Tagore, R., 'Introducing Oneself' in *Quest. A Quarterly of Inquiry, Criticism and Ideas*, Calcutta, May 1961.

Tagore, R., *The Religion of Man*, London etc., Unwin Paperbacks, 1988.

Tagore, R., *Selected Poems*. Translated by W. Radice, Harmondsworth, Penguin Books, 1987.

Tagore, R., *Short Stories*. Translated with an introduction by W. Radice, Harmondsworth, Penguin Books, 1994.

Thompson, E., *Rabindranath Tagore. Poet and Dramatist*. With an introduction by H. Trivedi, Delhi, Oxford University Press, 1991

5

Ethnicity in Modern Indonesian Literature
The Novels of Abdul Moeis and Pramoedya Ananta Toer

Mason C. Hoadley

Indonesia differs from the general pattern of ethnic identity reflected in literature. Despite the existence of hundreds of ethnic/linguistic groups and significant numbers of members of major world religions within a self-identified Moslem society, Indonesian writers are remarkably silent on the subject of ethnicity. The high priority given to nation-building makes this understandable. Less so is the apparent reluctance to come to terms with a recent past based upon a racially segregated social system, namely that of the Netherlands East Indies between 1850 and 1942.

During that period Dutch colonial practice produced an intricate system of hierarchial, artificial, and near water-tight categories – each characterized by its own legal and social norms – for the various ethnic groups residing in what would after 1945 become the Republic of Indonesia. Topping the list was the political, administrative, and economic elite consisting of 'Europeans' regulated by a recognizable variant of Dutch law promulgated especially for the Indies. To this group could be legally appended, on arbitrary and artificial grounds, individuals from other ethnic groups. This could be both involuntarily, as by birth to a 'European' father, or voluntarily, as via the status of 'gelijksteld' (lit. 'of equal status' but more colloquially something like 'honorary white'). Japanese and educated Indonesians provide striking examples of such voluntarily acquired status.

The vast majority of the Indies inhabitants were classed as 'natives.' Their legal obligations were regulated by the contents of one of the seventeen variants of the local customary law (*adat*) officially recognized by the Dutch East Indies government. Complicating the formal ethnic system was a social one characterized by a division between the new arrivals or pure *totoks* within the Chinese and Dutch groups and those born in the Indies or who were products of mixed marriages, the so-called *perakanan* and Indos/mestizos. To cite a prominent Dutch sociologist, W. F. Wertheim,

> About 1850 the colonial stratification based on race had assumed a fixed form in Java, which was reflected in the laws. The Europeans formed the ruling stratum, resembling a caste. In contrast with the situation in the British colonies, people of mixed blood belonged to this upper stratum if they descended from a white man in the male line and were either legitimate or recognized by the father.
>
> Over against this upper layer stood the Indonesians, referred to as Inlanders (natives) and representing the subject stratum. The gulf between the two layers was practically unbridgeable. Apart from one or two exceptional cases, transfer from the lower to the upper stratum was impossible. Discrimination was made on a racial basis in almost all departments of justice and social life....
>
> A person's position depended not on what he was himself but on the population group to which he belonged. Punitive measures were framed to ensure that the colour line should not be over-stepped – it was forbidden to dress otherwise than in the manner customary in one's own population group. The colonial rulers even succeeded in large measure in forcing the Indonesians themselves to accept the system of values based on race.... [1]

Despite the blatant 'racism' of society under Dutch rule, literary works in Bahasa Indonesia dealing with relations between Europeans and Natives are rare. Particularly so, are those dealing with the marriage of a 'European' woman to a 'native' man. Only a few writers have focused explicitly on the issue, the most important of whom are Abdul Moeis (1890-1959) and Pramoedya Ananta Toer (b. 1925), two of Indonesia's most prominent authors.

---

1) W.F. Wertheim, *Indonesian Society in Transition*, Bandung, Sumur Bandung, 1956, pp. 118-119.

Broached possibly as early as 1913, Moeis developed upon the theme throughout his career. It forms the major issue in his masterpiece of 1928, *Salah Asuhan* (Wrong Upbringing), considered one of the highlights of pre-war Indonesian letters. The novel was seen as revolutionary in so frankly dealing with ethnic boundaries of contemporaneous colonial society. Moeis returned to the theme in the post Indonesian Revolution era with his novels *Surapati* (1950) which may have originated forty years earlier and its sequel *Robert Anak Surapati* (1953). In contrast to Moeis, Toer turned to the ethnic issue only in later years, in particular during his detainment between 1965 and 1979. The issue is explicitly addressed in *This Earth of Mankind* (*Bumi Manusia*) and *Glass House* (*Rumah Kaca*), the first and last of his tetralogy also including *Child of All Nations* (*Anak Semua Bangsa)* and *Footsteps* (*Jajak Langkah*).

By way of tackling the problem, or what should have been a problem, in Indonesian letters, the essay is divided into three parts. These deal in turn with ethnicity as protest, ethnicity as contributory to the independence struggle, and ethnicity and modern Indonesian society.

Ethnicity as Protest

The 'Ethical Policy' (1890-1920)

Ironically, the apartheid-like ethnic order in the Indies was the result of a Dutch policy bearing the name 'Ethical Policy'. Fundamental to the thinking of the Ethici, as supporters of the Policy called themselves, was the eradication of what they considered to be lacks in the Indonesian social system. According to them, its social, political, and economic institutions were insufficiently developed to preserve it from disintegration in the face of negative foreign influences. The latter included exploitation by the Dutch themselves – under company, public, and private enterprise – along with seductive influences spread by 'disturbers' preaching the advantages of Islam, democracy, socialism, etc. By way of sheltering them from the pernicious effects of these influences, the native population was divided into a number of 'circles' on the basis of their own customs and regulations, the *adat*, as interpreted and enforced by Dutch civil servants.

Thus each 'race,' including minorities such as the Chinese, Arabs, *peranakans*, etc., lived under its own laws and regulations. For certain crimes and for all conflicts of law, European-derived Indies statute law automatically applied. Individual natives who were considered sufficiently developed to cope with European status could be admitted to equivalent status or 'gelijksteld.' Once so admitted, there was no return to one's roots, even in death[2]. The remainder of the population were to be educated by the Dutch East Indies government in association with enlightened Europeans. In this way the natives would gradually be brought to a point where they could handle their own affairs. Although never explicitly stated, the assumption was that this would occur when their laws and customs were raised to the level of the civilized world, envisaged by Dutchmen at some time in the very distant future.

Ethical Policy in Practice

In theory the Ethical Policy should have reversed the preceding centuries of unlimited economic exploitation; in practice, it brought about a new ethnic exploitation. Expectations that the Policy's ideals formulated at Den Haag by *totok* Dutchmen could be transformed into reality in a colony administered mainly by 'local' Dutchmen or Indos – especially when it threatened the latter's privileged position as *peranakans* – was naive in the extreme. Fundamental incompatibility between the ideal and the application was obvious to all by the 1920s. The Ethical Policy raised the expectations of Indonesians who participated in its educational programs without fulfilling them. Discovery of the true nature of the resultant ethnic system did not encourage greater efforts on behalf of the Dutch overlords.[3] By 1928 the Ethical Policy was history and the bankruptcy of association

---

2) This is the origin of the controversy over whether Hanafi, the hero of *Salah Asuhan*, was to be buried in a native or government (Dutch) cemetery (see Abdullah Taufik, 'Historical Reflections on Three Novels of Pre-War Indonesia' in *Papers of the Fourth Indonesian-Dutch History Conference*, Yogyakarta, Gadjah Mada University Press, 1985: 215ff).
3) Tham Seong Chee, 'The Social and Intellectual Ideas of Indonesian Writers, 1920-1942' in Tham Seong Chee, (ed.), *Essays on Literature and Society in Southeast Asia*, Singapore, Singapore University Press, 1981: 101-103.

between Europeans and Indonesians was illustrated by two events that year. The second Indonesian Youth Congress took the symbolic step of proclaiming a pan-Indonesian nationalism in the pledge 'one nation, one flag, one language and Balai Pustaka (the government publishing house) published *Salah Asuhan*.

Ethical Policy in Salah Asuhan

Examples of the failure of the Policy in *Salah Asuhan* are legion. This has led to at least one interpretation of the novel in biographical terms.[4] The frustrations and exclusion experienced by the novel's chief figure, Hanafi, both at the office and in social life, is supposed to derive from those of the young Abdul Moeis in the pre-war years.[5] Although undoubtedly correct, a biographical interpretation does not adequately account for the function of ethnicity in the novel. Moeis came not to praise, or even to criticize, the Ethical Policy but to bury it. Indonesian letters contain few more explicit condemnations of its failures than in the following vignette towards the close of the novel.

> A fellow [ship] passenger was reading aloud from a Dutch newspaper published in Batavia which was known for its vindictiveness towards Natives. The paper related the case of the engagement of an Indonesian youth studying in the Netherlands to a young lady who was a class comrade at the same High School. Not a little was the newspaper's censure and abuse of Natives educated under the auspices of the Ethical Policy; not a few were the names of prominent Dutchmen at Batavia who were likewise sullied. Although the writings were vile, even more so were the words of the passengers surrounding the reader.
>
> Hanafi, who lounged in a nearby deck-chair studying the blue of the sea, could not stand to listen to the censure and vilification. He pressed his hands to his ears. But he could still see the movements of those who continued to discuss this 'evil' [Ethical Policy]. Among them were those who got up from their deck-chairs and paced the deck like caged tigers

---

4) See David de Queljoe, *Marginal Man in a Colonial Society: Abdoel Moeis' 'Salah Asuhan'*, Athens, Ohio, Center for International Studies, 1974.
5) See Robert Van Niel, *The Emergence of the Modern Indonesian Elite*, Dordrecht, Foris Publications, (1960) 1984, p. 53.

and [those who] argued and punctuated their opinions by pounding the table.

Even less now did Hanafi have the strength to listen but rose from his deck-chair and went to his cabin. He could still hear the person pounding the table saying:

'For the European race, our world here has greatly shrunken. Everywhere we are put upon, pushed – we must be lenient. And in the matter of tax it is just we who must pay through the nose! What is wrong is none other than the Ethical Policy.' [6]

The Ethical Policy had not allowed for the strong reaction against a change of policy toward the Indonesian population by the Indies Dutch/Indo society which was directly in competition with the newly-educated, upwardly-mobile Indonesians.

The Ethical Policy in Bumi Manusia

Difference in the time point of writing and the resultant perspectives give another portrayal of the Ethical Policy in Pramoedya Ananta Toer's *Bumi Manusia*. Here the emphasis falls on its failure from the start. The book takes as its starting point the different legal/social status of the major characters. The hero, Minke, as well as his mother-in-law, Nyai Ontosoroh, are Natives and as such come under Javanese law. The proviso for changing to 'honorary white' status was not yet in vogue. Against them stand Annelies, Nyai Ontosoroh's daughter by a Dutchman named Mellema, later married to Minke, her brother Robert, and her half-brother Engineer Mellema, a son of Mellema by his Dutch wife. They are all Europeans thanks to the peculiar laws found in the Indies. The crux of the novel comes when Annelies' debauched father dies, leaving his estate and guardianship of Annelies to his Dutch son. Since Annelies had been declared 'European,' she is a minor under European law and thus cannot have really married Minke. In addition, she was married by Islamic ceremony which was non-existent for Europeans. Her known co-habitation with Minke is immoral and possibly illegal as the Surabaya court considers charging her mother with compliancy in the rape of a European girl by a Native.

---

6) *Salah Asuhan*, pp. 212-3.

Early Ethici appear in the novel via the characters of Minke's Dutch teacher, Magda Peters, the controller at his father's regency, Herbert de la Croix, and a number of friends and colleagues from the Surabaya journalistic world. All are shocked by the court order to dissolve a marriage legally sanctioned by Islamic law; all are equally effectively silenced by the colonial government. Magda Peters is banned from the colony for what were considered subversive activities, de la Croix is pressured by his superiors into silence, and those sympathetic to Minke and Annelies are shown to be powerless in preventing this travesty of European justice.

Here it seems clear that Toer's opportunity of hindsight – he was writing decades after the end of colonial society – allowed him to make a more realistic appraisal of what must be considered an 'ethical' parenthesis in Indies history. In *Bumi Manusia* the Ethical Policy was an impossibility from its origins. Association and enlightenment of natives – here it should be remembered that Minke, one of a dozen Natives in Dutch High Schools, was placed second highest in the all-Indies exams and that Nyai Ontosoroh was in some ways even more educated – could only lead to desire for freedom. At this time the desire was expressed merely by a, as it turns out, naïve, plea for a more just colonial society. The key may lie in Wertheim's phrase that 'The colonial rulers even succeeded in large measure in forcing the Indonesians themselves to accept the system of values based on race.' Moeis' questioning the worth of the 'reforms' initiated by the Ethical Policy should be supplemented by Toer's of why anyone could have believed in it in the first place.

Ethnicity in Rumah Kaca

In the remainder of the tetralogy – *Anak Semua Bangsa, Jajak Langkah*, and *Rumah Kaca* – ethnic inequality resulting from the Ethical Policy functions as background rather than plot. It is simply a fact of early twentieth-century life in the colony. As such, it calls for little further comment. A couple of points with regard to *Rumah Kaca*, however, provide noteworthy exceptions. Of lesser importance is the fact that Pangemanann (with two n's) as the chief architect of the campaign against Minke is a European *peranakan* who clearly identifies with the interests of his Dutch (*totok*) masters. In like manner, the chief of the gang of thugs employed by Pangemanann, Robert, is also a *peranakan*. Their ethnic identity was not the major factor in their actions against Minke. Pangemanann was motivated by the necessity to keep his 'white' status through serving the Dutch and Robert had a personal grudge to settle with Minke as he had earlier been an unsuccessful suitor to Annelies. Even so, their willingness to act derives from a need to hold the colour line against the potential threat of Natives. This was all the more so in the weakened state the Indies government found itself during the enforced isolation from Europe resulting from World War I.

More significant in this respect is Toer's representation of ethnicity as an instrument of colonial politics. As a last resort in curtailing growing Indonesian nationalism, Pangemanann sets his hired thugs to inflame inter-ethnic tensions. By setting fire to Chinese quarters and passing it off as the work of Natives, the intention was to drive a wedge between the various ethnic groups. Perhaps more accurately, this was a desperate attempt to prevent the realization of a Chinese-Javanese cooperation. This had been a bogeyman for Dutch colonial rulers since the early eighteenth century.[7] In Toer's tetralogy this is represented by Minke's relation to Ang San Mei and her 'friend', as well as the holding up of the Chinese political associations as a model for Indonesian action. Toer could have also pointed to the now recognized important contribution of Chinese Malay-language newspapers to both the national movement and to Indonesian letters.[8]

Ethical Policy v. Integration

A perhaps more fundamental hindrance to the Policy lay on the emotional plane, especially that of the Indies-born Dutchmen, mestizos, and *perakanans*. Moeis chose as his spokesman for this point of view Piet, a *totok* Dutchman fresh from Holland. After his divorce from Corrie, Hanafi had hired a room with Piet and his wife, herself a *peranakan*. Hanafi could not understand why he was ostracised by Dutch colonial society, especially in view of his Dutch education. To this Piet replies:

---

7) Mason C. Hoadley, 'Javanese, Peranakan, and Chinese Elites in Cirebon: Changing Ethnic Boundaries' in *Journal of Asian Studies* 47, 1988: 503-18.
8) See C. Salmon, *Literature in Malay by the Chinese of Indonesia. A Provisional Bibliography*, Paris, Edition de la MSH, 1981.

Hanafi you are truly an educated person but in the area of feelings and emotions it is if you are blind and dumb. I should not have to spell out everything in detail. You should realize that according to the emotions of my race you are still a Native; they refuse to accept you when you push yourself forward to enter that race. In their opinion your position would be higher as a human being if you remained faithful to your own race but showed deference towards theirs, the European race. If you had conducted yourself in that manner, i.e. showing yourself as a Native with modesty and learning, their respect for you would certainly be much greater. But the manner in which you conduct yourself now is totally unacceptable to them. All this is, of course, emotion but emotions cannot be controlled, especially not by those afflicted by them.[9]

In other words no matter how hard an Indonesian tried to become a Dutchman, or even be accepted within colonial society, the task was impossible. This was due to what Moeis elsewhere calls the sickness of racial pride. More important is what he does not say: there is no logical or rational bridge to bind the races together. Even though western education is valued for its logical and rational methods, when it comes to ethnic reactions the otherwise so attractive guidelines to enlightenment no longer function. To the extent that Moeis drew conclusions from this, then association of equals, the ultimate goal of the Ethical Policy, was by definition impossible. Natives had to conduct themselves as servile and separate but 'with modesty and learning.' Should one decide otherwise, the only alternative was non-association, i.e. Indonesian independence.

Ethnicity as Motive for Independence

Realization of being victimized by unjust racial boundaries need not remain passive. Under certain circumstances it can transform itself into a call for political action, ultimately contributing to the idea of an Indonesian independence movement. Such is probably the case for Moeis' historical novel *Surapati*. 'Probably' because

---

9) *Salah Asuhan*, p. 190.

the exact date of composition of *Surapati* is in some doubt. While the date of first printing by Balai Pustaka in 1950 is confirmable, an advertisement in *Hindia Serikat* of 1913 that a *Surapati* by Abdul Moeis was about to appear[10] means that the theme, or even a manuscript, dates from some three and a half decades earlier. In addition, the historical novel *Surapati* drew upon earlier works for the general outline of the real events portrayed in the late seventeenth century.[11] As a result, a number of questions concerning date, textual integrity, and sources remain to be resolved.[12] For present purposes, the text as published in 1950 can be used for the problem at hand.

Even the choice of subject was provocative. Few figures in the long history of Dutch-Javanese relations call forth such strong reactions as that of Surapati. The historical facts concerning Surapati, also known as *Untung* (The Fortunate) can be summarized in a few lines. Most likely of Balinese origins, as a child he had been sold as a slave to a Dutch merchant; as an adult he ran afoul of Dutch authority at Batavia. (The *Babad Tanah Djawi* attributes this to his relation with Suzanne, the merchant's daughter who according to the fictional version in o.a. Moeis was the mother of Robert, Surapati's eldest son.) Gathering a band of loyal followers, Surapati subsequently fled to the mountainous

---

10) C.W.Watson, 'Some Preliminary Remarks on the Antecedents of Modern Indonesian Literature' in *Bijdragen tot de Taal-, Land- en Volkenkunde 127*, 1971: 425.

11) See C.W. Watson op. cit. and W.V.Sykorsky, 'Some Additional Remarks on the Antecedents of Modern Indonesian Literature' in *Bijdragen tot de Taal-, Land- en Volkenkunde 135*, 1980: 502.

12) Crucial among these is the relation existing between Moeis' *Surapati* and *Robert, Anak Surapati* and that published by Marie Sloot (ps Melati van Java) as *Soerapatih; Historisch Romantische Schets uit de Geschiedenis van Java*. At very least one can say there is a remarkable similarity in plot almost undoubtedly transmitted via a Malay translation of Sloot's novel by F. Wiggers in 1898 entitled *Dari boedak sampe djadi radja*. (I am indebted to Mrs. Mary Bakker, Department of Languages and Cultures of South-East Asia and Oceania, Leiden University for this information from her doctoral paper on Surapati.) However Moeis' characterization of particularly Raden Pengantin – Surapati's son by Raden Gusik, a Javanese princess, who is also half-brother to Robert born of Suzanne, the Dutch merchant's daughter – differs sharply from Sloot's. Thus regardless of the origin, Moeis has consciously given his figures personalities whose analysis can shed light on the question of ethnicity in Indonesian letters.

tract of West Java.[13] Around 1678 he was recruited into the Dutch East India Company army with the rank of Lieutenant and he carried out at least one crucial mission. Upon being unjustly treated by a subordinate, Surapati quit the Company. With his band he proceeded first to Cirebon and then to Kartasura where he was welcomed by the Susuhunan of Mataram and granted a village near the *kraton*. In 1686 Dutch troops under Commander Tack, were dispatched to Kartasura in order to intimidate the Susuhunan and to arrest Surapati. They were, however, defeated and Tack was killed, after which Surapati moved on to East Java where he founded a kingdom at Pasuruhan. Repeated Dutch attempts to oust him were to no avail. He ruled more or less undisturbed until 1705. That year Surapati was mortally wounded in a pitched battle near Surabaya but on his deathbed counselled his sons to continue the struggle. This they did with effect until well into the 1720s when the last of them finally succumbed. A gauge to the threat posed by Surapati comes from the fact that when the Dutch forces were finally victorious they desecrated his grave, burned his remains, and scattered the ashes.[14]

A number of reasons can be given as to why Surapati became such a strong symbolic figure for Indonesians. As even Dutch historians have pointed out, Surapati's accomplishments are unique. Not only did he inflict decisive defeats on the troops of the 'invincible' Dutch Company, at the same time killing its commanders, but also he remained undefeated in the field. The fact that the struggle continued under the leadership of his sons also points to how deeply rooted the cause was among his followers. Another unique feature of the struggle was that Surapati could draw upon his experiences with the Dutch army, as well as those with the Javanese. This made him a particularly dangerous opponent. And finally, the fact that he could come from slavery and establish a sizeable kingdom for several decades attests to both his talents as a leader and organizer and the response of Indonesians, not just Javanese. In short the kingdom was unusual in that it was a multi-ethnic one which attracted Balinese, Javanese, Madurese, etc. under the same banner. This aspect is also emphasized by the

---
13) See Leonard Blussé, *Strange Company. Chinese Settlers, mestizo women and the Dutch in VOC Batavia*, Dordrecht, Foris Publications, 1986, pp. 195-6.
14) H.J.deGraaf, *Geschiedenis van Indonesie*, The Hague, W.van Hoeve, 1949, pp. 234-41.

Babad Tanah Djawi in mentioning that 'he attracted people to Pasuruhan.' A more fitting hero or model for an emerging national identity, or even struggle for independence, would be hard to find.[15]

Ethnicity and Modern Indonesian Society

In turning to the question of ethnicity and modern Indonesian society, the centre of focus must first be narrowed to the basic theme of the three novels summarized in Appendix 1, namely *Salah Asuhan, Surapati,* and *Bumi Manusia*. The ethnic issue in all three revolves around that of the result of a marriage between an Indonesian man and a 'European' woman. In merely describing the works' contents one is automatically entangled in the question of ethnic identity, at least according to Dutch colonial standards. None of the 'European' heroines are, in fact, *totok* European. Rather they are Indos or *peranakans*, i.e. children of European fathers and Indonesian mothers. Their status was relatively problem-free. They were simply decreed by the political elite as being 'European' with all the rights and responsibilities adhering thereto. These differed, however, from those of their mothers who remained simple 'natives' enjoying a sort of concubine status with the Europeans but belonging to the 'native' category. Despite the disparity in temporal setting of the three novels – the 1920s, the 1680s, and the 1890s respectively – basic continuity is provided by ethnic exclusiveness.

Thus the novels in question deal with a particular variant of 'mixed marriages.' Their counterparts between Indonesian women and Europeans are a much more common feature of the literature of the archipelago in the form of the 'Nyai' novels both in Malay and Indonesian.[16] Why the marriage of a European woman to an Indonesian man provoked such a reaction is eloquently explained by Corrie's father, himself married to a local woman. In contrasting the former with the latter, he points out that

---

15) Mohd. Ali, *Perdjuangan Feodal*, Bandung, Ganaco N.V., 1963, pp. 149-58.
16) Watson, 'Some Preliminary Remarks on the Antecedents of Modern Indonesian Literature'.

There is truly a difference, Corrie, a great difference. The reason is none other than the sickness 'racial pride.' Westerners came here with the knowledge and feelings that it was they who were to rule over people here. If they came to this land without bringing wives of their own race with them it was not seen as lowering themselves when they took local concubines (*nyai*). If these *nyai* then came to bear children, in the eyes of the westerners this was to do a service in improving the people and blood-stock here.

According to him, in the reverse situation the opinion of the Europeans was very different indeed. Such a girl was seen as throwing herself away. Moreover,

> ....this European girl who married a 'native' as long as she was in the hands of her husband she was stripped of her rights as a European. If the girl went so far as to have a child she was seen as taking part in undermining European status.[17]

Thus this type of double moral regarding marriage and sexual relations between 'Europeans' and 'natives', the definition itself being problematic, as well as the results of such liaisons form the major theme of the works under discussion.

Analysis

For purposes of analysis we can here expand the usual duality Traditional – Modern to include an ethnic dimension, namely European – Native. Using the two pairs to define the boundaries, the major characters of the novels under discussion here can be plotted on the grid. The resultant model shows the characters' relation to one another. It also graphically illustrates their standing vis-a-vis European-ness/Native-ness (vertical axis) and Modern-ness/Traditional-ness (horizontal axis). Even admitting the relativity of value judgments, a model might look like Figure 1 (overleaf).

---

17) *Salah Asuhan*, p. 15.

European

For convenience's sake discussion can begin with the category of 'European.' As shown in Figure 1, only the minor figures of Corrie's father, along with Herman Mellema and Herbert de la Croix, are pure European. The other 'European' figures of the novels, that is Suzanne, Robert, and Corrie, belong to the category only by official colonial definition.

Figure 1: Ethnic-Social Orientation Matrix

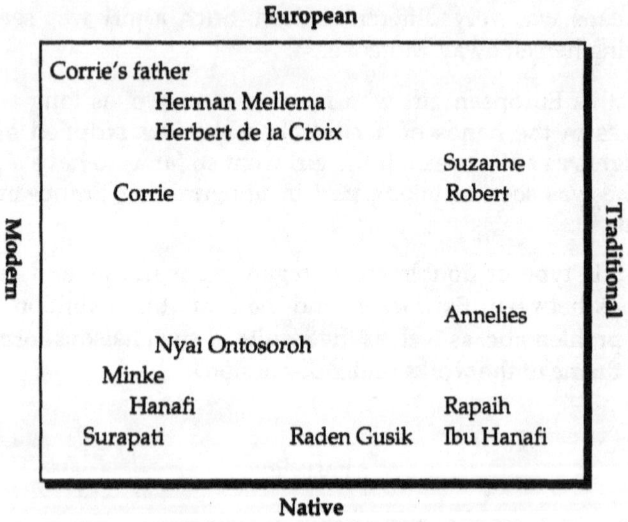

```
                          European

  ┌─────────────────────────────────────────────┐
  │ Corrie's father                             │
  │     Herman Mellema                          │
  │     Herbert de la Croix                     │
  │                                   Suzanne   │
  │     Corrie                        Robert    │
M │                                             │ T
o │                                             │ r
d │                                             │ a
e │                                   Annelies  │ d
r │                                             │ i
n │     Nyai Ontosoroh                          │ t
  │  Minke                                      │ i
  │     Hanafi                        Rapaih    │ o
  │  Surapati         Raden Gusik     Ibu Hanafi│ n
  └─────────────────────────────────────────────┘
                           Native
```

More striking with regard to the European category is the spread along the modern-traditional axis. Here the intention is to enable a judgment as to the modernity with reference to the characters time period. Thus only Corrie's father can be unreservedly seen as a modern figure, although for convenience (and perhaps colonial censorship) Moeis makes him a French nobleman. In contrast, Corrie is modern only in terms of the early twentieth century. By the same token, Suzanne and Robert are traditional within their temporal boundaries.

Native

In turning to the 'native' category one must admit that the characterization is considerably better. This in itself is hardly surprising in that the authors concentrated upon the Indonesian figures which could be modelled from living experiences. Just because they are less stereotyped there arises the resultant difficulty in categorizing them. Even so, clearly the most traditional of this category is Hanafi's wife and mother. Indeed the Hanafi-Rapaih (Ibu Hanafi) section of the triangle is a purely modern-traditional one. Yet as far as modernity goes, Hanafi and even Corrie are modern only in comparison to Rapaih and Ibu Hanafi. Despite their education they come nowhere near the level of a Minke, a Nyai Ontosoroh, or a Surapati, again the judgment being made in relation to their own temporal sphere.

The final group of characters belongs to the major figures of Toer's *Bumi Manusia*. They tend to cluster nearer the centre than those of Moeis. One reason is that Moeis tends to give his figures stronger personalities, with the attendant trend towards stereotype. Toer's, in contrast, are harder to pigeon-hole as to their position vis-a-vis the two axes utilized here. Minke is clearly a quite modern figure in that he studied within the Dutch system and takes an interest in developments around him through his journalism. This is despite his traditional elite background, a glimpse of which is given on the occasion of a visit to his father's regency of Bodjonegara. At the opposite extreme is his bride. Even though she, tragically so, is officially a European, she is far less so than say Corrie or Suzanne, almost less so one is tempted to add than her mother, Nyai Ontosoroh. She is also very traditional in her views, although in all fairness the reader has little chance to form an opinion as she is such a vague and in some respects unconvincing figure. This leaves the otherwise imposing figure of Nyai Ontosoroh. Were one to judge merely on character or will power alone, she would be further along the 'modern' axis. Yet she also has a clear picture of the strength of the walls supporting the colonial ethnic system. She is all too aware of the system to challenge it, and lose, as a female Surapati, or even helpmate and instigator, as Raden Gusik. In fact, Nyai is one of the few figures showing a real-life ambivalence. She understands (sees through) the 'modern Dutch' way but rejects its inhumanity against Natives. At the same time, she rejects native values for giving in to Europeans, i.e. selling their daughters into sexual slavery. Ultimately she opts for 'modern', but in French terms. In *Rumah*

Kaca she acts as the European conscience against Dutch colonial political provincialism.

Static observation – dynamic change

The model utilized thus far is a static one. That is, it helps to classify the major figures both in relation to one another and to the modern-traditional and European-Native axes. When one raises the question of the dynamics of the situation, including social changes through time and individual character development, the model changes form.

Modern = European

Constituting a two-dimensional grid, Figure 1 is utilized for plotting the co-ordinates of character-types by way of illustrating the major theme of the novels discussed here. But were these axes in fact really so regular? Without labouring the point, it seems clear that in practice the grid resembled more a parallelogram with the acute angle on the upper left-hand and lower right-hand corners. By this is meant that the poles of 'modern' and 'European' in practice were the same thing. Under colonial circumstances one could not be, or even strive to be, 'modern' without at the same time being, or striving to become, 'European.' The two were identical. Thus by absorbing Dutch learning and manners Minke or Hanafi became modern or in an attempt to become modern they had to do so via the vehicle of 'European = Dutch.' Toer raises the question by putting it into the mouth of van Kollewijn, a political Ethici who in *Jajak Langkah* asks rhetorically:

> Is it actually possible for a Native to develop a personality, a character, of his own? Aha, I am sure this is an issue that none of you have ever really considered. The development of a personality, of individual character, is a sign that a man and his times are in harmony.[18]

Similarly no matter how inherently conservative her social ideas were – she detested native customs and culture – in an absolute sense, because Corrie is 'European' by definition she is modern.

---

18) See translation, p. 21, original, p. 20.

This also raises the question as to whether Hanafi's attraction to her is based on the one or the other.

Traditional = Native

At the opposite corner of the parallelogram one observes a similar merging of poles, here native and traditional. The inhabitants of the corner, Rapaih and Hanafi's mother, are traditional by birth and choice. They are also 'Native,' as are Hanafi, Minke, and Surapati, although the latter aspires to European orientation = modernity. Thus in the confluence of native/traditional Rapaih and Ibu Hanafi are unaffected. Those directly affected are types such as Raden Gusik who to an extent shares the modern ideas of Surapati but because of her 'native-ness' is forced towards the traditional. Her counterpart would be Annelies who aspires to both native-ness and traditional-ness but because of her involuntary 'European' status is forced into the modern-European mould.

Traditional-European and Modern-Native: Non-Existent

If modern was becoming indelibly European and native traditional, what about the remaining categories at the other two corners. The combination European and traditional in colonial society simply was not possible. European-ness was by definition the wave of the future for colonial society. Here no matter how conservative, and there were plenty of examples such as Hanafi's fellow travellers or Piet's wife, Europeans were part of the ruling class to which all progress or modernity was ascribed. The same would hold true for the opposite corner. Modern – Native was simply a contradiction in terms. There was no possible image of a modern Indonesian society, other than one modelled on Europe.

At this point we are indebted to Moeis' novel *Surapati*. In it one is presented with these last two categories as viable alternatives; alternatives which otherwise are hard to visualize just because they were eliminated by the advent of colonial society. Within the setting of the late seventeenth century the categories modern and European (Dutch) and traditional and Indonesian were distinct. Moeis can realistically portray the figures of Suzanne and Robert as extremely traditional Europeans.

Traditional is used here in the sense of 'resistant to change' or even an inability or unwillingness to conceive change outside one's own cultural boundaries. Typical of this attitude are the contents of Suzanne's letter to Surapati pleading for him to 'become' a Dutchman as the only respectable course of action. In a similar manner, the reader witnesses Robert's conscious rejection of his father's offer of a high place within the newly-established Pasuruhan kingdom in favour of his modest position as a soldier of the Dutch Company. Again one has the feeling that the decision is motivated more by blind cultural/ethnic loyalty than a choice between viable alternatives.Hence Suzanne and Robert could be interpreted as providing the counter foil to the modernizing figure forced to be traditional by his/her native-ness: here it is their European-ness which imprisons them in traditionalism.

At the opposite end of the scale stands Moeis' Surapati. On several occasions he is forced to debate the pros and cons of European-ness unencumbered by the question of modernity. To the former belong the chances of winning back Suzanne and his son Robert; to the latter slavery, cultural and/or actual. To this weighing of alternatives Moeis adds, possibly spuriously, nationalistic feeling. Thus in many respects Surapati appears as a quite modern figure in his multi-ethnic following and his principled resistance to the Dutch. This contrasts sharply with his contemporaries' opportunism which at the same time tended toward an ethnic exclusiveness that on occasion rivalled that of the Dutch. The details can be of course debated. Yet the perspectives offered by the historical novel form allow speculation upon the question of identity, European or Indonesian, without the overlaying considerations of modern v. traditional.

Conclusion

Ethnicity as protest and as a contributory factor to shaping the idea of an independent Indonesia are powerful in themselves.Yet it is the contention here that the final question, i.e. that of ethnicity in the development of a modern society, motivated the writings considered above. The threat of the pairing of European with modern and Native with traditional, first expressed under the Ethical Policy, caused Moeis to take up the ethnicity theme in

Surapati two decades after the 1928 declaration of Indonesian national identity and Toer some three decades after colonial society's demise. For both writers a continuation of the twin concepts of modern-and-European v. traditional-and-Native would in the long run lower the value of their land's struggle for freedom. This would be especially so if it was won at the price of subverting an Indonesian society for one aping European models.

A couple of points can be brought forward to support the contention. First, both writers were deeply engaged with the situation of the 'little man', that is the vast majority of Indonesians. Modernization should, among other things, raise their standards of living through better agricultural techniques, financing, etc. If the formula above held true, would this mean that the peasant would become a farmer in the European model? More important, how would the governmental services supporting such development appear and what would happened to the traditional social structure as a result? Confirmation that their fears were not exaggerated comes from the observation that the Indonesian farmer of today tends to imitate the rational, decision-making type found in Europe with all the accoutrements of modern, scientific farming. As a result, Dewi Sri, the traditional rice goddess, is 'dead' without mourners.

The other point worth considering is that both Moeis and Toer sought models of modernity outside the strict European sphere. For Moeis Islam was a rational force which held considerable attraction. In addition, a stream of Fabian socialism can be detected in his political work, as well as in the figure of Surapati with his concern for the people's welfare. In Toer socialism of the communist variety had greater appeal but one which was adapted to Indonesian circumstances. Had the events of 1965 not intervened one can only wonder if his and Moeis' views of a modern Indonesia, but one that was not a mere copy of Europe, would have emerged.

Appendix 1. *Salah Asuhan (1928)*

The novel's main character, Hanafi, has been given a western education but without absorbing the underlying values and norms of that education. As a result, he develops a strong dislike for his own culture, hence the novel's title 'Wrong Upbringing.'

His attempts to become part of European society revolve around his attraction to Corrie du Busée, an 'Indo' child of a French father and Minangkabau mother. Corrie and Hanafi have been brought up together since childhood.

When Corrie returns home after several years at school in Batavia she is no longer Hanafi's little sister but an attractive young lady with whom he falls in love. Fearing that she herself is too strongly attracted to Hanafi, Corrie flees to Batavia. Intellectually, she realizes that a marriage with Hanafi would be disastrous for them both. In one of the book's key speeches her father points out that marriages between 'European' girls and 'native' men aroused the worst prejudices among Europeans because of 'the sickness of racial pride.'

Disappointed in love, Hanafi finally accedes to his mother's persistent pleas that he marry Rapiah, a match which was arranged through customary channels. The marriage is a failure. Hanafi feels that the wife given him by his mother is an embarrassment in front of his European friends.

When he is forced to seek treatment in Batavia, Hanafi accidentally meets again with Corrie. In the meantime, her future had become uncertain due to the death of her father. Hanafi decides to remain in Batavia, at the same time divorcing his wife and actively courting Corrie. Needing time to think, Corrie goes to a friend's house in East Java. After a few weeks she writes Hanafi to come there so that they can announce their engagement at the friend's house. This is prevented when the host finds out that Corrie's intended is a 'native' and will have nothing to do with their plans. The two return to Batavia where they are married.

This marriage, too, is a failure. The ostensible cause is gossip and misunderstandings; in reality it has its roots in the tensions and ill-will between husband and wife due to their exclusion from European society, itself stemming from their mixed marriage. Corrie finally leaves Hanafi, feeling herself humiliated and insulted by her husband and finds work in a orphanage in Semarang. Full of remorse, Hanafi follows her in order to ask her forgiveness. He arrives too late, finding Corrie dying of cholera.

After her death Hanafi is despondent and returns home to Sumatra and his mother. There he only succeeds in destroying the close relationship which had grown up between his mother and wife and child who had been living together at his mother's village. Seeing no other way out, he takes his own life. Even here ethnic complications are not over as considerable controversy arises over whether he should be buried in the village cemetery as a 'native' or in the government one as a 'European'.

Plot: *Surapati*

The novel focuses on what little is known of the career of Surapati. At the novel's opening in 1680, Surapati, or Untung 'the Fortunate' as he was known at that time, was the household slave of the Dutch merchant in Batavia. He had been raised together with Suzanne, the merchant's daughter, presumably born of a local woman. Their relation develops from elder brother – younger sister to one of love, ultimately fulfilled in marriage. On learning of their marriage, Suzanne's father has Untung cast into prison. There he befriends several of the inmates who form the core of Untung's following.

Following their escape from Batavia, Dutch pursuit of Untung's band is interrupted by more important political considerations, namely persuading the last of the Banten rulers to submit peaceably to the Company. The mission is entrusted to Untung who carries it to fulfilment, seeing in it a way to win back a place in (Dutch) society and thereby his wife and son. These hopes are dashed when the Dutch renege on their promise and themselves take credit for capturing the Banten prince. Just at this time Untung receives a letter from Suzanne who after her father's death had gone to Holland. She pleads with Untung to give up his ways, become a Dutchman, and submit to the 'Honourable Company'. The letter effectively destroys any remaining illusions as to the acceptability of his 'native-ness', as well as motivation for co-operating with the Dutch.

Accompanied by Raden Gusik, the Banten prince's youngest wife who would not submit to the Dutch, Untung and his band are pursued by Dutch troops across West Java. They first come to Cirebon where Untung is given the title Surapati, but are forced to leave because of the Sultan's impending submission to the Company. They come to Kartasura where they are somewhat better received, the Mataram ruler being ambivalent as regards Dutch rule. When Dutch troops, under Commander Tack, attack the kingdom it is defended by Surapati and Tack is killed in the melee.

Surapati then withdraws to East Java where he rules a small fief which attracts people from all over the archipelago who want to resist the Dutch.

The story then jumps to 1706 and Dutch preparations to attack the remaining strongholds of Mataram in East Java. As part of this, Robert, who is unaware that he is Surapati's son, is sent out to spy on his father. He is discovered by his half-brothers, brought into his father's presence where his real identity is revealed. Robert is then offered the place as second in command of the kingdom but refuses to abandon his 'race', i.e. the Dutch. Although Surapati's army initially withstands the Dutch attacks, he is mortally wounded in the battle. On his death-bed Surapati in vain tries to persuade Robert to stand with his half-brothers. When this fails, he then turns to his (Javanese) sons and exhorts them to continue the struggle. He dies praising Allah that he could exit life standing shoulder to shoulder with his sons in defence of the fatherland.

Plot: *This Earth of Mankind (Bumi Manusia)*

The novel relates the discovery of the harsh realities of the colonial world created by the Dutch in turn-of-the century Indies by Minke, an eighteen-year-old Javanese. He is the only Native in the Dutch High School at Surabaya. The story opens with Minke's enchantment with the great advances in technology by Europeans, among them the ability to reproduce and print pictures as, for example, one of the young Queen of the Netherlands, Wilhelmina, Minke's favourite. It ends with Minke's wife being taken from him and forcibly sent to Holland, all sanctioned by the government of that selfsame queen.

Through a classmate, Minke comes into contact with the *Borderij Buitenzorg*, a dairy farm outside of Surabaya run by the remarkable Nyai Ontosoroh. (A *nyai* is a native concubine of a European with a recognized position in Indies society.) Nyai Ontosoroh, who was sold into concubinage by her parents, is not only learned, reading and speaking fluent Dutch, but also an extremely capable businesswoman. With the help of her daughter, Annelies, she astutely managed the business after her husband, Herman Mellema, had essentially gone mad and moved to the neighbouring house of prostitution. Although already married in

Holland, and thus unable to marry Nyai, Mellema had legally recognized his two children by her. Thus her, son Robert, who followed in his father's degenerate footsteps, and Annelies were in the Indies 'European.' Their mother was only a 'Native' and as such fell under separate legal and social conventions.

During the course of the novel Minke falls in love with Annelies and moves to the farm while studying at the Dutch High School. Despite this, he is supported by his language teacher, a radical Dutch lady named Magda Peters, and the Controller of the district in which his father is *Bupatih* (regent), Herbert de la Croix. The latter is firmly convinced of the ideas propounded by the so-called Ethical Policy. (The Ethical Policy ca. 1890s–1920s was aimed at associating the Natives with Europeans through education.)

The dramatic climax of the novel is ushered in by the death of Herman Mellema under mysterious circumstances at the Chinese house of prostitution where he had been living for the past few years. Police inquiries into the circumstances result in publicizing Minke's relationship to the 'European' Annelies, as well as public disgrace for Nyai Ontosoroh. The case attracts the attention of Mellema's Dutch son. An Amsterdam court awards him ownership of the *Boerderij Buitenzorg*, as well as guardianship over the (under Dutch law) under-aged Annelies. Upon receiving the Dutch court order, the Surabaya authorities considered charging Nyai with complicity in the rape of her daughter by a Native, despite the fact that Annelies and Minke had been legally married in an Islamic ceremony several months previously. In the ensuing battle with the Dutch colonial authorities, Minke and his supporters are either defeated or otherwise silenced by the government which orders Annelies to be sent to Holland on order of her legal guardian, i.e. her half-brother.

References

Primary sources:

Abdul Moeis, *Salah Asuhan*, Jakarta, Balai Pustaka, 1928.

——, *Surapati*, Jakarta, Balai Pustaka, 1950 (1905).

———, *Robert, Anak Surapati*, Jakarta, Balai Pustaka, 1953 (1915).

Pramoedya Ananta Toer, *This Earth of Mankind*, Penguin Books, Australia, 1982.

———, *A Child of All Nations*, Penguin Books, Australia, 1985.

———, *Footsteps*, Penguin Books, Australia, 1986.

———, *Glasshouse*, Penguin Books, Australia, 1987.

———, *De pionier: biografie van Tirto Adhisoerjo*, (Trans. uit het Indonesisch door Marjanne Termorhuizen), Amsterdam, Manus Amici/Novib, 1988.

Secondary Sources

Ali, Moh., *Perdjuangan Feodal* [Feudal Struggle], Bandung, Ganaco N.V., 1963.

Anderson, Benedict (trans.), '*Perburan* 1950 and *Keluraga Gerilya* 1950. Pramoedya Ananta Toer' in *Indonesia* 36, 1983:24-48.

———, *Fantasy and Revolution in the Age of Mechanical Reproduction*, Cornell University, 1986.

Azmi., *Abdul Muis*, Jakarta, Departemen Pendidikan dan Kebudayaan, 1984.

Balfas, M., 'Wrong Upbringing: Characterization in an early Indonesian Novel' in *Journal of the Oriental Society of Australia* 6, no 1/2, 1968/1969:5-15.

Blussé, Leonard, *Strange Company. Chinese Settlers, Mestizo Women and the Dutch in VOC Batavia*, Dordrecht, Foris Publications, 1986.

Foulcher, Keith, '*Bumi Manusia* and *Anak Semua Bangsa*: Pramoedya Ananta Toer enters in 1980s' in *Indonesia* 32, 1981:1-15.

Graaf, H.J. de., *De Moord op Kapitein Francois Tack* [The Murder of Captain Francois Tack]. Amsterdam, 1935.

———, *Geschiedenis van Indonesië* [History of Indonesia], The Hague, W. van Hoeve, 1949.

Hoadley, Mason C., 'Javanese, Peranakan, and Chinese Elites in Cirebon: Changing Ethnic Boundaries' in *Journal of Asian Studies* 47, 1988: 503-18.

Klooster, H.A.J., 'Abdul Moeis' roman over Surapati' in *Jambatan* 3-1, 1984:3-15.

Kumar, Ann, *Surapati, Man and Legend. A study of three Babad traditions*, Leiden, E. J. Brill, 1976.

Lukács. Georg, *The Historical Novel*, Harmondsworth, Middlesex, Penguin Books, 1981.

Metali van Java [ps N. Marie C. Sloot], (3rd edn), *Soerapatih; Historische Romantische Schets uit de Geschiedenis van Java*. Schiedam, H.A.M Roelants, 1928-29.

Queljoe, David de., *Marginal Man in a Colonial Society: Abdoel Moeis' "Salah Asuhan"*, Athens, Ohio, Center for International Studies, 1974.

Ricklefs, M.C., *Modern Javanese Historical Tradition: A study of an original Kartasura chronicle and related materials*, London, School of Oriental and African Studies, 1978.

Salmon, C., *Literature in Malay by the Chinese of Indonesia. A Provisional bibliography*, Paris, Edition de la MSH, 1981.

Sykorsky, W. V., 'Some Additional Remarks on the Antecedents of Modern Indonesian Literature' in *Bijdragen tot de Taal-, Land- en Volkenkunde 136*, 1980:498-516.

Taufik Abdullah, 'Historical Reflections on Three Novels of Pre-War Indonesia', *Papers of the Fourth Indonesian-Dutch History Conference*, Yogyakarta, Gadjah Mada University Press, 1985.

Taylor, Jean Gelman, *The Social World of Batavia. European and Eurasian in Dutch Asia*, Madison, 1983.

Teeuw, A., *Modern Indonesian Literature*, The Hague, Martinus Nijhof, 1967.

——, 'The Impact of Balai Pustaka on Modern Indonesian Literature' in *Bulletin of the School of Oriental and African Studies 35*, 1972:111-127.

——, *Pramoedya Ananta Toer. De Verbeelding van Indonesië* [Pramoedya Ananta Toer, Indonesian Imagination], De Gens. Breda, The Netherlands. 1993.

Tham Seong Chee, 'The Social and Intellectual Ideas of Indonesian Writers, 1920-1942' in Tham Seong Chee, (ed.), *Essays on Literature and Society in Southeast Asia*, Singapore, Singapore University Press, 1981.

Van Niel, Robert, *The Emergence of the Modern Indonesian Elite*, Dordrecht, Foris Publications, (1960) 1984.

Watson, C. W., 'Some Preliminary Remarks on the Antecedents of Modern Indonesian Literature' in *Bijdragen tot de Taal-, Land- en Volkenkunde 127*, 1971:417-433.

——, 'The Sociology of the Indonesian Novel', M.A. Thesis, Hull University, 1972.

——, '*Salah Asuhan* and the Romantic Tradition in the Early Indonesian Novel' in *Modern Asian Studies 7, 2*, 1973.

Wellek, René and Austin Warren, *Theory of Literature*, Harmondsworth, Middlesex, Penguin Books, 1985.

Wertheim, W. F., *Indonesian Society in Transition*, Bandung, Sumur Bandung, 1956.

6

'I Felt like a Car without a Driver'
Achdiat K. Mihardja's novel *Atheis*

Hendrik M. J. Maier

Published in 1949, at the end of the physical revolution, at the start of political independence of the Republic of Indonesia, Achdiat K. Mihardja's *Atheis, roman* ('The Atheist, a novel')[1] could be regarded as the first national novel of Indonesia. The book appeared under the aegis of the government-controlled publishing house of Balai Pustaka in Jakarta, a place of hegemony, the metropolis which was soon to retrieve its authoritative position in the political and intellectual life that opened up in the new state.

Atheis, roman was immediately hailed as a milestone in the development of modern literature in Indonesian. Readers of a wide variety of ideologies felt addressed, and they reacted accordingly. In the introduction to the second edition of 1953, Achdiat expressed his pleasure with some of the reactions on his book; referring to the opinions of Hidding, Hamka, Pramoedya Ananta Toer and a Malay journalist in Singapore who, each in his own voice, had warmly praised the author's courage to problematize human existence, he concluded that 'the problem that has been woven into the story of the novel is a problem which remains of acute importance in the life of human beings of all times'. These positive reactions could not be but a cause of great pride and pleasure for the author who, being close to the centre of literary authority of the early fifties and at the time working himself for Balai Pustaka, made up part of the Jakarta intelligentsia and shared the desire with many of his fellow authors

---

1) Achdiat K. Mihardja, *Atheis, roman*, Jakarta, Balai Pustaka, 1949.

not only to please but also to teach his public. In the 1953 introduction, the negative reactions that had come from orthodox Muslim circles were passed over in silence, and so were the critical remarks that had been made about the allegedly Freudian analysis of the protagonist's inner turmoil. *Atheis* was to remain the subject of many debates and discussions, in close correspondence with the many voices that emerge from the novel itself: communists, Muslims, nationalists, activists, merchants, civil servants, males, females. Polyphony on two levels, in short: in the novel itself – fragmented and disjunctive – and in the conversations about it – undecided and unresolved. Time and again, up to the present day, in essays and textbooks, in surveys and criticisms reference is made to *Atheis*. A monument. A standard. A compass.

Polyphony plays on yet another level: for the Jakarta intelligentsia, the production of Achdiat's novel, Idrus' short stories and Chairil Anwar's poetry in the years after the 1945 Proclamation of Independence were ample evidence that literature in Indonesian had reached the stage of maturity. This was work that was really worthy of the name of *kesusasteraan Indonesia* (Indonesian literature), a term which had emerged in the newly-constructed Indonesian of the thirties and was now being substantiated in an appropriate manner. As a matter of course, the most respected authors of the new generation whose work started to appear in the tumultuous years of the revolution were not very eager to show much admiration for the prose and poetry that had been published in the late colonial days. Idrus was of the opinion that the older authors were narrow-minded and very provincial in outlook; for Chairil Anwar, Rivai Apin and Asrul Sani it was difficult to be more positive than that. However, such disclaims were too emphatical to be accepted at face value.

Atheis, Achdiat K. Mihardja's first full-blown literary work in Indonesian, was written and published in the last year of the physical revolution; that is not to say, however, that the author felt particularly close to these angry young men. Born in 1911 and raised in a Muslim family, Achdiat had attended the AMS, a Dutch-language secondary school; he had moved in journalistic circles before starting to assist St. Takdir Alisjahbana and Armijn Pane in their work of editing *Poedjangga Baroe*, the journal which had enjoyed great respect among pre-independence intellectuals.

Poedjangga Baroe (established in 1933) had mainly published poetry and essays; in performing its self-assigned task of offering ideas and concepts about modern culture, language, literature, and society, it could not but create an 'avant-garde' aura around the people who ran it. And thus it had to face the fate of every avant-garde: sooner or later its ideas and sentiments acquire a certain familiarity in leading circles and that is the beginning of an often painful end – that is exactly what happened to *Poedjangga Baroe* after Independence.

In 1948 Achdiat edited *Polemik Kebudajaan*, a collection of essays which intellectuals around *Poedjangga Baroe* had published about the new Indonesian culture-under-construction in the last years of colonial rule. *Polemik Kebudajaan* can be read in two ways. It may have been meant to gain control over discussions about the newly created state, and from that perspective, Achdiat's book shows an amazing lack of appreciation of the cultural and societal dynamics which were beyond control at this time of revolutionary turmoil. On the other hand, *Polemik* can be read as a well-intended attempt to provide intellectuals and politicians with some useful and sophisticated ideas about life and institutions in a newly-created state. In both readings, *Polemik Kebudajaan* suggests that Achdiat had a warm sympathy for the older guard to which he belonged not merely in terms of age. His sympathies are even more self-evident if we agree with Umarjati that Anwar, one of the main characters in *Atheis*, is modelled on the *poete maudit* of the young generation, Chairil Anwar; the picture is a very negative one – Anwar is presented as a destructive, egotistic and vain man who in daily life does not live up to the ideals with which he tries to impress the other protagonists of the narrative.

There is yet another reason why Achdiat should be regarded as a member of the older intelligentsia: where the short stories of Idrus, the main prosaist of the new generation, invite a smile and a grimace because of their poignant sarcasm, *Atheis* asks for a patient reading and an admiring gaze. The novel is meticulously con-structed in a language that is well-chosen (not to say studied), full of odd but appropriate metaphors and similes, full of explicit and conflicting ideas about society – in form as well as thematics closer to novels like Armijn Pane's *Belenggoe* (1940), Takdir Alisjahbana's *Lajar terkembang* (1936) and Abdoel Moeis' *Salah Asoehan* (1928) than to the short stories and sketches of Idrus and his successors.

The younger authors – in retrospect they were given the name Generation '45' (*Angkatan 45*), and Achdiat was one of the first to use that name, it seems, in order to create a distance from them – may have been derogatory and dismissive about their predecessors, yet there was at least one thing they had in common with them: the intellectual background of Chairil and Idrus, Asrul Sani and Rivai Apin was as European as Armijn's and Takdir's. No matter how angry or patient, no matter how young or old, they all had to come to terms with the very same shadow of European 'high culture' with which they had become familiar during their upbringing. Operating from the hegemonic aura of Jakarta, the pivot of the new Republic, developments in art and culture in Europe (and the USA) continued to serve as a model of thinking, a standard for activities for these intellectuals; in their urgent efforts to determine the role and function of art, culture and education in the new state they could not but operate against the background of their fascination with the achievements of 'Europe', of Picasso and Rodin, Mann and Dostojevsky, Marsman and Rilke. Their knowledge of European art and philosophy – fragmentary and selective – formed the basis of most of the discussions that were taking place; the differences in political agenda and ideological stance could only add the spice that was needed to make the discussions as lively as they often were.

Not all intellectuals, artists and politicians, however, seem to have been sufficiently down-to-earth to be aware of the fact that these discussions had to be related to a new native state of which the pillars were still thin, shaky, and breakable. Knowledge of the Indonesian language – a version of Malay – was limited; illiteracy was considerable; paper shortage was an everyday problem; the system of formal education was under construction; most members of the new state did not have the leisure time, let alone the habit, to carefully read a two hundred and fifty page novel in an unfamiliar language. Discussions tended to be as lofty and abstract as they had been in the *Poedjangga Baroe* days – and those who wanted to join in but did not have a solid knowledge of European achievements were not taken seriously. In a movement that betrayed arrogance as well as self-confidence, the new establishment soon tended to shut these ignoramuses out. As a result some youngsters felt compelled to have discussions on their own, looking for their inspiration to Eastern Europe, China, and regional cultures, and soon enough counter-ideologies developed which, on the rebound, tried more carefully to be in tune with local cultures and traditions than with 'world culture'. Their point was a sensible one: what could Picasso and Rilke, Steinbeck and Dostojevsky tell Indonesian workers, farmers and soldiers?

Illustration from Atheis, roman *(2nd edition), Balai Pustaka*

The Republic was young, its creation generated vigour, hope and enthusiasm, and many discussions were spent on the question of how to effectively define and implement terms like 'Indonesian culture' (*kebudajaan Indonesia*) and 'Indonesian identity' (*kepribadian Indonesia*). The metropolitan intelligentsia, close to politicians and policy-makers, believed that the *bahasa Indonesia*, the Indonesian language, was to play a predominant role in the life of all citizens of Indonesia. 'Indonesian' was to be the unifying motor of the new state's cultural life which still had to be filled with vitality and creativity; the newly-formed national language was to be the repository from which authority was to spread through a complex of molecular processes, intervening in these processes whenever it was deemed necessary to keep the situation under control, to put it in Gramscian terms.

Within the discursive formations that were taking shape in this national language, literature (*sastra* or *kesusasteraan*) was given a pivotal place. In the late colonial days, prominent thinkers and politicians like Sjahrir had claimed that 'literature' was the only element of the national culture that had already taken a distinct form and should therefore be given a predominant role in the building of the new nation-to-be. In this, Indonesian intellectuals followed a pattern that can be found in many of the newly-created states in the nineteenth and twentieth centuries and could be summarized as follows: an urban intelligentsia, close to political power, close to textbooks and newspapers, close to the capital, tries to appropriate 'literature' as a tool of nation-building and formulates a cultural and educational policy in which it is given a central place. Sjahrir and his comrades tried to be even more specific: what really counted within *kesusasteraan* was the novel whose intention is to picture society in its complexity and fragmentation and which should be seen as the climax of literary art. Here too, Indonesian intellectuals followed the pattern: by exploring questions of racial heterogeneity, socio-economic inequality, urban life versus rural life, the novel in particular was expected to play the role of creating a cultural fiction that could make a substantial contribution to holding a nation together as an imagined community. [2]

Published in the centre of power, hailed by taste-making intellectuals like H.B. Jassin, Hamka, Soedjatmoko and Pramoedya Ananta Toer, *Atheis* was clearly in tune with authoritative discourse in Jakarta. Here was a novel that was strong enough to be given a place of importance in the intellectual life that was developing in the New Republic. Here was an author who had a place of honour and respect, and played his role with dedication: modest, wise, erudite, idealistic and, for a time, the main editor of the government publishing-house of Balai Pustaka, at that. Moreover, in discussions and seminars he expressed his political and cultural stance in a clear and convincing manner. And was he not the one who had edited *Polemik Kebudajaan*, the book that had been so warmly discussed in the early years of the New Republic? A man of stature.

---

2) See Benedict R. O'G. Anderson, *Imagined Communities. Reflections on the Origin and Spread of Nationalism*, London, Verso, 1983, Timothy Brennan, 'The National Longing for Form' in Homi K. Bhabha (ed.), *Nation and narration*, London, Routledge, 1990: 44-70., and Jean Franco, 'The Nation as Imagined Community' in H. Aram Vesser (ed.), *The New Historicism*, London, Routledge, 1989: 204-212.

Atheis was made part of the canon of *kesusasteraan Indonesia*, on a par with novels like *Siti Noerbaja* (1922), *Salah Asoehan* (1928), *Lajar terkembang* (1936), and *Belenggoe* (1940). Domesticated in textbooks. A source of national pride and self-confidence. An example of the 'universal art' to which Indonesian nationalists were eager to make their own distinct contribution.

* * *

Atheis is situated in the years and days preceding Inde-pendence – that is, the last years of Dutch colonial rule and the Japanese period. It pictures life in the big city of Bandung, southeast of Batavia, in the heartland of the Sunda-speaking area of Western Java – lively, busy, noisy, modern – as well as life of the little community of Panjederan, deep in the Sunda country-side – quiet, 'traditional', pastoral. The descriptions of both places must have been recognizable for its contemporary readers. Realistic, that is, similar to the realism which can be found in so many pre-war Malay novels with which Achdiat must have been as familiar as with the novels of Tolstoy, Dostojevsky, Ivanov, and Gide he claimed to have read as a young man in Dutch translations. The narrative forces in *Atheis, roman* easily lead to a realistic reading – about a modern man in Bandung; they equally produce an allegorical reading, about life and death in this world.

Theoreticians like Jameson[3] have claimed that all third-world texts could be read as national allegories; others have rightly argued that such a claim is a dangerous simplification. It cannot be denied, however, that at first sight many of the Balai Pustaka novels that were published under Dutch supervision before the Japanese period (take *Karena mentoea, Siti Noerbaja,* or *Apa dajakoe karena perempoean)* do easily lead to an allegorical interpretation. Their main protagonists are not just individuals with personal desires who have all sorts of adventures; they are also representations of some more abstract phenomena which are usually referred to in sociological or culturological terms, like 'tradition', 'feudalism', 'capitalism', 'modernity', 'static', 'dynamic'. In most Balai Pustaka novels the main protagonist moves from the safe countryside (usually somewhere in the Minangkabau) to a big city (Padang, Batavia, Semarang, Medan) where he is confronted with

---

3) Frederic Jameson, 'Third-world Literature in the Era of Multinational Capital' in *Social Text* 15, Fall 1986: 65-88.

people from other cultural backgrounds as well as with fragments of modern life, like newspapers, trains, clocks, bureaucrats. These confrontations are disruptive experiences and deeply affect him. Upon his return home, to his wife or fiancee, he feels as if he is being strangled by the pressures of tradition, of the community – the conflicts that he has to solve in his community could be interpreted in terms of a clash of personalities but also in terms of a clash between 'tradition' and 'modernity'.

It is possible to present *Atheis* as a continuation of these explorations into the conflict between modernity and tradition; actions and thoughts of its protagonists, it could be argued, read like concretizations of certain ideas, concepts, philosophies, like representations of the predominant currents in Indonesian society. For *Atheis, roman* the argument could run like this: Rusli is the self-confident communist, Hassan the doubting Muslim, Anwar the wild anarchist, and together they weave a story of love and hate around Kartini, the young, attractive, and courageous woman who stands for the Indonesian nation that has been liberated from tradition but needs advice as to how to operate in the new world. By keeping the four protagonists in their distinct moulds – in particular the discussions in the narrative could be read to this effect – *Atheis* offers a consistent representation of the tensions that are generated by modernity and tradition and could be read as an allegory more effectively than any of the Dutch-sponsored Balai Pustaka novels. A climax in allegorical writing, in other words; its thematic pluralism is confirmed in its formal experiments, innovative in comparison with pre-war Balai Pustaka novels (a framed first-person story, presented from a number of perspectives).

Where do so-called Chinese-Malay writings come in, the corpus of narratives which, originating in circles of people of Chinese descent, generated so many more experiments than the corpus of the novels that were published under Dutch supervision? At no time has Achdiat ever explicitly acknowledged his gratitude towards the authors who operated in the Chinese-Malay tradition, and it would not be easy to prove direct links. In the project of *kesusasteraan Indonesia* upon which Armijn Pane, Takdir Alisjahbana, and others were embarking in the wake of their Dutch masters, Chinese-Malay novels were not given a place. They were disposed of with judgments like 'superficial', 'irrelevant', 'mediocre', and textbooks and surveys tend to spend only a few words, if any, on them. It makes the genealogy of modern Malay literature a thin and indistinct one; *Siti Noerbaja, Karena mentoea, Lajar terkembang, Belenggoe,* and then *Atheis*. The real *roman*, the national novel, taking European examples for its model rather than 'native' forms of discourse, either Sundanese or Malay, was real 'literature'!

These were days of hope and shocks, full of expectations and optimism. Order and tradition were questioned, challenged, tested. These were the years in which individual responsibility and personal morality were intensely explored in new forms of language, new words, new expressions. Disjunctures, fragments, polyphony. In its fragmentary form, with its questions about morality, ethics and religion, *Atheis* must have touched a sensitive chord in its urban readership. The climax of a genre, let us say, opening up new vistas to readers and writers. It had the power to enter 'great time', to use another Bakhtinian term: it was meant to have the potential of breaking the boundaries of its own time and to live in other ages, other places, intensely and fully, to be universal, and pluralistic.

A summary of the narrative[4]

In the final years of the colonial period, the main protagonist, *saja* (I), a nameless blackmarketeer in Bandung, is visited by Hassan, a young and nervous man who confides in him and asks him to read the notes he has made of his life so far. Intrigued by the picture Hassan gives of himself, *saja* wants to share Hassan's personal notes with the readers:

The son of a good family in the countryside, Hassan is given a strictly Islamic upbringing; on top of this, he follows a Dutch education, falls in love with a local girl whom he is not allowed to marry, becomes a mystic and eventually decides to leave the village. He finds a job at the Water Board in Bandung and meets an old school friend, Rusli. Rusli, a communist activist, well-read and self-confident, introduces him to his friends and comrades who, in turn introduce him to new ideas and concepts; the most prominent of these friends are Anwar, a bohemian artist, and Kartini, an emancipated divorcee. Hassan gradually loses his Muslim

---

4) In the following, use was made of the 5th edition of 1969.

faith and this causes him great pain; his father's curse further aggravates his burden of remorse and fear. He marries Kartini but their marriage is far from happy. Hassan's notes end with a careful description of the despair and doubt he is experiencing not long before his separation from Kartini – the loss of his religious feelings, the failure of his marriage, the condemnation by his father, his unfocused reading. Here the notes end.

Hassan visits *saja* once more, and they have a long discussion about life, the future, society, but after that he does not show up again; *saja* concludes that Hassan has been killed by the Japanese and decides to finish the manuscript's narrative himself. Partly on the basis of the information he acquires from people close to Hassan, he describes how Hassan, sick, desperate and full of remorse, is wandering through Bandung and is eventually killed in an air-raid at the end of the Japanese occupation.

The beginning of the novel provides us with the end of the story: the blackmarketeer describes how Rusli and Kartini pay a visit to the headquarters of the Japanese army in Bandung shortly after the Japanese capitulation. They are told that Hassan is dead but it remains unclear to them what exactly caused his death: criminal behaviour of the Japanese, or a combination of tuberculosis and maltreatment.

* * *

A summary is a reduction, a deduction, an interpretation – always deceptive, selective, and therefore always inappropriate: it closes off the narrative forces rather than giving them the space they try to create for themselves. *Atheis* is constructed in a very complicated manner. There is a first-person narrative (*aku*, Hassan) that is pushed along by the force of a young man's remorse and fear – remorse about losing his tradition, fear of hell and damnation. This narrative is embedded in the framework of another first-person narrative (*saja*, the blackmarketeer) that is moved along by curiosity, arrogance and desire – curiosity about other people's problems, arrogance about worldly knowledge, desire to complete the narrative and life at once.

The narratives of these two first-persons begin with the end of the story: on pages 7–11 *saja* describes how Kartini, Hassan's ex-wife, and Rusli, his closest friend, conclude that Hassan must be dead; pages 12–236 tell us what happened to Hassan and how

Kartini and Rusli (and *saya* and we, the readers) come to their conclusions. To make things even more complicated, the narrator (*saja*), admits that he has blurred the distinction between *Wahrheit* and *Dichtung* – and this not only applies to his own narrative but also to Hassan's manuscript (pages 16 –184).

A *Rahmerzählung* (the marketeer tells us about Hassan who tells him about himself) the frame of which itself is broken to pieces: chronologically speaking, at the end of the story but at the beginning of the novel, the author sees (and knows) Kartini and Rusli who are informed that Hassan is dead; chronologically speaking, before this but in the novel after it, *saja* comes to know Hassan; then there is Hassan's narrative about his own experiences and recollections which are moving back and forth in time; on top of all this, the wanderings and eventual death of Hassan are presented in a separate layer at the end of the novel – and the narrative's last page suggests that he is shot dead whereas we have already been told in the first pages that he died of tuberculosis and maltreatment.

A manuscript within a manuscript, narrators who are struggling with questions of truth and fiction, and an author who plays with the problems of writing, composition, construction, perspective. Of course Multatuli's *Max Havelaar* comes to mind; the fact that Achdiat K. Mihardja had a Dutch education makes it not improbable that he drew inspiration from one of the greatest Dutch novels of all time.[5] Many perspectives, many layers of time: it is impossible to determine what 'really' happened and to organize the narrative in a summary. This holds true even for Hassan's diary: it could have been the simple report of events described by a single person, authentic, from a single perspective. But, then, the blackmarketeer tells us that he has the impression that Hassan mixed *Dichtung* and *Wahrheit*, and this, he tells us, is a reason for him to have no qualms either about further brushing up Hassan's notes so as to make them look more interesting and coherent. After all, he remains a blackmarketeer and hence unreliable, keen on profit and gain, trying to turn these notes about misery into an interesting commodity that can be sold. A blackmarketeer as a teller of fragmentary and unreliable tales – an effective literary device indeed; on another level, the same could

---

5) See Subagio Sastrowardoyo, *Pengarang modern sebagai manusia perbatasan*, Jakarta, Balai Pustaka, 1989.

be also said of presenting Hassan as working for the Water Board: everything is in a flux.

* * *

> What is the meaning of regret if there is no longer any hope to correct errors? To expiate sins?
>
> But then, could regret vanish because the hope to expiate sins has vanished? Or is the reverse the case, and does the pressure of regret become the stronger, once hope begins to vanish?

Sin (*dosa*), regret (*sesal*), and hope (*harapan*) are words of morality, ethics, religion; they occur several times in these very first paragraphs of *Atheis*. If only for that reason, they offer themselves as keywords in an effort to organize an interpretation of the narrative in terms of right and wrong: the protagonists' actions are clearly presented as errors committed towards God, towards fellow man and, concurrently; thus, the awareness of sin is created and then of regret, of remorse even. *Atheis* is a narrative about man's search for how to overcome regret; the key that opens the door to hope and liberation, however, remains hidden.

The protagonists Kartini and Hassan are searching for a solution to all mistakes, errors, faults, sins which they are making. They do not know where to look for it. They keep circling around one another, around words that remain unfound. Neither is able to conceptualise or name actions and words that could relieve them from their despair and misery. They are not even able to answer the question of why some deeds are thought to be errors and sins and others are not. Not focused, not centered; concurrently, actions, discussions, thoughts seem constantly out of place, misplaced, displaced. *Atheis* is the narrative of people who are in search of something and do not know what it is, how to name it, and how to find it.

From *saja*'s (the blackmarketeer's) perspective, Hassan as well as Kartini are fully aware of their shortcomings; they are pictured as feeling oppressed by regret about what they regard as their personal wrongdoings towards their fellowmen, their community, their Lord, their partner. Similarly oppressed by errors they have made, they are driven by a strong desire to relive experiences from their recent past so as to correct these errors, only to realize that errors cannot be corrected – and that time can not be turned back, let alone be overcome. Worst of all: neither Hassan nor Kartini is able to disentangle and fathom the precise definition of the word *kesalahan* – the word that refers to 'error' as well as to 'guilt', that is, to an action as well as to the feeling about that action. A search to correct an error – or is it a search to correct guilt? A single word that covers two concepts which are successive in time and causal in meaning. An ambiguous goal, in short; no wonder that the search remains undecided.

* * *

In the first pages of the novel, situated at the end of the Japanese occupation, the words 'sin', 'error' and 'regret' are invoked and problematized. Rusli, the novel's most balanced protagonist, offers Kartini the conclusive solution to it all: 'Life of man is short, life of mankind is long, as people say; try to forget your sadness, and work harder than you ever did. Work for humanity'. *Kemanusiaan*, uses the Indonesian for the last word of this quotation, and the dictionary tells us that this word refers to a variety of English words: humanity, humanism, humanitarianism and mankind at once. Another complexity: should Kartini work for people, for mankind, for humanity, for humanism maybe, or for humanitarianism, whatever that may be?

In all, a multiform solution – *kemanusiaan* – to an ambiguous problem – *kesalahan*, and hence in tune with the polyphony and fragmentation of the novel as a whole. Reading a novel should be done from its beginning to its end; reading *Atheis* from beginning to end means that we are first of all told that in 1945 the narrative ends and real life starts with a resounding *kemanusiaan* for those who survived the ordeals of the Japanese and Dutch occupation: narrators, readers and protagonists have to live with 'humanism' as their compass. *Kemanusiaan* is the encompassing answer to all questions that protagonists and readers alike will have in real life after 1945 as well as in the next two hundred pages of the book. It should have been the solution for Hassan, a personification of tradition, who is as dead as the past; it could still serve as a solution to the problems of Kartini, the personification of the Indonesian nation which is given a chance for renewal in the future.

Hassan, the man who tries so hard, fails to make the definite step from tradition to modernity. Urban life has uprooted him from his Islamic certainties. In his search for a new stability he explores the reach of words like 'fear' (*takut*), 'nervous' (*bimbang*) and 'restless', 'excited' (*gelisah*) – only to realize, to his horror, that these words are lacking the stable content for which he is so desperately searching. Altogether, these words refer to modernity, as described by Berman in his breath-taking book on the subject: 'to be modern is to find ourselves in an environment that promises adventure, power, joy, growth, transformation of ourselves and the world – and, at the same time, that threatens to destroy everything we have, everything we know, everything we are. (modernity) pours us all into a maelstrom of perpetual disintegration and renewal, of struggle and contradiction, of ambiguity and anguish.'[6]

His failure to grasp the meaning of the word *kesalahan* leads Hassan towards his disintegration; confronted with anguish and ambiguities, grasping for renewal, he falls into the abyss of a depression which eventually leads to his death. Kartini, the woman who tries so hard but fails to convey her feelings to her husband goes through a similar crisis. For literary reasons her emotions remain rather hazy; the two I-narrators, Hassan and the black-marketeer, offer us little information about her, yet it is obvious that she feels as depressed, as disintegrated as Hassan. First she has followed tradition by marrying the man her parents chose for her; but then she revolts and is uprooted from tradition, just like Hassan. She too is depending on others to overcome her insecurity, leaning on others, haunted by thoughts of regret and sin, by melancholia. She too does not manage to come to terms with these ambiguities of error and guilt, of mankind, humanism and humanity.

* * *

It is no coincidence that these feelings of sin, guilt, and remorse around the unnameable are explored in the city of Bandung; in urban life the individual is exposed to a variety of stimuli and experiences, a polyphony that easily shatters beliefs, hope, convictions. Not only can this be deduced from the protagonists' deeds and thoughts – Hassan's actions and words suggest anguish about many as yet unnameable things, events, emotions –

---

6)   See Marshall Berman, *All That Is Solid Melts into Air – the Experience of Modernity*, London, Verso, 1985, p. 15.

but also from the descriptions of the city which breathe this modern sensibility. It is equally manifest in the comparisons and metaphors that are used ('to see people praying gave them as much pleasure as a movie addict has from watching a movie' and: 'when my beloved's marriage took place... I felt like a car without a driver'). Casual comparisons but certainly effective: tradition is pushed aside by machines, motors, movies.

The description of one of Hassan's many bike-rides to his friend Rusli's home reads as a vignette of big city life and the emotions it creates:

> A beautiful evening. The roads that had been empty from two thirty to four thirty now become crowded again. People who are going to play ball or to walk around in Pasar Baru, the main square, or Braga are flocking along the sidewalks, bathing in the sunlight which is bidding a farewell. The bells of horse-drawn carriages are clanging, as if they do not want to yield to the claxons of the motorcars that are following or passing them on all sides, as though the product of a caged spirit does not want to yield to the product of a free spirit. Bikebells are tinkling and ringing; bikes are easily slipping in between these products of two centuries. The beauty of the evening makes me even more cheerful. Among these thousands of people who are wandering around on the roads probably nobody but me wanted to submit to infidels.[7]

Hassan rides through the crowd, the chaos, the traffic; he experiences all sorts of sounds and colours in an environment that 'promises adventure, joy and transformation of ourselves'; rather than being in continuous shock, he observes things in the pleasantly indifferent manner that makes it possible for a city-dweller to survive: the capacity to evade shocks and yet to have an occasional deep thought. The awareness of time, of machines, mechanics. A vague feeling of bliss.

The depression is felt at home, in the loneliness which is caught between four walls, far away from the bustling streets, full of time, machines and newspapers.[8] Hassan's ties with tradition, however, are still strong. In his autobiographical notes he offers us not only emblematic pictures of life in the city but also of life in

---

7) *Atheis, roman,* p. 58.
8) Franco Moretti, 'Homo Palpitans – Balzac's Novels and Urban Personality' in *Signs Taken for Wonders,* London, Verso, 1988: 109-129.

the countryside, first his recollections about his pious childhood, later his experiences as a grown-up who makes a visit to his parents in the company of the anarchist Anwar who ridicules everything he sees. In his recollections, Hassan realizes that his upbringing was essentially based on a single sentence: *Allahu akbar*, a formula that tried to close him off from the world of everyday life. Under the umbrella of this sentence, life in the village was pastoral, quiet. But pastorality was disturbed, and as it turned out, the world can no longer be summarized in a single sentence: the Lord's authority is being questioned, the tradition ruined, the community broken to pieces; on second sight the village is a static place, depressing and totalizing. In the miserable solitude of his Bandung house Hassan tries to organize his life once more around tradition, around that once all-powerful sentence; he tries some mystical exercises, but the result leads him to despair: he loses his head. 'My head reeled but my body felt as buoyant as that of a boy who had just alighted from a merry-go-round'. Another fine image of modernity, by the way – machines, motors are strong enough to overcome tradition.

* * *

Of course this disintegration is closely linked with language. Hassan is taught, and then talks, in the forms of language that are used by Rusli, Anwar and Kartini, and subsequently a puzzling variety of dialogues (in which 'all that is solid melts into air') is substituted for the all-conclusive monologue of *Allahu akbar*. Hassan is forced to translate his experiences in a discourse with which he is unfamiliar; this is another reason why he is having problems in effectively defining and naming his new reality. What exactly does *kesalahan* refer to? And all those other words? Disruption. Confusion. Loneliness.

Kartini is given the word *kemanusiaan* for a compass in life and language by Rusli after Hassan's death, at the start of a new world; Hassan was given the same word *kemanusiaan* by the blackmarketeer halfway to his downfall:

> What should be our compass in our efforts to perfect our relations? For me, the only criterion is humanity. Humanity is central in feelings of mutual love, mutual compassion, mutual sympathy among the creatures of this world. Really, my friend, together with love, compassion and sympathy,

humanism is the prime basis of our life, eternal, it has to have a fertile life in the heart of everyone of us. And with this humanism for a compass and basis, we use our rationality and common sense, the most important tools we have for reaching perfection.[9]

Kartini as well as Hassan are given the advice to take 'humanism' ('mankind', 'humanity', 'humanitarianism') as the alternative to tradition, to country-life, to monologic Islam, as the key to modern civil society; it is not the only correspondence between the two main protagonists in the drama that is unfolding in the novel.

Again and again, Hassan as well as Kartini are given suggestions by others as to how to live, how to act, how to survive. More than that: they need the others to maintain themselves in society. 'Sin', 'regret', 'remorse' and 'hope' drive Hassan towards his lethal depression at the end of the book, Kartini to her shriek of despair at its start. These words form part of a more comprehensive movement which they are trying to make in the shadow of Rusli and Anwar: the attempt to leave tradition behind and become modern individuals. 'Regret' (*sesal*) and 'sin' (*kesalahan* and *dosa*) are words that refer to individual emotions and personal anguish. They are words of modernity, explored by those who are trying to escape the pressures of their community and become obsessed by their personal search for meaning; they pour us into Berman's maelstrom of disintegration and, hopefully, renewal.

Sesal, *kesalahan* and *dosa* are words that already occur with great regularity in the Balai Pustaka novels in which protagonists are in conflict with custom, tradition and religion. In these novels, however, they are the effect of the protagonists' actions and do not ask for a solution. *Atheis* is different: here the same words are not the result of actions and events but rather their starting point, the motor, so to speak, which makes the protagonists realize that they actively participate in a greater whole: Rusli's sophisticated teaching in politics and culture tells them that they form a part of a country, a nation, which tries to get rid of Dutch and later Japanese repression – and of insecurity and despair – by way of *kemanusiaan*.

---

9)   *Atheis, roman*, p. 193.

***

In giving this strong emphasis on the awareness of an 'imagined community' *Atheis* becomes part of a political project: the newly-formed nation of which Hassan, Kartini, Rusli, Anwar and the others are part should be built on humanity, humanism, mankind – which word should be used? According to Rusli, the black-marketeer, the author, *kemanusiaan* should be the myth, the hook on which all political and cultural values should be hung – and the citizens of the new state of Indonesia, like Kartini and Rusli, should see to it that this myth be implemented.

Polemik Kebudajaan, the collection of essays on modern culture, was published in 1948, edited by Achdiat K. Mihardja who also wrote an introduction.[10] *Atheis* appeared in 1949, and it is self-evident to make a link between the two. In the Introduction to *Polemik* is written: 'Modern time does not allow us to live by looking backward and follow the *adat* institutions that tie the human soul; we have to look forward and use intellect and free thinking to analyse the facts. If there is something that ties us, it should only be our obligation and responsibility for the progress of Humanism (*kemanusiaan*) in the real sense of the word'. It reads like a summary of *Atheis*.

In the new state that came into being shortly after Kartini was told about 'humanism' and 'humanity' as the solution to all problems, the same word *kemanusiaan* was going to have great authority. 'Humanism' was one of the pillars of the state ideology of the new nation as conceptualized by Sukarno and his political friends, and the word appears in all sorts of pamphlets, treatises and statements. It was to emerge again and again in the political writings and speeches of a wide variety of politicians. It echoed in terms like 'humanisme universal', 'humanisme nationalis', and so on and so forth. *Kemanusiaan* resounded in the metropolis in the fifties and early sixties; the question of how to fill it up with meaning was to lead to increasingly virulent confrontations. Achdiat K. Mihardja, the author who had made the term a keyword of his novel, left his homeland in the early sixties; it is tempting to interpret his departure as an indication that the project he helped to start had failed.

---

10) Achdiat K. Mihardja, 'Introduction' to *Polemik Kebudajaan*, Jakarta, Balai Pustaka, 1948.

Achdiat's introduction to *Polemik Kebudajaan* could steer the interpretation of *Atheis* in yet another way. No doubt, many of his sentences were composed against the background of the writings of socialist thinkers like Takdir Alisjahbana and Sjahrir, the only two names that are explicitly mentioned. 'Within the emprisonment of customary law, the mind of an individual is unable to develop freely; thinking can not be critical, emotions can not develop according to the individual will' and then follows a Takdir Alisjahbana-like comparison between static and dynamic societies. 'In the confrontation with the capitalism of western culture, people with open eyes emerge from the depths of a static and feudal society. They carefully look at the culture with which they are confronted, they analyse it, study it, compare it with their own culture, and for the first time ever conflict and unrest emerge in this static culture'. It fully applies to Hassan and Kartini as well as to Rusli, Anwar and the blackmarketeer: all of them are used as pawns in the presentation of the conflict between static and dynamic, tradition and modernity, belief and analysis, custom and individuality, superstition and rationality. Achdiat speaks, it seems, through Rusli and the black-marketeer, the two protagonists who realize that a new world is emerging, in the novel, in Indonesian reality. As the *Polemik* 's introduction formulates it: '... we use the slogan... "know in order to see and act towards the future" because modern time does not allow us to live by looking backward and follow the adat institutions that tie the human soul; we have to look forward and use intellect and free thinking to analyse the facts.'

* * *

Atheis presents its readers with human beings who have to cope with all sorts of personal problems and uncertainties, thus representing elements of a new society that are never to attain a solid coherence. Tradition – personified in Hassan, doubtful, hesitating – is killed by the Japanese. For anarchism – in the person of Anwar – modernity has no place. The responsible modern individual – Rusli – is the man who comes up with a solution for the new situation in which Kartini, the Indonesian nation, is to survive and prosper. The novel could very well be read like a national allegory: nationalism, Japanism, communism, Islam, anarchism, individualism and communalism, many of the ideologies with which people in the young Republic were familiar are sketched and then tentatively unified by a single word, a single slogan. The fact that these very ideologies were to become increasingly incompatible in the fifties and collided in the sixties should only intensify our willingness to give *Atheis* the status of a 'national novel'; under the keyword of *kemanusiaan* it could function as a starting point for further thoughts backwards and forwards into time about the construction of a nation, a state.

* * *

Atheis is presented to us as a *roman*, the Dutch word for novel; writing a 'roman' implies joining a western-oriented project. In the eyes of a Dutch-educated intelligentsia, the publication of *Atheis* was a proof that the new nation was now creating literary art that could and should be universally appreciated and interpreted. Indonesia had acquired a place of its own in the world of nations also in terms of culture, and this novel, source of pride and self-confidence, could be read as part of a political project of creating a national literature, with claims of universal validity: this was a novel as a novel should be. Among intellectuals, few would reject that claim or express amazement about the solution it offered; only fierce nationalists, Muslims and communists had the courage to question the relevance of such a 'universality' in a new state like Indonesia which still had so many internal problems to solve and was so different from the rest of the world. The novel, with its polyphony and confusion, may well be seen as the richest and most sophisticated genre in western literature, but did that automatically imply that it suited Indonesia as well? And should the production of novels really be the main criterion of measuring the success of this project of *kesusasteraan Indonesia*? What was the point of such a project of 'universality' at all within the context of Indonesia, within the wealth of local cultures with their own literary genres, within the construction of *kebudajaan Indonesia*?

Judging from the number of editions that have appeared since its first publication in 1949,[11] we may safely assume that *Atheis* did not really reach a large public; therefore, it could be argued that it failed in spreading the message of *kemanusiaan* as the starting point of political and cultural action. Of course, the

---

11) Editions appeared in 1949, 1953, 1957, and 1956.

influence and impact of texts can never be measured by quantitative criteria alone. The fact that *Atheis* is presented in textbooks as an essential part of the literary canon suggests that it may have had a considerable impact on political and cultural thinking in Indonesia. To say the least, *Atheis'* message was in perfect tune with the vehement discussions about *humanisme universal* that were to dominate political and cultural life in the fifties and early sixties.

Let us stick to the ancient adage that literature can save us, and novels in particular. In the fifties, the novel – *roman, novel, nobel* – was to return to its subterranean role in the discursive formations of Indonesian. The older novels were losing their direct relevance, only very few new and complex novels emerged that could take their place. Intellectuals expressed their worry about this; they started to speak of a crisis in the national project of *kesusasteraan Indonesia*. Now Bakhtin has taught us that the novel is an unfinished genre, the genre of becoming, without finality, without definite form, in an ongoing interplay with other forms of discourse as well as with societal developments, continuously challenging discursive formations, revealing their limits, their artificial constraints, and inviting to surpass them.[12] Obviously, writing in Indonesian continued and expanded; 'novelization' continued with it, although almost invisible and impercept-ible.The limits and constraints of Indonesian literature continued to be questioned, challenged, parodied – in spite of all sorts of direct and indirect forms of censorship.

It was to take another thirty years before some really strong and complex novels came to the surface, in a limited number of pages representing the confusion, the polyphony of this world, and of Indonesia in particular. They were to give new fuel to the motor of the novelization of Indonesia and its culture.

References

Anderson, Brenedict R. O'G., *Imagined Communities. Reflections on the Origin and Spread of Nationalism*, London, Verso, 1983.

---

12) See Tony Bennet, *Outside Literature*, London, Routledge, 1990, pp. 96-7.

Achdiat K. Mihardja, 'Introduction' to *Polemik Kebudajaan*, Jakarta, Balai Pustaka, 1948.

——, *Atheis, roman*, Jakarta, Balai Pustaka, 1949.

Bakhtin, M.M., *The dialogic Imagination – four Essays* (ed. Michael Holquist, translated by Caryl Emmerson and Michael Holquist), Austin, University of Texas Press, 1981.

Bennet, Tony, *Outside literature*, London, Routledge, 1990.

Berman, Marshall, *All that is solid melts into air – the experience of modernity*, London, Verso, 1985.

Brennan, Timothy, 'The national longing for form', in Homi K. Bhabha (ed.), *Nation and narration*, London, Routledge, 1990.

Franco, Jean, 'The nation as imagined community', in H.Aram Vesser, (ed.), *The New Historicism*, London, Routledge, 1989.

Frisby, David, *Fragments of Modernity – Theories of Modernity in the Work of Simmel,Kracauer and Benjamin*, Cambridge, MIT Press, 1986.

Jameson, Frederic, 'Third-world Literature in the Era of Multinational capital' in *Social text* 15, Fall, 1986.

Moretti, Franco, 'Homo Palpitans – Balzac's Novels and Urban Personality' in *Signs Taken for Wonders*, London, Verso, 1988.

Subagio Sastrowardoyo, *Pengarang modern sebagai manusia perbatasan*, Jakarta, Balai Pustaka, 1989.

Umarjati, Bun S. *Roman Atheis. Satu Pembitjaraan*, Jakarta, Gunung Agung, 1962.

From Huaqiao to Minzu:
Constructing New Identities[1] in Indonesia's Peranakan Chinese Literature

Thomas Rieger

Introduction

The territory of present-day Indonesia has known, for approximately the last 1000 years, communities of Chinese immigrants, the oldest of which are presumed to be those of Java which preceded the establishment of such immigrant communities in other parts of Southeast Asia by a considerable period of time. Although never achieving large-scale demographic significance like in Malaysia and Singapore, these Chinese communities have been of considerable importance in urban society. By inter-marriage of the almost exclusively male Chinese immigrants with local women and a steady trickle of new immigrants, in the course of centuries the so-called *Peranakan* communities, the commu-nities of local born Chinese, were established.[2] Links with China, especially since the mid-seventeenth century, were very weak, as the policy of the Manchu discouraged emigration and prohibited emigrants and their descendants from re-entering China. While retaining some Chinese customs, the majority of these Peranakan Chinese was not able to speak or write Chinese. Assimilation of a non-

---

1) The problem of identity poses the question of ontological definition as such. Identity, in the opinion of the author, cannot be defined ontologically, but only as the chosen and assigned (which need not always be the same) place of an individual or group within a set of overlapping and interlinked social systems, each embedded into a historical dynamic.
2) First generation immigrants or those still predominantly Chinese speaking are referred to as *Totok* Chinese.

negligible proportion of this community into the indigenous societies certainly occurred, but new immigration as well as the segregationist policy of the colonial authorities ensured its survival as a relatively distinct group.

This situation began to change only in the second half of the nineteenth century, when the weakened Manchu regime had to make concessions to European powers and America, ceding to them control over major Southern Chinese port towns, and a wave of emigration on an unprecedented scale, partly 'voluntary' to escape poverty and political turmoil, partly through deceit and outright force by the infamous coolie-traders, occurred.

The political crisis of the Manchu, awakening Chinese nationalism which by new immigration and improved means of communication more easily filtered through to the Dutch East Indies, as well as their domestic grievances, all contributed to a certain 're-sinisation' of the Peranakan communities. Peranakan Chinese were among the first non-Dutch to engage in newspaper publishing, to found modern organisations and to publish books in romanized Malay.[3] Along with Pan-Islamism, Pan-Asianism or Christian mission and other forms of western penetration, reformist Confucianism and emergent Chinese nationalism played their role in the reshaping of the intellectual landscape of a predominantly urban community which for a time played such a prominent role in what has been called Indonesia's 'age in motion' (Shiraishi) in the late nineteenth and early twentieth century. Though, as Suryadinata in his study on Peranakan Chinese politics on Java in the 1917-1942 period remarked, the 'Chinese nationalism in colonial Indonesia was not simply a manifestation of Chinese nationalist sentiments; it was also used to improve their social condition and community status in the Dutch East Indies.'[4] Likewise, when from the mid-1920s onwards a growing proportion of Peranakan Chinese opted to be regarded as one group among what was called 'Dutch subjects' and to be regarded

---

3) For the Peranakan Chinese's role in the birth of the Indonesian press see A. Adam, *The vernacular press and the emergence of modern Indonesian consciousness (1855-1913)*, unpublished Ph.D. thesis, London, SOAS, 1984; for their activities in the field of early book publishing see C. Salmon, *Literature in Malay by the Chinese of Indonesia. A Provisional Annotated Bibliography*. Paris, Edition de la MSH, 1981.
4) L. Suryadinata, *Peranakan Chinese Politics in Java*, rev.ed., Singapore, Singapore University Press, 1981, p. 169.

as part of the Indies' society, it was the *construction* of a new identity for new political purposes rather than any dramatic changes in language, customs, basic norms or values that brought about this shift.

Although to a lesser degree than in the case of Malaysia, this reorientation had some significance for the process of nation-building in Indonesia as well. As the phenomenon can be regarded, moreover, as sharing some typical traits with developments in Malaysia and other Southeast Asian countries, we propose here to use the categories established by Tan Liok Ee in her work on Chinese political discourse in Malaysia,[5] where Huaqiao denotes adhesion to/orientation towards the Chinese nation, i.e. a self concept of an overseas member of that imagined community,[6] whereas Minzu denotes a self-concept of the descendants of Chinese immigrants where they place themselves within the framework of the nation on whose territory they have their residence, although as a distinct group bearing cultural traits conceived as being Chinese.

It should be noted here that, as the Indonesian Peranakan community's political discourse was predominantly in Malay, the Huaqiao-Minzu dichotomy is not to be observed in the same form in their political discourse. The word *Huaqiao* is used there fairly inconsistently denoting anything from somebody identifying him/herself as a member of the Chinese nation staying abroad to somebody feeling a part of the nation controlling his/her territory of residence, but also feeling some vague cultural attachment to the land of his/her ancestors. The phenomenon as such, however, definitely existed in Indonesia too, and Tan's categories seem to be an appropriate description and furthermore a valuable point of departure for future comparative analysis.

On the level of organisations or the press, quite a lot of research has been done over the period in question, but very little with regard to another discourse, politically so important at the

---

5) Tan Liok Ee, *The Rhethoric of Bangsa and Minzu: Community and Nation in Tension, The Malay Peninsula, 1900-1955*, Working Papers No. 52, Monash University,1988.

6) The term is Anderson's. See Benedict R. O' G. Anderson, *Imagined Communities. Reflections on the Origin and Spread of Nationalism*. London, Verso, 1983.

time, i.e. literature. The present article should be seen as a preliminary attempt at starting to fill this gap.

1905-1924: Constructing the Chinese Nation in Bazaar Malay Literature

It has been only little more than a decade since the long term conceptual exclusion of works by Peranakan writers from Indonesian literature was dealt a lethal blow by the pioneering work of C. Salmon, *Literature in Malay by the Chinese of Indonesia. A Provisional Annotated Bibliography*.[7] This question has obviously a lot to do with identity too, i.e. that of the Indonesian nation as a whole, but it cannot be dealt with here.[8] It should be noted, however, that Indonesia's Peranakan Chinese community played a major role in the formation of a literary discourse as such in the country[9] and also had a certain influence on the process of 'writing the nation'[10] in Indonesia. Before going into details of identity construction in literary works, a number of peculiarities of this literary production will be briefly touched on here.

Historically speaking, the notion of 'traditional literature' is a very misleading oxymoron, because the very act of producing texts in romanized Malay, belonging to this new discourse, had a lot to do with delineating identity. It meant placing oneself in the context of the emerging urban middle class public of the Indies of the time. Without being necessarily openly anti-colonial, the very act of producing texts in a language other than that of the col-

---

7) Cf. footnote 3.
8) Recently the issue has at last been taken up, however, by the scientific community in Indonesia as the conference on Sino-Malay literature at the Universitas Indonesia in early 1992 shows.
9) The present day concept of sastra is roughly identical to the post-romantic western concept of literature as a discourse in the Foucaultian sense. This state of affairs, however, is not the product of a universal striving of humanity towards the creation of textual beauty but the process of a profound restructuration of the Malay discourse system in the latter half of the nineteenth century; for a more detailed analysis see T. Rieger, *Le récit du movement nationaliste avant 1942 dans la littérature indonésienne*, Ph. D. thesis Ecole des Hautes Etudes en Sciences Sociales, Paris, 1992, pp. 25-39.
10) The concept is Bhabha`s. See Homi K. Bhabha, 'DissemiNation: time, narrative and the margins of the modern nation' in Homi K. Bhabha, (ed.),*Nation and Narration*, London, Routledge, 1990, pp. 291-322.

onisers and also different from the brand of Malay promoted by the colonisers, had a strong emancipatory aspect, clearly felt by the Dutch as their continuous, if vain, efforts to curb this development show.[11]

Furthermore, this literature, constructing a 'Chinese' identity, was never written in Chinese. It was written in urban colloquial Malay of the time which is sometimes referred to as Bazaar Malay. To the knowledge of the author, not a single Chinese language novel had been produced by Peranakan writers at the time![12]

In choosing the texts of this period to be treated in this preliminary study we have limited ourselves to original works, thus excluding the translations into colloquial Malay of Chinese classics flourishing at the time, which found themselves transformed into entertaining literature and certainly had their share in the construction of Chinese identity. We moreover concentrate on texts where clear allusions to political topics relevant to the Peranakan Chinese public are found. It is obvious, however, that other, ostensibly 'less political' texts are not necessarily less im-portant for the construction of identity under review and will have to be included in a more extensive analysis.

There are three major topics, which are the crucial points for delineating Peranakan identity as Huaqiao:

- 'Pan-Chinese' issues, i.e. issues affecting Chinese in as well as outside the Dutch East Indies, like the current of confucianist reformism or the cutting of the pigtail;
- questions affecting the Indies' Peranakan status of national-

---

11) For a most interesting account of this cultural counterinsurgency programme launched by the Dutch mainly through their colonial publishing house see D. Jedamski, *Die Institution Literatur und der Prozess ihrer Kolonisation. Enstehung, Entwicklung und Arbeitsweise des Kantoor voor de Volkslectuur/ Balai Pustaka in Niederländisch Indien zu Beginn dieses Jahrhunderts*, Unpublished Ph. D. thesis, Hamburg University, 1991.

12) Nor, by the way, did the new immigrants from China, of whom at least the better educated would be in a much better position to do so, produce any such works. There are later works on Indonesia produced by *Huaqiao* in the Chinese language – but published well after their return to China. See C. Salmon, 'A Chinese View of the Indonesian Revolution: The Adventure of Gao Yangtai (1982)' in B. Eberstein/B. Staiger, (eds), *China. Wege in die Welt – Festschrift für Wolfgang Franke zum 80. Geburtstag*. Institut für Asienkunde, Hamburg (1992), 1992.

ity, like the Dutch Nationality Law *(Wet op het Nederlandsch Onderdaanschap)* and compulsory militia service;
- issues of Chinese cultural identity, like the defence of Chinese values against the encroachment of Christianity or of certain traditional customs against western concepts.

As for the first group, we find the motive of the schools of the *Tiong Hoa Hwe Koan* (THHK)[13] providing/having provided education for the heroes of the stories told, imbuing them with Chinese values and pride of their nation. Instances of this type of allusions are numerous, an instructive example being provided by Kwee Seng Tjoan's novel *Tjerita anak prampoean di bikin sebagi parit mas atawa iboe jang doerhaka* (The Story of a daughter transformed into a source of revenue or The Wicked Mother) published in Jakarta in 1917. The story's hero is Keng Hok, a young immigrant from Fujian province living in a Peranakan milieu of down town Batavia (Jakarta) and, after having gone to a traditional vernacular school attached to the local temple, is sent by his father to the newly established THHK-school. The author describes first the general importance of the foundation of the THHK for the Indies Chinese (p. 23):

> After our people here in the Indies have been united and have realised that education is extremely useful in order to earn a living, but under conditions where one has to learn a difficult foreign language in order to enrol in a school which is anyway so expensive that only children of the rich can afford it, it was under such circumstances that they founded the Tiong Hoa Hwe Koan.[14]

It is thus ONE school for ONE people, the people of the young hero, and that is the Chinese people, comprising the Peranakan

---

13) The Chinese Association, founded in 1900, the first and principal of the Pan-Chinese organisations in the Dutch East Indies and the first modern Indonesian organisation; the most comprehensive account of its history is given by Nio Joe Lan, *Riwajat 40 taon dari Tiong Hoa Hwe Koan-Batavia 1900-1939*, Batavia, THHK, 1940.

14) 'Tapi setelah kita poenja bangsa di ini Insulinde soeda bisa bersatoe hati dan dapet taoe djoega bahoewa pladjaran ada sanget bergoena boeat orang mentjari pengidoepan, sementara boeat bladjar bahasa asing terlaloe soesa boeat bisa di trima didalem itoe sekola serta pembajarannja ada sanget mahal, djika boekan anaknja orang hartawan atawa orang jang dapet gadji besar soeda tentoe tida bisa dapet itoe pladjaran, maka itoe ia orang soeda berdiriken Tiong Hoa Hwee Koan.'

which were in fact the dominant force in the foundation of the THHK.[15]

This orientation becomes even clearer in another scene (p. 77), where the school's director is delivering a speech on the occasion of rewarding the most successful students – among them, of course, the hero of the story – at the end of the year:

> You, the students, should not forget, that we have established this school with tremendous effort, hoping that this effort will bear fruit in the future by enabling our people here in the Indies to use its own language and writing. When all Huaqiao can read Chinese characters, only then can love for our fatherland blossom in our hearts and we will again be able to strengthen our ties with China! Study diligently, in your own interest and that of your nation![16]

This blend of traditional Chinese 'culturalism' and newly emerging nationalism in the political discourse of Peranakan authors is quite typical for this early period of the reshaping of the overall intellectual and political landscape of the Dutch East Indies transforming eventually into Indonesia.

Salmon[17] has analysed a lengthy narrative poem, the *Sair Tiong Hwa Hwe Kwan koetika boekanja Passar derma* by Tjia Ki Siang (1905) which abounds in evocations of the advantages of a THHK education, that is a reformist Confucianist education in Mandarin, not Chinese vernacular, Malay or Dutch, for the 'Chinese nation', the Peranakan of the Indies. There are numerous other examples where through the place of the THHK motive in the narrative structure or in certain semantic isotopies, the positive Chinese

---

15) Cf. the analysis of the backgrounds of early THHK-Batavia leaders by Lea E. Williams, *Overseas Chinese Nationalism. The Genesis of the Pan-Chinese Movement in Indonesia, 1900-1916*, Glencoe, The Free Press, 1960, pp. 137-142.
16) 'Dan sekarang moerid-moerid moesti inget, jang kita orang soeda berdiriken ini roema pegoeroean dengen soesa dan boewang banjak tanaga dengen harepan boeat dapetken boeahnja di kemoedian hari, jaitoe soepaja kita poenja bangsa di ini Insulinde bisa mengenal hoeroef dan bahasa sendiri. Djika semoewa Hoa Kiauw bisa batja soerat Tionghoa, di itoe waktoelah baroe bisa timboel kita orang poenja ketjintahan hati pada kita poenja tanah aer dan djoega kita orang poenja perhoeboengan dengen Tiongkok bisa djadi rapet kombali! Bladjarlah dengen soenggoe-soenggoe ini ada kebaekan boeat sekalian moerid-moerid poenja diri dan djoega boeat kebaekan kita poenja bangsa!'
17) C. Salmon,' Le Sjair de "l'Association Chinoise" de Batavia', *Archipel* No. 2, 1971, pp. 55-100.

identity of positive characters is reinforced, sometimes even more markedly by ascribing non-Chineseness or a lack of Chinese identity to the wicked opponents of such characters. To name just a few, there are the novels *Souw Leng Tat atawa Korban dari Akalan* (Souw Leng Tat or The Victim of Deceit) by Hwa Kim Pit (1920) and *Soeami jang boeta* (The blind husband) by Njoo Cheong Seng (1923) or the piece *Allah jang palsoe* (The false god) by Kwee Tek Hoay (1919).

The other pan-Chinese issue to be found in the literary works to be considered here is the fight for cutting the pigtail. Although the issue is a very complex one in the Indies[18] it can be safely stated, that fairly early in this century it was, at least in the more progressive-minded circles of the Peranakan community, agreed that the pigtail or thauwtjang was a disgrace to the Chinese nation.[19] In 1905 there appeared a narrative poem, again by Tjia Ki Siang, entitled *Boekoe sair kabaikannja orang jang hendak melepas thauw-tjang, dari fihak kaum moeda* (The *syair* about the advantage of cutting the pigtail, according to the modernists). The pigtail is first branded as a symbol of Manchu reign and Chinese misère (stanza 7), then the example of the Japanese – enjoying prestige because of their recent victory against Russia – is presented to prove the advantage of being a nation on the path of progress (stanza 24) and finally all this is linked to the organisational efforts of the Indies Chinese striving to carve out new ways independently from the Dutch (stanza 58):

Koetika Beng Tiauw pegang kwasa,
Tersohor tjina gaga perkasa,
Sedari Tjheng-tiauw Thauw-tjang di paksa,
Sampe sekarang djadi binasa.

---

18) Under Dutch colonial law each ethnic group was supposed to dress in its customary way, to the effect that wearing the pigtail was compulsory for the Chinese. Semarang's tycoon Oei Tiong Ham is the first reported case of a Chinese, who by permission of the governor general, had his pigtail cut in 1889 (See Liem Thian Joe, *Riwajat Semarang 1416-1931*, Semarang, Ho Kim Joe, 1933, p. 154.), but he did so when quitting the Chinese quarter to live in the European one; on the other hand until the victory of the Chinese revolution in 1911 there were still conservative Peranakan wearing this symbol of the Manchu; a paper of the author on these subjects is forthcoming.
19) For the voice of a Chinese reformist of that time see for example Oei Tiang Seng, 'Thowtjang' in *Bintang Hindia* vol. 1, (1903), No. 23, 14.11. 1903, pp. 247 f.

Orang sekarang lebi mengarti,
Di timbang betoel jang tela misti,
Liatken djepang mendjadi boekti,
Lepaskan Thauw-tjang traboleh mati.

Dapet ingetan bikin koempoelan,
Hendak atoerken sewaktoe djalan,
Kita sendiri ada oengkoelan,
Troesa di toeroet boewatannja holan.[20]

The theme of the pigtail is again linked very explicitly with the question of Peranakan identity when Tjia urges his fellow Peranakan to use the Chinese language:

Bitjara tjina hendak di pake,
Soepaja njata toeroenan sengke,
Djikaloe ada jang matjam bike,
Ripoe lah dia temengke-mengke.[21]

---

20) 'When the Ming reigned/China's strength and power was well known/ Since the Manchu [have risen to power] the pigtail has been enforced/and until now we're down. Now people understand better/they consider what has to be done/look at the Japanese, they give proof/if you cut the pigtail you won't die. We've got the idea of building an organisation/to determine our destiny (?)/we are the greatest/and need not to copy the ways of the Dutch'.
21) 'The Chinese language should be used/To make clear that we are of Chinese stock (lit. are descendants of the newly immigrated)/If any of us hides his Chineseness/he will be the most miserable creature.' The exact translation of the last two lines of this stanza poses some difficulty and the solution that we propose might be contested. In the third line we interpreted 'bike' as consisting of 'bi' 匿 (See J. J. C. Francken and C. F. M. de Grijs, *Chi-neesch-Hollandsch Woordenboek van het Emoi Dialekt*, Batavia, Bataviaasch Genootschap van Kunsten en Wetenschappen, 1882, p. 25), or 密 (p. 26) 'to slip in clandestinely' or 'to hide'. The element 'ke' should be interpreted parallel to 'sinke', but not too narrowly as 'immigrant' but in a larger sense as 'Chinese', as 'toeroenan sinke' in the second Line is also meant as 'of Chinese stock' and not just literally as 'descendants of the newly immigrated'. The term 'bike' then might be interpreted not as 'clandestine immigrant' but as 'somebody hiding his/her Chineseness'. We have not been successful in tracing the term temengke-mengke (nor any root, or grammatical/phonetical variations of it) in any Malay or Javanese dictionary. As the author renders the final [ŋ] of a syllable with a consecutive [g] in the initial position of the next syllable not as ngg (cf. 'oengkoelan' in the previous stanza = 'unggulan' in present day Bahasa Indonesia spelling) as convention went even in most colloquial Malay texts of the time, it might be derivated from the root 'mengga' (complete, perfect). Ripoe lah... temengge-mengge might thus mean something like 'most miserable'.

The Chinese republican and nationalist revolutionary movement itself is dealt with lengthily in Tan Boen Kim's novel *Nona Kim Lian* (Miss Kim Lian) (1916), but only isolated references are made to the situation in Java where that movement was also present in the form of the *Soe Po Sia* (Reading Rooms) branches in many major cities.[22] One reference is to be found in a footnote on p. 314, where a Chinese language anonymous brochure of the revolutionaries, distributed on Java, is mentioned. Interestingly enough, the love story between a young revolutionary journalist, Kwee Tiong Boen, and Kim Lian, a well educated but poor girl, is written in a style which sounded probably very familiar to the average Peranakan reader. Names of characters are all according to Hokkian pronunciation, as are most of the other Chinese words (forms of address etc.). Were it not for occasional Chinese toponyms, the setting could just as well have been in the Indies. This style of familiarity differs markedly with the style of the exotic used in later stories with a Chinese setting. The congruence from the shift from direct identification with China towards an Indonesia-centred identity is certainly not a matter of chance.

Interestingly enough, the topic of this novel, the life of young lovers involved in the nationalist movement, was to become an extremely popular one among Sumatran (and some Javanese, but all non-Peranakan) nationalist writers in the late 1930s. Even the combination – a male journalist with a well-educated girl – was to be the same.

A central issue of Peranakan politics during the period under consideration here, was the question of the nationality status of the Peranakan community. China, after centuries of total disregard or even hostility towards emigrated Chinese, had made a sharp turn in 1909 by declaring all persons of Chinese descent to be Chinese nationals.[23] This was answered by the Dutch, fearing a loss of control over an important group of the population of their colony, by promulgating the Dutch Nationality Law which declared the Peranakan to be Dutch subjects. The Chinese nation-

---

22) For an account of Soe Po Sia in the Indies cf. Lea E. Williams, *Overseas Chinese Nationalism. The Genesis of the Pan-Chinese Movement in Indonesia, 1900-1916*, pp. 103-109.
23) See L. Suryadinata, *Peranakan Chinese Politics in Java*, p. 25f.

alists conducted a vigorous campaign against this law, urging the Peranakan to declare themselves aliens, i.e. Chinese nationals.[24]

We have so far traced only one literary work, where this motive is to be found, but there it is clearly linked with other constitutive elements of a Huaqiao identity of a Peranakan hero. Tan Kioe Gie, the hero of Kwee Tek Hoay`s *Allah jang palsoe* (1919), idealistic young Peranakan journalist, excelling in all Confucianist virtues, choosing a Chinese educated wife etc., quits his well paid job as editor in chief of a Peranakan newspaper when the owner tries to force him to take an apologetic attitude towards the plans of the Dutch government to make the Peranakan Dutch subjects and to make them serve in an Indies militia (p. 59). The last point, also linked to the question of nationality, seems to have figured in a number of other works which have not been at our disposal or which are currently no longer available. These include Phoa Tjoen Hoat's novel *Ah soeda kasep. Tjoe Ka Lam satoe journalist jang djadi milicien* (Ah, it's too late. Tjoe Ka Lam, a journalist who became militia member) (1918) and Kho Tjoen Wan's *Boekoe sair Indie Weerbaar* (1917).

A third category of motives delineating Huaqiao identity are connected with issues of Chinese cultural patterns. Tan Boen Kim, pioneer journalist and one of the most outstanding Peranakan novelists of the time, portrays in his novel *Nona Lan Im* (Miss Lan Im) (1919) the love story between a young Peranakan girl, Lan Im, firmly adhering to what is regarded as Chinese values and a young Peranakan man from a Christian family background, Kim Leng. The latter finally abandons his 'alien' faith and marries Lan Im, but not in a way violating the principles of filial piety so dear to Confucianist thought: when his uncle (who has brought him up) dies practically at the very moment that Kim Leng is supposed to marry the girl that the family has chosen for him, he reaches an agreement to break off this engagement as it may incur further bad luck (p. 156). And only after his aunt dies a short time later, does he finally break with the Church (p. 157). Kim Leng`s rupture with Christianity and his embracing of what are conceived as Chinese values has a deeper symbolic significance for the demarcation of Peranakan identity. It is the emanci-pation of Chinese nationalism in the Indies from the Christian mission to

---

24) For a detailed account of this issue cf. ibid pp. 25-38.

which it owed – paradoxically even in the field of reformist Confucianism – historically not little of its initial impetus.[25]

Another theme that was of some relevance for ascertaining one's Chineseness may be a specific aspect of sexual morale, i.e. the taboo of marriage between people of the same surname (*she*[26]). Hardly anybody, even at that time, would have branded such a marriage as incestuous, but it was against the exogamic marriage pattern believed to be central to the Chinese culture and therefore opposed by many. In Kwee Tek Hoay's piece *Allah jang palsoe* (The false god) (1919) one of the means of portraying the hero's antagonist as the 'bad guy', the one who has ceased to be a Chinese, is to let him marry a widow of the same surname. The question, however, was not so clear-cut at the time; Phoa Tjhoen Hoay, a journalist from Bogor, who linked the question of customs to the cause of nationalism in a preface to his novel *Tjhik tjhik Boeng Nona Kampoeng* (1918) also dealing with that topic, refused explicitly to pass a judgement on the issue.

In conclusion it can be stated, that – at least in part – the Peranakan literature of the time was engaged in the effort of constructing a Huaqiao identity of the Peranakan, uniting them with the other Chinese (newcomers to the Indies as well as in China herself), making them part of the imagined community that constitutes the Chinese nation.

1925-1942: Reorientation towards an Indies Identity

At the Semarang-conference in 1917 the Huaqiao nationalists of the SIN PO-group gained a victory when their line of non-participation in colonial political institution, on the grounds that Peranakan were Chinese aliens, was accepted by the representatives of the major Chinese organisations.[27] This date marked

---

25) For a discussion of the link between Christian mission and the early Confucianist reformism in the Indies see Charles A. Coppel, 'From Christian Mission to Confucian Religion: The Nederlandsche Zendingsvereeniging and the Chinese of West Java, 1870-1910' in D. P. Chandler and M. C. Ricklefs, (eds), *Nineteenth and Twentieth Century Indonesia. Essays in Honour of Professor J. D. Legge*, 1986, pp. 16-39.
26) Xing (性) in Standard Chinese.
27) An account of the conference is found in L. Suryadinata, *Peranakan Chinese Politics in Java*, pp. 14-20.

in a certain sense the high tide of Huaqiao sentiments among the Peranakan of Indonesia.

Towards the mid-1920s a gradual shift began to occur. Friction between Peranakan and Totok (China born or Chinese speaking immigrants) was more openly discussed, some originally Huaqiao-minded intellectuals became disenchanted with their former ideals[28] and the Indies-oriented forces started to organise.[29] Things in China had not improved like the revolution had promised, there was still no strong Chinese government in a position to protect its citizens in the Indies. The Dutch colonial authorities had removed a number of particularly discriminatory regulations affecting the Peranakan, in particular the segregationist settlement pattern, the limitations on travelling, the obligation to dress in traditional way and to wear the pigtail. Perhaps even more important, at least for middle class Peranakan plenty of educational facilities were provided by the Dutch, making the THHK-schools increasingly the domain of Totok-Chinese.

This being in broad terms the general political background to the shift in the identity, the self-concept of the Peranakan, there are a number of general observations to be noted regarding their literary production, before we go into the details of the way the new identity was constructed in literary texts.

The characters from the mid-1920s increasingly have at least partly western names and are educated in Dutch schools. The Dutch educational facilities for the Peranakan, the HCS (Dutch Chinese Schools), were producing a sufficiently large, westernised, young reading public to sustain a new type of entertaining novel with westernised characters with whom the reader could identify.

It is interesting in this context that translations of Chinese classics had a proportionally less important weight within the totality of textual production than in the preceding period, whereas the proportion of entertaining novels (both original ones

---

28) For example, Liem Koen Hian, the later champion of Peranakan involvement of the fight for Indonesian independence took up a job at the *Soeara Poebliek* newspaper in 1925 and changed his view from a China-orientated view towards his concept of Indies citizenship (Ibid, p. 129).

29) Important dates in this respect are the Chung Hwa Congres in Semarang, April 1927 (Ibid, pp. 49 ff.) and the foundation of Chung Hwa Hui at the second Chung Hwa Congres again in Semarang, April 1928 (Ibid, pp. 57-63).

and translations from popular contemporary fiction from China) rose dramatically.[30]

The main relevant motives for the construction of the new Minzu-identity were among others:

- The description of the crisis of Chinese organisations
- The presentation of China as the 'Other'
- The appearance of Indies-based utopias

These are only the most prominent of the motives used in the construction of the new identity, naturally any given piece of literary discourse could contain all or part of these 'ingredients' in the new cocktail.

While during the preceding period Chinese organisations, be they Peranakan or Totok dominated – making this difference was, off course, carefully avoided – were presented as the key to Chinese progress and Chinese unity, as a means of Chinese nation building, we now find some very down-to-earth accounts of what happened in the ordinary organisational life of these associations. The motive of 'Chinese organisation in crisis' can be found in numerous works, sometimes simply depicted or deplored, sometimes combined with scathing criticism of what was conceived of being their weaknesses. One of the earliest examples was the piece *Korbannja Kong Ek* (Victim of Social Commitment)[31] of Kwee Tek Hoay (1925). In this piece, modelled on Ibsen's *An Enemy of the People*,[32] Kwee presents a mismanaged Chinese school to offer a scathing criticism of the functioning of the Chinese organisations of the time in general. In particular the Huaqiao nationalists are presented as a bunch of irresponsible hypocrites, opposed to the selflessly working activist of a local orientation. The piece marks for the author, one of the most outstanding Peranakan intellectual of the pre-war period, the break with the SIN PO-group.

---

30) See C. Salmon, *Literature in Malay by the Chinese of Indonesia. A Provisional Annotated Bibliography*, p. 62f.
31) The work has been described in T. Rieger, *Kwee Tek Hoay sebagai dramawan*, unpublished thesis submitted for the Sarjana Sastra degree at the Universitas Indonesia, Jakarta, 1987, where also a summary of the plot is to be found (pp. 138 f.)
32) C. Salmon, *Literature in Malay by the Chinese of Indonesia. A Provisional Annotated Bibliography*, p. 211.

In a similar vein is Ong Siauw King's novel *Terloenta-loenta* (Suffering)[33] (1927), one of the rare Peranakan publications from Sumatra (Palembang), which describes the fate of a Huaqiao activist organising support for the victims of natural disasters in China, but marginalised in Palembang Peranakan community

Cover and front page of Ong Siauw King's "Terloenta-Loenta"

when his business runs into trouble because too long neglected for the sake of his community work. Enthusiasm has died, selfishness reigns, sacrifice for the cause of the Chinese nation doesn't pay off: this is in brief the message the two authors try to convey to their public.

Presenting China as the 'Other' is another textual innovation of this period contributing to the construction of a new identity available to the Peranakan community. Surely the most important instance for this phenomenon is the topic of the Sino-Japanese War in numerous novels of Peranakan authors between 1932-

---

33) For brief summary see T. Rieger, *Le récit du mouvement nationaliste avant 1942 dans la litterature indonésienne*, p. 191.

1941.[34] Although some of these novels, especially those by Tjie Tek Goan, display a strong measure of Han chauvinism, China is nevertheless presented in all of these novels as the 'Other': there are hardly any Peranakan characters to identify with, Mandarin variants of names in place of Hokkian versions are given (which used to be the other way round during the preceding period, cf. Tan Boen Kim's *Nona Kim Lian*) and the whole plot is presented as something far away from the reader. It is no longer 'us' involved in fighting, but 'them', no matter how sympathetic the account may be vis-à-vis the Chinese side.

In at least one case, the motive of criticism of Chinese organisations overlaps with that of the Sino-Japanese War, i.e. in Kwee Tek Hoay's novel *Pendekar dari Chapei* (The Fighter/Warrior from Chapei), a lengthy novel published in 1932, in which Kwee once again attacks vigorously the Huaqiao nationalists and their efforts to help China through boycotts of Japanese goods and collection of funds.

Interesting enough in this regard is the fact that in a number of novels by non-Chinese Indonesian nationalist writers one finds Totok activists in Indonesia raising funds, like in Ananta Gs.'s *Tjong Kuo Kuo Ko* (1940), or Muslim Chinese in China fighting hand to hand with the Japanese invaders, like in Jusuf Sou'yb's *Pengorbanan di medan perang* (Sacrifice at the battle field), but again there are no Peranakan characters. The sense of a common anti-imperialist cause among certain Indonesian nationalists seems thus to have been stronger than the feeling of belonging to the Chinese nation among the majority of Peranakan.

This last observation reaffirms the significance of a variation on this motive, the description of the efforts of a Peranakan in linking up with China as being in vain. This point is very clearly made in another piece by the extremely prolific Kwee Tek Hoay, *Korbannja Yi Yung Thoan* (A victim of the 'Brigade of Courage') published in serialised form in Kwee's own review Panorama in 1928 and aimed, once again, at his foes from the SIN PO-group of Huaqiao nationalists. Yi Yung Thoan was a short-lived organ-

---

34) For a more detailed account of the topic of the Sino-Japanese war in Indonesian literature in general (thus including the works of Peranakan authors) see T. Rieger, 'Le guerre sino-japonaise dans la litterature indonésienne' in C. Salmon, (ed.), *Le moment "sino-malais" de la littérature indonésienne, Cahier d'Archipel* No. 19, Paris, Archipel, 1992.

isation of Huaqiao nationalists close to SIN PO which was founded to organise the dispatch of a volunteer brigade of Indies Peranakan to aid Chiang Kai Shek in his campaign against the warlord government of the North in 1926. The project was a failure, however, when a number of young people sent to China suffered considerable hardships there and SIN PO was criticised for having lent support to an irresponsible endeavour. SIN PO however pointed to the fact that participants in the project had left their assignment in order to evade the hardships of military life or to otherwise enjoy themselves.[35] The publication of the piece was accompanied by the publication of interviews with and letters from those returned in order to prove Kwee's point, that involvement into China's politics was futile and Peranakans could only be the losers when turning to China in place of striving to improve their lot in the Indies.

The appearance of Indies-based utopias is another indicator of a shift towards an Indies-centric identity and also a means of constructing such an identity. Perhaps the two most outstanding examples of such utopias in the works of Peranakan authors of the period are those to be found in Liem Khing Hoo's *Berdjoeang* (Fighting) (1934) and in Kwee Tek Hoay's *Drama di Boven Digoel* (Drama in Boven Digoel) (1929-1932, as feuilleton).

Liem's novel, published as part of the popular Surabaya-based TJERITA ROMAN series, describes a community of jobless Peranakan youth during the economic crisis of the early 1930s who, through their collective effort in Kalimantan, build themselves a new existence.

The novel is extraordinary in many respects and constitutes a landmark in the shift from a Huaqiao to a Minzu pattern of identity. Among the new features are:

- in place of rejecting Dutch citizenship, rather, demanding that concrete rights for Peranakan Chinese should flow from this status (pp.19,37,68);
- placing the evolution of the Peranakan community and its culture *expressis verbis* into the framework of Indonesian history (p. 8, 11);

---

35) For a brief account of the affair see L. Suryadinata, *Peranakan Chinese Politics in Java*, pp. 44 f., for an account on its literary treatment see T. Rieger, *Kwee Tek Hoay sebagai dramawan*, pp. 103-113 and T. Rieger, *Le récit du mouvement nationaliste avant 1942 dans la litterature indonésienne*, p. 154.

- demanding land for the Peranakan Chinese as a stable economic basis, thereby implicitly giving it a territorial basis (p. 72);
- referring to the Malay language as the future language of Indonesia, and, still more important, as the mother tongue of the Peranakan community (p. 100);
- as a remedy against the devastating effects of the economic crisis on the Peranakan Chinese community of Indonesia no help from China, nor the perspective of returning there is ever offered, instead the necessity of reliance on the Peranakan community's own efforts within Indonesia is repeatedly stressed;
- placing oneself within the political structure of the colony by adopting the administrative structure prevailing in the Javanese countryside (p. 45);
- adopting Indonesian nationalist discourse: the Dutch East Indies are constantly referred to as 'Indonesia', fellow members of the hero's organisation (a Peranakan Chinese youth organisation) are addressed with 'soedara'[36], reference to the detainment camp of Boven Digoel is made (p. 58), the local retail shop is said to function as a co-operative (p. 69), repeatedly sayings of Gandhi are quoted (pp. 11, 70).

Also some of the above mentioned motives are to be found, like referring to Amoy and Canton, the place of origin of most Chinese immigrants to Indonesia, as 'abroad' (p. 69)

Kwee's novel,[37] *Drama di Boven Digoel*, a 700-page-long *chef d'oeuvre* set in the aftermath of the abortive 1926/1927 communist led anti-colonial uprising, treating the theme of men's karma and the futility of efforts to escape one's fate flowing from that karma, offers as the point of culmination of the plot a scene where the

---

36) This applies only to formal discopurse, in informal speech situations Hokkian forms of address are used like *(e)nko* for male peers/slightly elder person or *(e)ntji* for female peers/slightly elder persons.
37) A detailed summary of the novel is to be found in M. Sidharta, *100 Tahun Kwee Tek Hoay. Dari Penjaja Tekstil ke Pendekar Pena*, Jakarta, Sinar Harapan, 1989, pp. 294-298, various aspects of it are treated by T. Rieger, 'Roman Drama di Bowen Digoel oleh Kwee Tek Hoay: sebuah ulasan ringkas' in M. Sidharta, (ed.), *100 Tahun Kwee Tek Hoay. Dari Penjaja Tekstil ke Pendekar Pena*, and T. Rieger, *Le récit du mouvement nationaliste avant 1942 dans la litterature indonésienne*, pp. 124-130.

heroine (an indigenous young woman) has a vision about the Indies future in which a mestizo people from indigenous Indonesian, Chinese, Arab, Papua and other descent will found a mighty empire in the archipelago:

> Within the next five hundred years in this part of New Guinea a mighty nation will be established which will rule all the islands to the East of Lombok and Borneo. It will also rule over Australia and the surrounding islands. Its territory will be larger and its population more numerous than those of present day Japan or the Netherlands. The predominant part of the population of that country will be a new people who consist of a mixture of Indonesians, Papuans, Eurasians, Peranakan Chinese and Arabs. This melting pot which brings about a new people, fitter to hold that enormous power, has already started to be formed in Java...[38]

Whatever we might think of the political content of these utopias, one thing is certainly remarkable: they were definitely located in the Indies, the return to China or a strong Chinese protection for the Indies' Peranakan no longer figured on the list, even of utopian options. In this sense, even fairly strange utopias, reflecting to some extent Dutch projects of the time for large scale colonisation of the Outer Islands through resettlement schemes (later revived in independent Indonesia and nowadays known as transmigration), do indicate the shift in Peranakan Chinese thought that we have been dealing with in this article.

This list of identity constructing features to be found in post-1925 Peranakan literature may be still far from complete, but the trend is obvious.

---

38) 'Dalem lagi lima ratoes taon di ini bagian dari Nieuw Guinea bakal berdiri satoe karadja'an besar jang memegang perentah atas semoea poelo-poelo jang terletak di sabelah timoer dari poelo Lombok dan Borneo, dan berkoeasa djoega atas benoea Australie dan laen-laen poelo di sapoeternja. Daerah ini negri bakal lebih besar, dan rahajatnja lebih banjak dari-pada jang dipoenjaken oleh Japan atawa Nederland sekarang ini. Jang berkoeasa di itoe negri ada satoe bangsa baroe jang terdiri dari satoe tjampoeran antara Indonesier, Papoea, Indo-European dan Paranakan Tionghoa dan Arab. Ini pengleboeran dara beberapa bangsa boeat mentjiptaken poela satoe bangsa baroe jang lebih pende dan tjakep aken pegang itoe kakoeasa'an besar sekarang soedah dimoelai di Java...'(p. 689 f.)

Conclusion

The pre-war Indonesian Peranakan Chinese literature contributed first to the construction of an identity as Huaqiao, available as one pattern of defining one's place in the world for its Peranakan readers. Various textual means are employed to support the idea of Indonesian Peranakan belonging to the imagined community that is the Chinese nation, thus being Huaqiao or overseas Chinese. Acquiring such an identity helped the Peranakan in the specific socio-historic context of the early years of this century in the Indies to advance their aspirations and reach the cohesion necessary for their collective struggle to improve their status. Internal and external factors, however, rendered this identity less practical in the 1920s and since the middle of that decade, an increasing number of literary works offered another construction for the Peranakan identity, namely that of a specific group within the framework of the Indies' society, one community with certain cultural traits among others, or in other words, a Minzu perspective within the Indonesian or Indies nation (depending on their stance with regard to the Indonesian independence struggle, which is, however, of less importance to our point here). In doing so, this literature, in a certain sense, helped to 'write the Indonesian nation'.

References

Primary sources:

Hwa Kim Pit, *Souw Leng Tat atawa Korban dari Akalan*. Surabaya, Han Soei Yang, 1920.

Kho Tjoen Wan, *Boekoe sair Indie Weerbaar*, Jakarta, Favoriet, 1917.

Kwee Seng Tjoan, *Tjerita anak prampoean di bikin sebagi parit mas atawa iboe jang doerhaka*, Jakarta, Kwee Seng Tjoan & Co, 1917.

Kwee Tek Hoay, *Allah jang palsoe*, Jakarta, Tjiong Koen Bie, 1919.

——, *Korbannja Kong Ek*, Semarang, Hap Sing Kong Sie, 1925.

Njoo Cheong Seng, *Soeami jang boeta*, Jakarta, Tjio Kim Siong, 1923.

Ong Siauw King, *Terloenta-loenta*, Palembang, Kamadjoean, 1927.

Phoa Tjoen Hoat, *Ah soeda kasep. Tjoe Ka Lam satoe journalist jang djadi milicien*, Semarang, Hap Sing Kong Sie, 1918.

Phoa Tjoen Hoay, *Tjhik tjhik boeng Nona kampoeng*, 1918.

Tan Boen Kim, *Nona Kim Lian*, Jakarta, Tjiong Koen Bie, 1916.

——, *Nona Lan Im*, Jakarta, Goan Hong, 1919.

Tjia Ki Siang, *Sair Tiong Hwa Hwe Kwan koetika boekanja Passar derma*, Jakarta, Yap Goan Ho, 1905.

——, *Boekoe sair kabaikannja orang jang hendak melepas thauw-tjang, dari fihak kaum moeda*, Jakarta, Kho Tjeng Bie, 1905.

Secondary sources:

Adam, A., *The Vernacular Press and The Emergence of Modern Indonesian Consciousness (1855-1913)*, unpublished Ph.D. thesis, London, SOAS, 1984.

Anderson, B.R.O'G., *Imagined Communities. Reflections on the Origin and Spread of Nationalism*, London, Verso, 1983.

Bhabha, Homi K., 'DissemiNation: time, narrative and the margins of the modern nation', in Homi K. Bhabha (ed.), *Nation and Narration*, London, Routledge, 1990.

Coppel, Charles A., 'From Christian Mission to Confucian Religion: The Nederlandsche Zendingsvereeniging and the Chinese of West Java, 1870-1910' in D.P. Chandler and M.C. Ricklefs, (eds), *Nineteenth and Twentieth Century Indonesia. Essays in Honour of Professor J.D.Legge (1986)*, 1986.

Francken, J.J.C. and C. F. M. de Grijs, *Chineesch-Hollandsch Woordenboek van het Emoi Dialekt*, Batavia, Bataviaasch Genootschap van Kunsten en Wetenschappen, 1882.

Jedamski, D., *Die Institution Literatur und der Prozeß ihrer Kolonisation. Enstehung, Entwicklung und Arbeitsweise des Kantoor voor de Volkslectuur/Balai Pustaka in Niederländisch Indien zu Beginn dieses Jahrhunderts*, unpublished Ph.D.thesis, Hamburg University, 1991.

Liem Thian Joe, *Riwajat Semarang 1416-1931*, Semarang, Ho Kim Joe, 1933.

Nio Joe Lan, *Riwajat 40 taon dari Tiong Hoa Hwe Koan-Batavia 1900-1939*, Batavia, THHK, 1940.

Oei Tiang Seng, 'Thowtjang', in *Bintang Hindia* vol. 1 (1903), No. 23, 14.11.1903.

Rieger, T., *Kwee Tek Hoay sebagai dramawan*, unpublished thesis submitted for the Sarjana Sastra degree at the Universitas Indonesia, Jakarta, 1987.

——, 'Roman Drama di Boven Digoel oleh Kwee Tek Hoay: sebuah ulasan ringkas', in M.Sidharta (ed.), *100 Tahun Kwee Tek Hoay. Dari Penjaja Tekstil ke Pendekar Pena*, Jakarta, Sinar Harapan, 1989.

——, *Le récit du mouvement nationaliste avant 1942 dans la littérature indonésienne*, Ph.D. thesis Ecole des Hautes Etudes en Sciences Sociales, Paris, 1992.

——, 'La guerre sino-japonaise dans la littérature indonésienne' in C. Salmon, (ed.), *Le moment "sino-malais" de la littérature indonésienne, Cahier d'Archipel* No.19, Paris, Archipel, 1992.

Salmon, C., 'Le Sjair de "l'Association Chinoise" de Batavia', *Archipel* No.2,1971.

——, *Literature in Malay by the Chinese of Indonesia. A Provisional Annotated Bibliography*, Paris, Edition de la MSH, 1981.

——, 'A Chinese View of the Indonesian Revolution: the Adventure of Gao Yangtai (1982)' in B. Eberstein and B. Staiger, (eds), *China. Wege in die Welt – Festschrift für Wolfgang Franke zum 80. Geburtstag*, Institut für Asienkunde, Hamburg (1992), 1992.

Shirashi, T, *An Age in Motion. Popular Radicalism in Java, 1912-1926*. Ithaca, Cornell University Press, 1990.

Sidharta, M., *100 Tahun Kwee Tek Hoay. Dari Penjaja Tekstil ke Pendekar Pena*, Jakarta, Sinar Harapan, 1989.

Suryadinata, L., *Peranakan Chinese Politics in Java*, rev. ed. Singapore, Singapore University Press, 1981.

Tan Liok Ee, *The Rhetoric of Bangsa and Minzu: Community and Nation in Tension, the Malay Pensinsula, 1900-1955*, Working Papers No.52, Monash University, 1988.

Williams, Lea E., *Overseas Chinese Nationalism. The Genesis of the Pan-Chinese Movement in Indonesia, 1900-1916*, Glencoe, The Free Press, 1960.

Identity in Modern Japanese Literature
The Case of Natsume Sōseki

Noriko Thunman

Natsume Sōseki (1867–1916) was active as a writer in the early twentieth century. He was already 39 years old when he published his first novel, *Wagahai wa Neko de aru*, (I am a cat), serialized in *Hototogisu* in 1905. Many novels appeared in rapid succession until his death in 1916 at the age of 49. Along with Mori Ōgai, Natsume Sōseki is considered to be one of the most outstanding writers of the Meiji and early Taishō eras. Sōseki[1] was also an outstanding intellectual, having studied English literature at the Tokyo Imperial University and later in London from 1900 to 1903. His wide knowledge of oriental and western philosophies and literatures made him an excellent critic of contemporary Japanese civilization.

The question of the 'self' was discussed during the Meiji and Taishō eras,[2] and could be paraphrased as a search for a new sort of modern identity of a man living in a new kind of society of enlightenment and industrialization. The swift shift of political and economical systems forced a man to define himself anew. It

---

1) I shall call him by his first name Sōseki in the following as is usually done in Japan.
2) For instance see Izawa Motoyoshi, 'Meiji no Seishin to Kindai-bungaku – Natsume Sōseki *Kokoro* o megutte' in *Natsume Sōseki*, Nihon Bungaku Kenkyū Shiryō Kankō-kai hen, vol. 1, Tokyo (1970) 1976. Izawa says in the article: 'It is often said that in the course of the development of modern (Japanese) literature the awakening of the notion of the self has played an essential role,' ('Kindai-bungaku no tenkai wa koga no kakusei o konkan to shite iru koto wa yoku iwareru tokoro de ari, mata sō nanode aru ga,') p. 227.

was not an easy task, but perhaps easier for a Meiji man such as Sōseki than for a man of the 1940s and 1950s such as Abe Kōbō, because Sōseki could define himself either against old values or against the new values that he recognized around him. Both new and old value systems could been seen more clearly then, because the old ones were still acting strongly and the novelty of the new ones rendered them easier to identify. The time when Sōseki was active, forty years after the Meiji restoration, seems to me a very appropriate distance for an analysis of what was won and lost by the changes.

My analysis of Sōseki's identity is based on his own writings, mainly his novels but also some of his articles and speeches. Having read his novels, I am confident that certain reflections in the novels are his own. If the same reflections are repeated in some of his public speeches, I judge this to reinforce my hypothesis. Sōseki wrote many reflections on life and on a desirable personality, all of which help to tell what notion of identity he had. There is always uncertainty as to whether the image of his own person he created in writing is a really the 'real' Sōseki. The question is unanswerable, but the important thing is that he wished to present his image and thoughts as he did, and we cannot doubt his sincerity. I also consulted Miyai Ichirō's two volume biography of Sōseki, Tokyo, 1982, which is the most comprehensive modern biography of Sōseki.[3] The biography may reinforce my hypothesis on some points. One should be careful when Sōseki is ironical; he could caricature himself. However, observing carefully the quality of his irony will also tell us something important about his personality.[4]

---

3) Miyai Ichirō, *Shōden Natsume Sōseki*. vol. 1, Tokyo, 1982.
4) As for the quality of Sōseki's caricature, see the study of Umehara Takeshi, 'Wagahai wa Neko de aru no Warai ni tsuite' included in *Natsume Sōseki*, Nihon Bungaku Kenkyū Shiryō Kankō-kai hen, vol. 1. Umehara compares the humour (*warai*) of Jonathan Swift seen in *Gulliver's travels (Travels into Several Remote Nations of the World, by Lemuel Gulliver)* and that of Sōseki's *Neko*, relating them respectively to Western and Oriental philosophical traditions; platonism on the one hand and taoism and zen on the other. Umehara's conclusion is that Swift places himself alongside of absolute values such as beauty and goodness, whereas Sōseki places himself in a lower position alongside of a cat which is not at all better than a mankind, and Sōseki himself is one of them who is laught at by the cat, perhaps most badly, too, and this, according to Umehara, because of the different traditions of the West and Orient – Platonism, and Taoism and Zen.

Sōseki and his individualism

Sōseki's 1914 speech to the students of Gakushūin, entitled 'Watashi no Kojinshugi' (My individualism), is included in volume 21 of *Sōseki Zenshū*. The speech is often quoted by scholars and is interesting in showing Sōseki's own standpoint. He spoke of the uncertainty he long felt concerning the question of what literature is, and of his vexed desire to accomplish something of value in his life without really being able to find out how. He recounted how, in 1901, while in London, where he had been sent by the Ministry of Education (Monbu-shō), he came to think that the notion of literature must be found out or established by himself, because he would never find a convincing theory in the writings of others, especially westerners. He must establish honestly (his own word) his point of view as a Japanese. Speaking of how to find one's own point of view, Sōseki used the word *jiko-honi* (egotism): the notion of what literature is should be gained only by relying on one's own self, thinking and judging according to one's own capacity which is unconditionally determined by social and historical factors. This is why Sōseki, a Japanese living in Meiji Japan, cannot possibly adopt a notion thought out by a European acting in a different context.

Jiko-honi (egotism)

The word *jiko-honi* was quoted by many scholars and critics as an important component of Sōseki's thought. When, after more than one year in London, Sōseki became aware of the importance of egotism, it meant a new departure (his own word in the speech) for him. Having acquired a firm footing, he knew in which direction to advance in his research of English literature, but realizing that it would not be possible to accomplish the task during his stay in London, he concentrated on buying books and gathering materials, preparing the work to be continued in Japan. It was intended to result in a new theory of literature of his own, but financial circumstances prevented Sōseki from accomplishing this after his return to Japan. He had to work as a teacher to earn a living for himself and his family, and only a part of the theory was published as *Bungaku-ron* (Theory of Literature), in 1908. Sōseki also spoke of the importance of respecting other people's egotism. However, Tamai Takayuki[5] said that, until the time of *Kokoro* (1914), Sōseki was not quite aware of the egotism of others. He said that in his novel *Michikusa* (1915), Sōseki showed, for the first time, that he really understood the rights of others to be individual, depicting the characters as equals of the main protagonist Kenzō, all being shown with their shortcomings and their own stubbornness. Tamai's article contains a fine analysis of the two novels, but it seems to me not adequate to judge Sōseki's own standpoint as he did. It is true that *Kokoro* and *Michikusa* show the differences, as Tamai pointed out; the former treating mainly a concentrated history of a man and his conscience[6], the latter showing conflicts and misunderstandings between the persons of the novel, mostly between the protagonist and his family members e.g. wife, parents and adoptive parents. However, in *Sanshirō* (1909) there was already depicted the young girl, Mineko, who had her own personality. Besides, the speech quoted and *Kokoro* appeared in the same year, 1914, and there was only one year between *Kokoro* and *Michikusa*. There seems to be no reason to say that Sōseki was not really aware of the right of others to be individualists, before the time of *Kokoro*.

The speech also stressed the question of power and money, two dangerous factors, because both could be used to compromise the freedom of others. Those possessing power or money must exercise this power with caution and have a strong sense of duty.[7] Sōseki stressed the differences between egotism and egoism and the importance of not confusing them. Discussing the same passage of the speech of Sōseki, Shimizu Ikutarō has pointed out that 'The society which existed around Sōseki was such that he couldn't use the word "individualism" without great caution.'[8]

---

5) Tamai Takayuki, '*Watashi no Kojinshugi* Zengo – *Kokoro* kara *Michikusa* e' in *Natsume Sōseki*, Nihon Bungaku Kenkyū Shiryō Kankō-kai hen, vol. 1, pp. 236–254,
6) It goes without saying that the 'I' (young man) of the novel and the wife of *sensei* (master) are also important persons in the novel, but the main theme can be said the question of the conscience of *sensei*.
7) Sōseki spoke of power and money, because his audience, the students of Gakushūin, were chiefly the sons of rich and powerful families. The same sort of argument can be found in his novels, for instance in *Nowaki*, see the speech of Dōya-sensei, *Sōseki Zenshū* vol. 4, Tokyo, (1957) 1979, pp. 312–317.
8) Quotation from Shimizu's article 'Jiko-honi no Tachiba' included in *Natsume Sōseki*, Nihon Bungaku Kenkyū Shiryō Kankō-kai hen, vol. 1.

The word could presumably easily be misunderstood as a synonym of 'egoism' and also as the opposite of 'nationalism' at the time.[9] He also spoke of a group-minded mentality and action of which he himself was a victim.[10] He defined the type of action as 'out-dated' (*jidai okure*) and feudal, which indicates that he regarded himself as up-to-date (modern) and non-feudalistic. Was he alone to be in possession of these qualities? Not theoretically, because he spoke of mutual respect between individuals; yet he also spoke of an inescapable loneliness, because it would be impossible to meet someone who would think as oneself. Thus each individual, in Sōseki's mind, existed as an isolated entity with no common quality shared with others.

Shimizu Ikutarō discussed Sōseki's egotism (*jiko-honi*) in the article 'Jiko-honi no Tachiba' (The position of egotism).[11] Shimizu compared individualism in Europe and in Japan; in Europe there was a universal being such as God, and each individual possessed the universal being in himself. It allowed an individual to assume that what was good for him was also good for others, and admitted some universal common values. In Japan, individualism was for some chosen elites, meaning most often those who had a university degree and had lived abroad for some time, and had experienced European culture. Hence also, an individual (egotist) of the time in Japan would not be understood by his surroundings which did not share his background and experience, and consequently a Japanese egotist would feel very lonely. Shimizu said that Sōseki's kind of individualism could only exist in an early stage of society regulated by natural law, where individualism, nationalism and cosmopolitanism can co-exist without any problem.[12] According to Shimizu, Sōseki's individualism was such that he could not come to terms with the reality around him. Shimizu seems to be saying that if Sōseki really wanted to change society, he should have adopted a more ideological standpoint,

---

9) On Sōseki and nationalism, see Ooka Shōhei's article, 'Sōseki to Kokkashugi – *Shumi no iden* o megutte' included in *Natsume Sōseki*, Nihon Bungaku Kenkyū Shiryō Kankō-kai hen, vol. 2, Tokyo, 1982.
10) Sōseki spoke of the publication of a critical comment on a person in a newspaper for which he was responsible, and of the ensuing attack from a literary group of which the person in question was a leader.
11) Included in *Natsume Sōseki*, Nihon Bungaku Kenkyū Shiryō Kankō-kai hen, vol. 1.
12) *Ibid.* p. 20. As for his analysis, see further his *Shakai to Kojin – Shakaigaku-seiritsu-shi*, vol. 1.

Natsume Sōseki

based not on individualism but on, for instance, some political and economic ideology.

This is a possible criticism of Sōseki's individualism, but apart from that, his egotism shows an interesting picture of a Meiji intellectual; a man who saw clearly the general historical conditions of Meiji society and searched for a new identity, one not only meaningful and worth living for himself, but also for others.

Miyai Ichirō pointed out in 'Shishiteki Bungaku', in Chapter 9 of his biography of Sōseki, quoting mostly Sōseki's letters to his devotees, that Sōseki had a strong sense of duty to be a good example for others. In a letter to Suzuki Miekichi sent on October 26, 1907 (the second that day), Sōseki spoke of the two kinds of literature; *kan-bungaku* (a leisurely literature) and another type created by an ardent spirit resembling *shishi* (a samurai fighting for his ideal). He said that he would not just be a leisurely writer, aiming only at beauty or the world of *haiku*, but he would also fight as a Meiji restoration *shishi*, seriously for life and death.[13] The expression might seem exaggerated, but Sōseki seems to have meant here that, even though he enjoyed the world of harmony and calm contemplation as described in his novel *Kusamakura*, it was also crucial for him to contribute to a better world and better human relations. Sōseki spoke in the letter of the ubiquitous enemies to be fought and the necessity of changing the world. It is important to remember Sōseki not only as a writer of *Kusamakura* but, above all, as the writer of numerous novels where he criticized the society and morals of the time, examining the mechanism working between people, in a family and between a man and a woman, thus trying to understand why people living in Meiji society were unhappy. Sōseki's individualism lacked perhaps a solid social base, as Shimizu pointed out. Sōseki was a solitary intellectual without money or power, and he could only influence society by words, as his fictional alter ego often tried. Had he even had a power to force his values onto others, he would never have done so, because it was against his principles to suppress the liberty of others. The influence he aimed to exercise should be wielded through sympathy and understanding. Despite the character of his individualism, his interest in contemporary reality was by no means negligible; on the contrary, as he wrote to Suzuki Miekichi, a writer must live in the midst of reality even if it meant a nervous breakdown or madness.[14]

Sōseki's stress on his own self was inherited strongly by the writers of Shirakaba-ha (the Birch school), and his introspective and reflective style could be found in the works of the group.[15] Shimizu's conclusion is that Sōseki was essentially a man of monologue and self-defence vis-à-vis his wife, brother, sister and the outer world in general: a man who escaped into the world of *haiku* as in *Kusamakura* and finally arrived in the world of *Sokutenkyoshi* (follow-heavenly-way-and-free-oneself-from-one's-own-self). Thus his egotism, in fact, resulted in an 'oriental nothingness'. According to Shimizu, it was a very Japanese type of individualism.

---

13) Miyai Ichiro, *Shōden Natsume Sōseki*. vol. 1., pp. 660–661.
14) See the same letter to Suzuki, included in *ibid*. vol. 1, p. 661.
15) Izawa Motoyoshi is of the same opinion. See his article 'Meiji no Seishin to Kindai Bungaku' in *Natsume Sōseki*, Nihon Bungaku Kenkyū Shiryō Kankōkai hen, vol. 1., p. 234.

Shimizu's conclusion seems to give a too one-sided picture of Sōseki. It is true that Sōseki needed *haiku*, Chinese poetry and painting, for the balance of his mind. Following work on a novel in the morning, he used to enjoy drawings or the composition of *haiku* and Chinese poetry in the afternoon in order to purify his mind. Novels were a frame of work where he treated reality with its ugliness, suffering, love and resignation, whereas the world of painting and poetry was for him a world of beauty lying closer to an ideal state of mind. In *Michikusa*, Sōseki analysed all the persons of the novel, including Kenzō who is generally considered to be his alter ego[16], keeping a distance from all of them. The novel is not at all a monologue or self-defence of Kenzō, as Shimizu seems to say, but the author is as critical of Kenzō as of his wife or anyone else. However, it is true that Sōseki was not religious, nor was he a believer in some sort of absoluteness such as eternity or truth. He was interested in Zen, but it is doubtful that he reached the enlightened state (*satori*). His novels give a negative answer. The only possible solution for him seems to have been to be one with the universe which is also the 'nothingness', and to be happy in a harmonious state of mind, as described in *Kusamakura*. But Sōseki knew that the harmonious state was simply a short pause in life. He had to search all his life for a solution to the problems around him, and he had to try to see clearly the forces working in the lives of his contemporaries. It seems, however, that 'nothingness' might have been one important feature in his personality.

The World of Nothingness

Sōseki's individualism was based upon his belief in *jiko-honi* (egotism) which in turn was based upon his trust in man's rationality. In the 'Watashi no Kojinshugi' speech, Sōseki explained that his individualism was logical and rational without any blind, group-minded and sentimental narrowness (*tōha-shin*).[17] Hence

---

16) *Michikusa* is generally regarded as an autobiographical novel. See for instance Aihara Kazukuni, '*Michikusa* no Seiritsu ni tsuite' in *Natsume Sōseki*, Nihon Bungaku Kenkyū Shiryō Kankō-kai hen, vol. 1., p. 255, Tamai Takayuki, '*Watashi no Kojinshugi* Zengo' in *ibid.*, p. 236.
17) See *Sōseki Zenshū*, vol.21, p.152.

Sōseki trusted each man's capability to think and judge what is right and wrong. On the other hand he did not think that man is a thoroughly rational being. On the contrary, he wrote repeatedly that there are sentiments and desires deeply hidden in a man so that he himself is not aware of them, but it is these hidden forces that make a man do things that he never dreamt of. Karaki Junzō wrote about an unknown X in Sōseki, quoting an early article published in 1897 in a school magazine, *Ryūnankai-zasshi*, where Sōseki said, 'Life cannot be synthesized logically,... Unexpected feelings come out of the depth of one's heart.'[18] Examples of the unknown X can be found amply in the novels of Sōseki.[19] Many scholars have discussed his two contradictory poles, which were named differently by different scholars. Komi-ya Toyotaka spoke of reality (ugliness) and dream (beauty and poetry), the two poles being expressed by works such as *Neko* (reality) and *Yōkyo-shū* (dream/poetry), both written in the same period.[20] For Etō Jun the satiric world of *Neko* coexisted with the world of *Yōkyo-shū* where Sōseki shows the reader his inner abyss.[21] Uchida Michio's analysis of *Yōkyo-shū* in the article 'Yō-kyo-shū no Mondai'[22] shows that Sōseki's interest lay in writing about the inexplicable forces that govern a human destiny.[23] Ac-cording to Uchida, the mind of Sōseki swayed like a pendulum between the worlds of *Neko* and *Yōkyo-shū* all his life. Karaki Junzō also mentioned the two different features in Sōseki and called them 'ethical' and 'haiku-like' (*haikai-teki*). Sōseki and the world of *haiku* has been discussed by many scholars,[24] and we know that Sōseki, as a friend of Shiki, wrote *haiku* all his life.

It seems quite adequate to speak of two coexisting characteristics of Sōseki expressed in different works; *Yōkyo-shū* and

---

18) See Karaki Junzō's article 'Sōseki to Ōgai' included in *Natsume Sōseki*, Nihon Bungaku Kenkyū Shiryō Kankō-kai hen, vol. 1., pp. 86–87.
19) For instance, in *Sorekara*, Daisuke tries to handle his love for Michiyo whom he helped to marry his best friend without being able to forget her.
20) *Natsume Sōseki*, 1938. See Uchida Michio, 'Yōkyo-shū no Mondai' in *Natsume Sōseki*, Nihon Bungaku Kenkyū Shiryō Kankō-kai hen, vol. 1, pp. 142-143.
21) *Natsume Sōseki*, 1956. See Uchida Michio, ibid.,p. 144.
22) *Ibid.*
23) Uchida Michio,'Yōkyo-shū no Mondai',p.148.
24) Just to mention some of them; Naruse Masakatsu, 'Shasei-bun no Bungakushi-teki-kachi ni tsuite no Ichi-teigen, Sōma Tsuneo, 'Sōseki to Shaseibun and Kamei Hideo 'Shasei-bun no imisuru mono' in *Natsume Sōseki*, Nihon Bungaku Kenkyū Shiryō Kankō-kai hen, vol.2.

Kusamakura on the one hand[25] and the novels from *Gubijinsō* to *Meian* on the other. Sōseki was not religious, but he was interested in Chinese philosophies such as Rōshi (老子/Lao Zi) and Sōshi (荘子/Zhuang Zi) and in 1893 wrote a long essay on Rōshi, 'Rōshi no Tetsugaku' (The philosophy of Rōshi).[26] Analysing the quality of the laughter of Swift and of Sōseki, Umehara Takeshi showed brilliantly the two different, underlying traditions of thought, the occidental and the oriental, analysing also the differences in quality of laughter in Rō-Sōshi (老/荘子) and in Zen. His conclusion is that the laughter of Rō-Sōshi originates from 'nothingness'; a man situated on the point of absolute 'nothingness' looks upon a man who is caught in a relative world, and because he knows that everything is equal before 'nothingness' and there exist no differences between 'I' and the others, there will be forever a calm smile on his lips. But the laughter of Zen is a little different; one bursts into laughter when one finds a solution to problems and contradictions, thus Zen laughter is more dynamic and includes a sort of absolute affirmation.[27] Umehara said that it is not so easy to define the origin of Sōseki's laughter, but he was rather confident that it lay closer to the nothingness-based laughter of Rō-Sōshi. Was it a Japanese cultural context that Sōseki could not free himself from? Despite his belief in man's rationality, Sōseki was at the same time aware of the existence of something irrational in a man. When he needed peace of mind, it was the world of ultimate harmony that consoled him for a while, where he was confidently embraced by nature and was himself one with nature. Nature considered as such seems devoid of human quality; no fear, conflict nor love. Is it not possible to call this nothingness? Umehara also pointed out that in Sōseki there coexisted the western idea of the self and the oriental nothingness whose ideal was the opposite of egotism; the disappearance of the self (*mushi/muga*).[28] Umehara's opinion seems justified, and the two poles coexisted in Sōseki.

---

25) It does not mean that the two works are of identical character; the former giving expression to Sōseki's hidden dreams (longings), and the latter to an ideal state of mind.
26) Included in *Sōseki Zenshū*, vol. 22. The essay was written as a report for examination at the University.
27) Umehara also says that the former is existential and the latter epistemological. See Umehara, *'Wagahai wa Neko dearu* no Warai ni tsuite' in *Natsume Sōseki*, Nihon Bungaku Kenkyū Shiryō Kankō-kai hen, vol. 1., pp. 136–137.
28) *Ibid.*, p. 140.

Enlightenment and Modernization

Another Sōseki speech, 'Gendai Nihon no Kaika' (Enlightenment and development in Japan today), 1912, is often quoted in connection with his critical view of Meiji Japan.

Sōseki started by defining the word *kaika* (enlightenment and development). *Kaika* is not static but moves forward all the time, and that is why it is difficult to define it adequately. *Kaika* is a process of positive and negative human activities. When a man does something because it is his duty, he will use as little energy as possible, and Sōseki called this a passive sort of activity, e.g. work one has to do to earn one's living. Sōseki also mentioned modernities such as the telegraph and the railway as useful means of reducing the burden of 'negative activities'. Whereas if a man does something he likes, for instance fishing, he will spend his energy gladly, and it is, according to Sōseki, a positive activity. Sōseki said that *Kaika* brought about rapid technical development, and, economically, the living standard had been raised so that more and more people could afford to have 'positive activities' such as hobbies, philosophy and literature. At the same time no one felt that living conditions had improved; on the contrary, competition had become harder, and life was at least as painful as before. Sōseki said that the greatest paradox of the enlightenment and industrial development of the time was that the development by no means led to people's happiness.[29]

Further he continued to discuss the special condition of Japanese modernization and industrialization. Western modernization and industrialization, he said, were brought about by inner forces and were a result of a natural development (*naihatsu-teki*), just like a bud, when the time comes, bursts into bloom (his own words).[30] But industrialization (*kaika*) in Japan was carried out under external pressure, and because Japan was forced to adapt to the demands of other countries (*gaihatsu-teki*). Sōseki said that Japan had to hurry to catch up with the west during the past forty, fifty years, and the situation would long remain the same.[31] The psychological effect of Japanese *kaika* would be dissatisfaction and uncertainty, and the feeling of emptiness, because *kaika* was achieved by swallowing new knowledge without really digesting

---

29) See 'Gendai Nihon no Kaika', *Sōseki Zenshū*, vol. 21, pp. 37–44.
30) *Ibid.*, p. 44.
31) *Ibid.*, pp. 44–47.

it. He criticized as hypocrites those who were proud of being modern.[32] Sōseki was pessimistic about the future of Japan, failing to see any given solution to change the condition of Japanese modernization and industrialization.[33] Sōseki's point of view seems well-founded, based as it is upon his knowledge of society in England.

How did Sōseki's opinion of *kaika* affect his identity? First Sōseki did not want to be identified with a majority of citizens who accepted all the novelties and materialism of the Meiji era. In his *Nowaki*, Shirai Dōya seems to have a good portion of Sōseki himself. Dōya[34] speaks of the Meiji *kaika* as the first step in the modernization of Japan, and the period lacks earlier historical equivalence. This implies that those born in a society which lacks an earlier example, must themselves make new examples. It also means that they possess great liberty which in turn obliges them to be responsible. Dōya continues to speak of the importance for youth of having an ideal and trying to realize it. He criticizes Meiji society where money means too much. Dōya is perhaps a little more militant, reminiscent of *shishi* of the Meiji restoration, than Sōseki himself; but the idea seems to be identical to Sōseki's. Sōseki seems to have presented, in Dōya, one possible solution of how to live. Dōya is critical of society, but he has not given up the struggle. He has no social position, but material difficulties do not bother him. He is content with his life and tries to do his best to influence others by writing books and lecturing. Takayanagi, a young person who sympathizes with Dōya, also has an ambition to write down his thoughts, but financial difficulties preclude this. He is always vexed because of this and very lonely. He has a complex about being poor, and feels unloved. He also seems to share a part of Sōseki's personality; vexation at never having the possibility of realizing his dream of writing a good novel as did Takayanagi, or the life-work on literature as Sōseki; [35] and the feeling of loneliness and of not being loved by anybody. The

---

32) *Ibid.*, p. 50.
33) *Ibid.*, pp. 52–53. As Sōseki mentioned in the speech, there were many at the time who were proud of Japanese modernization and asserted that, after the victory in the Russo-Japanese war, Japan had joined the most advanced counties. Eighty years after the speech, it seems to me that Sōseki was right.
34) The first name Dōya is used as his name in the novel, and I do the same.
35) See Miyai Ichirō, *Shōden Natsume Sōseki*. vol. 1., pp. 506– 509, where Miyai quotes a passage of *Michikusa*, which tells about the vexation of Kenzō over the difficulties to get time for writing.

narrator of the novel explains the differences between the two saying that Dōya is working to change society, not thinking much about himself. He is a leader and a real egotist, believing in his mission and not bothering about what others might think of him (for instance his poverty and lack of imposing titles). Takayanagi, on the other hand, feels lonely because he still sees himself through others' eyes, and because he is still a materialist. Sōseki presented in Takayanagi an example of the dissatisfaction and uncertainty he spoke of in 'Gendai Nihon no Kaika', and in Dōya a possible solution to the problem.[36]

It is, however, evident that Dōya was not the solution to the problems raised by modernization. However, a Dōya-type solution seemed to have been dear to Sōseki and it reappeared in *Sanshirō* in the person of Hirota *sensei* (magister Hirota). Hirota is less militant than Dōya and enjoys the life of a detached, intellectual man. He lives by the principle of *jiko honi* (egotism) and has found spiritual harmony. Hirota shares some qualities with Sōseki, but Sōseki could never live long in a harmonious state of mind like Hirota could. He felt dissatisfaction and uncertainty just as Takayanagi did, and the old values represented in *Sanshirō* by the mother of Sanshirō existed closely around him in his wife, sister, brother and parents. In *Michikusa*, Sōseki depicted the suffering of all the persons in the novel, and Kenzō, the egotist, far from being free of suffering, perhaps suffered most, because he wanted things to be different, and he could see clearly the egoism of the others. Modernization and industrialization did not mean happiness, but merely augmented the suffering of an awakened, modern egotist who had to handle old thinking and an old set of values, while at the same time trying to realize his ideal. Thus Sōseki's protagonists are often pessimistic and resigned. Japanese modernization gave Sōseki no hopeful vision, and unfortunately, history bore this out. Sōseki treated the question from the point of view of an individual, not from a wider perspective, and Shimizu's criticism was to the point in this respect. This did not prevent Sōseki from being very critical of the new social tendencies such as the valuing of worldly power, status

---

36) In Nakano Sōseki showed a person who lives with his time without much reflection; Nakano is a son of a rich man, modern, well-adapted and playing a serious and playful love-game with a beautiful woman (She is just called 'Onna' (woman) in the work.)

and money. He was an idealist who wanted to believe in the possibility of changing historical conditions through the power of the spirit. He was rather resigned, but not so much as the writers of the Taishō era, who almost from the start, gave up trying to change society. Their individualism was more harshly limited.[37] It is true that there existed an *atarashiki mura* movement which aimed to create a utopia. But Musha no Kōji Saneatsu[38] himself was, in my opinion, less interested in the social and historical conditions of Japan since the Meiji restoration than was Sōseki.

Conclusion

Sōseki's notion of his own identity consists, in my opinion, of three major factors discussed above; *jiko honi* (egotism/individualism), Oriental nothingness and the critical view of Meiji society. Vis-à-vis society, the position of an individual is quite painful; he cannot really succeed in changing society and people living in it. His effort must be made from outside the established society which was governed according to different value systems than his own. Besides, there still existed so many old values which made life difficult for a modern egotist. His novels such as *Michikusa* and *Meian* give a good insight into the problems. The painful, contradictory society forces a rational and conscious egotist to be an outsider. Does this imply that Sōseki considered himself an outsider? He worked first as an English teacher, later as a lecturer at Tokyo Imperial University, and *Neko* made him a very popular writer. His novels since 1908 were published in the *Asahi*. Even though he had his own social position, it is possible that Sōseki felt rather an outsider. He refused to accept the doctorate offered to him in 1912. It can be understood that he, an individual with no impressive title, had managed very well and would not need one in the future either.[39] However, his position as an outsider seems to me a little different from that of the Taishō (1912–1926) writers.[40] In spite of his stand-point, Sōseki had a

---

37) Here I am thinking of the naturalists in Japan.
38) The leader of the 'Shirakaba-ha' who was behind the movement.
39) See Sōseki's letter addressed to the Ministry of Education on the 21 February 1912. Included in Miyai, *Shōden Natsume Sōseki*. vol. 1., p. 246.
40) Here, too, I am thinking of the naturalists who consisted the stream of of Japanese literature during the Taishō era.

very clear picture of his time and its historical conditions. He tried, in his novels, to study relationships between people, presenting the problems caused by a new individualism and the influences of the west. Perhaps it is more appropriate to speak of a committed intellectual with a vision, though rather disillusioned from the start, who believed in/hoped for the possibility of exercising some influence through his writing. This is perhaps why there are so many passages of reasoning in his novels.[41]

Sōseki considered himself an egotist with a certain role in society. His 'self' needed to pause from time to time and rest in the world of oriental nothingness. Perhaps the sense of nothingness lay deeper in his personality, and it is possible that it even coloured his egotism. Because he believed in no universal value, but in the sincerity of a person, a rational egotism could be dissolved into a relative world which he could contemplate from the point of view of nothingness (*Michikusa*). There were such moments in his novels; but for the most part, it seems that he himself was a victim of egotism and suffered worse than any of his characters.

References

Aihara Kazukuni, 'Michikusa no Seiritsu ni tsuite' in *Natsume Sōseki*, Nihon Bungaku Kenkyū Shiryō Kankō-kai hen, vol. 1, Tokyo (1970) 1976.

Izawa Motoyoshi, 'Meiji no Seishin to Kindai-bungaku – Natsume Sōseki *Kokoro* o megutte' in *Natsume Sōseki*, Nihon Bungaku Kenkyū Shiryō-kai hen, vol. 1, Tokyo (1970) 1976.

Kamei Hideo, 'Shasei-bun no imisuru mono' in *Natsume Sōseki* Nihon Bungaku Kenkyū Shiryō Kankō-kai hen', vol. 2 Tokyo 1982.

Karaki Junzō, 'Sōseki to Ōgai' in *Natsume Sōseki*, Nihon Bungaku Kenkyū Shiryō Kankō-kai hen, vol. 1, Tokyo (1970) 1976.

---

41) See Masamune Hakuchō, 'Natsume Sōseki-ron in *Natsume Sōseki*, Nihon Bungaku Kenkyū Shiryō Kankō-kai hen, vol. 1, p. 1, where Hakuchō says: 'I was quite bored by the logical reasoning that can be found amply on every page.'

Masamune Hakuchō, 'Natsume Sōseki-ron' in *Natsume Sōseki*, Nihon Bungaku Kenkyū Shiryō Kankō-kai hen', vol. 1, Tokyo (1970) 1976.

Miyai Ichirō, *Shōden Natsume Sōseki*, Tokyo 1982.

Naruse Masakatsu, 'Shasei-bu' no Bungakushi-teki-kachi ni tsuite no Ichi-teigen' in *Natsume Sōseki*, Nihon Bungaku Kenkyū Shiryō Kankō-kai hen, vol. 2 Tokyo 1982.

Natsume Sōseki, '*Gendai Nihon no Kaika*', 1912, included in *Sōseki Zenshū*, vol.21, Tokyo (1957) 1979.

—— *Gubiji'sō*, included in *Sōseki Zenshū*, vol. 5, Tokyo (1956) 1979.

—— *Kokoro*, 1914, in *Sōseki Zenshū*, vol. 12, Tokyo (1956) 1979.

—— *Kusamakura* in *Sōseki Zenshū*, vol. 4, Tokyo (1956) 1979.

—— *Meian* in *Sōseki Zenshū*, vol. 14–15, Tokyo (1956) 1979.

—— *Michikusa*, 1915, in *Sōseki Zenshū*, vol. 13, Tokyo (1957) 1979.

—— *Mon* in *Sōseki Zen'shū*, vol. 9, Tokyo (1956)1979.

—— *Nowaki* in *Sōseki Zenshū*, vol. 4, Tokyo (1956) 1979.

—— 'Rōshi no Tetsugaku' in *Sōseki Zenshū*, vol. 22, Tokyo (1957) 1979.

—— *Sanshirō*, 1909, in *Sōseki Zenshū* vol. 7, Tokyo, (1956) 1979.

—— *Sorekara* in *Sōseki Zenshū* vol. 8, Tokyo, (1956) 1979.

—— *Wagahai wa Neko de aru*, 1906, in *Sōseki Zen'shū*, vols 1–2, Tokyo (1956) 1978

—— 'Watashi no Kojin'shugi' in *Sōseki Zenshū*, vol. 21, Tokyo (1957) 1979.

Ooka Shōhei, 'Sōseki to Kokkaishiki – *Shumi no iden* o megutte' included in *Natsume Sōseki*, Nihon Bungaku Kenkyū Shiryō Kankō-kai hen, vol. 2, Tokyo 1982.

Shimizu Ikutarō, 'Jiko-honi no Tachiba' included in *Natsume Sōseki*, Nihon Bungaku Kenkyū Shiryō-kai hen Vol. 1. Tokyo (1970) 1976.

Sōma Tsuneo, 'Sōseki to Shaseibun' in *Natsume Sōseki*, Nihon Bungaku Kenkyū Shiryō Kankō-kai hen', vol. 2, Tokyo 1982.

Tamai Takayuki, 'Watashi no Kojinshugi Zengo – *Kokoro* kara *Michikusa* e' in *Natsume Sōseki*, (1970) 1976.

Uchida Michio, '*Yōkyo-shū* no Mondai' in *Natsume Sōseki*, Nihon Bungaku Kenkyū Shiryō Kankō-kai hen, vol. 1, Tokyo (1970) 1976.

Umehara Takeshi, '*Wagahai wa Neko de aru* no Warai ni tsuite' included in *Natsume Sōseki*, Nihon Bungaku Kenkyū Shiryō Kankō-kai hen, vol. 1, Tokyo (1970) 1976.

9

Framed by Fiction
Malay Literary Characters in the Literatures of Europe, the United States and Asia

Muhammad Haji Salleh

There has been quite a substantial amount of historical writing from the early period on Malaysia and the Malay Archipelago by Fa Hsien and I-Ching (China), Sulaiman (Middle East), the anonymous author of *Jataka* and *Kartha Sarit Sagara* (India), Ptolemy and Pliny (Greece), Pigafetta (Italy) and of course the Portuguese and British, in the forms of records and personal sketches.

As intercontinental communication became speedier and more convenient in the nineteenth and twentieth centuries, the number of stories, novels and poems set in Malaysia grew surprisingly large. The writers were from different countries: the United Kingdom, France, Italy, Japan, Australia and the USA. Some came as rubber estate managers, like the French Henri Fauconnier; as ship captains, like the Polish-British Joseph Conrad; as colonial administrators and adventurers, like Hugh Clifford; as tourists, like Somerset Maugham; as housewives, like Agnes Keith and even as university lecturers, like Paul Theroux. The variety of their professions and the types of experiences have provided us with a rich anthology of perspectives.

This article attempts to study the literary portrait and identity of Malay characters in some of the European, Japanese and American works and to trace the mind and cultural frameworks of their writers. The limited space will necessarily force me to concentrate on the more important works and touch quite superficially on the others. So this article cannot do justice to the variety of perspectives and literary forms and talents. Also, I have no linguistic access to some of the literatures and I have therefore, left the work to other more competent scholars.

To write about a people is to assume a certain responsibility to that people. Thus the talent to describe or fantasize about a people is not enough. Writers must, to my mind, try to discover the soul of their characters, the rhythm of their environment, and perhaps also the personality of a nation.

Most of the writers who came our way were blessed by the colonial government or influenced by its way of thinking and can be categorised in three different groups. In the first we would include major writers like Joseph Conrad, Henri Fauconnier and perhaps also Hugh Clifford, who because of their talents were more independent of the colonial frame of racial perspectives than others. They have not only tried to sketch the surface character of the Malays, within their (the authors') limitations of knowledge and experience, but have also allowed themselves and us as readers to taste a bigger and thicker slice of their lives, through descriptions of the *adat*s, customs, beliefs and daily life, though with characteristically western logic and slant. While some of these works give glimpses of human beings quite free of prejudices, others are obviously marked by a pre-determined mould of racial conceptions and/or the colonial frame of mind.

The second group of writers has had less experience of the life and environment in Malaysia than those in the first group (in this way perhaps Conrad, too, may belong here, but for his greater talent and more extended use of Malay characters so that we have included him in the first category) and have only captured a thin, dry crust of life in their description. Malays are seen from the outside, often through a cultural framework which produces stereotypical prejudices. In this group we would include for instance W. Somerset Maugham.

The third group of writers has never stepped onto the shores of Malaysia or seemed to have written from an archipelago created by their readings and/or truly rich imagination. Two names come to mind immediately here: Emilio Salgari and Pierre Boulle (the latter was in the archipelago only for a short time). Both preferred story and adventure to the real Malays and have given a front stage to their fictionalized heroes.

The perspectives of these authors raise a fundamental problem of point of view. During the colonial years, especially in the late nineteenth and early twentieth centuries, the perspectives were those of writers who generally grew up in a surrounding of colonial arrogance. Usually, the act of describing is an attempt to define the unknown. The European author in describing the Malays, for example, is trying to recreate in words a 'reality' that contained their lives. And once immortalised in books the Malays are almost described for good. In that way, the more important writers are the more dangerous, if their works are prejudiced or unconsciously derogatory.

The rich orature (oral literature) and the classical literature of the Malays contain a great number of portraits of the people, from the servant to the minister, from the judge to the rajas, from the ancient to the very contemporary periods, which together form the amorphous identity of the Malays. No doubt in these works the Malays were judging themselves through their own biases, in many cases also with sharp criticism of the greed of rulers and nobles, the failures of states and statesmen and the people as a whole. But during the colonial, and often also during the postcolonial periods the literatures of the West are privileged even in the colonised countries, referred to as achieving greater heights while the native literatures are full of fantasy, rooted to the oral tradition and belonging to the past. And for readers of the west who have no access to local works in the local languages, the colonial descriptions remain current and become the standard descriptions of Malaysia. Thus is Winstedt's *A History of Classical Malay Literature* (first published in 1940), even with its biased colonial sense of approach to literature and a limited knowledge of the literatures of the Malay world, the main text for the study of Malay literature around the world, sometimes also in Malaysia. And with our bias for the European scholarship, the book will be a source of reference for a long time still, for Malaysians and Europeans alike.

In writing this article many questions are forthcoming. For example: are the Malays the 'other' of the western writers in their attempt to create a literary identity for them and therefore so described in their works? Is it possible for the sympathetic writer to be entirely free from colonial prejudices? Is it possible to be fair to a people if one writes from another racial context, from an ethnocentric experience or judgement? Is the European language, whichever it may be, however rich in its own land, sufficient to describe a new situation and a different people? These are some of the important questions which must be considered. Further-more, if the Malay is considered the 'other' is there only one 'other' and may there not be many 'others'? In the question of identity, the Scottish worker in Britain, for example, might even appear to be the 'other' of the London shop-owner. So is the Malay raja's slave his 'other'. Like the London shop-owner, the Malay raja has not only 'others' in his own country, but many more 'others' in Europe and all around the world, including those living in invaded societies, to use the term by Ashcroft, Griffith and Tiffin.[1] It is with these questions that we must approach the problem of the literary identity of Malay characters, created by the different writers of Europe and elsewhere in the various works.

From lists of fictional works on Malaya by Donn Hart[2] and Lewis Hill[3] and my own search[4] there are more than three hundred literary works in English, French and Japanese that have Malaysia as their setting. Malaysia is defined here as the countries of the Malays, including the Peninsula, the coast of Sabah, Sarawak and parts of Sumatra. Only a few writers have been able to capture the Malays in the literary medium as round characters, full and serious, to see them against their natural and social environments, beliefs and their intellectual life. Joseph Conrad, Hugh Clifford and Henri Fauconnier are among the few who tried to study the Malays, sketch their ways and follow the flow of their minds and emotions. The range and variety of characterization is quite broad. We meet in these literary works those from the feudal, aristocratic circles who live out their lives in leisure, or are involved in reclaiming their independence and dignity as in the characters of Joseph Conrad, to peasants who are sketched in the field mud and upstream villages and also at the edges of the palaces, as in Hugh Clifford's stories, to the flat background characters who appear in Maugham's verandahs and halls.

---

1) Ashcroft, Bill, Gareth Griffith and Helen Tiffin, *The Empire Writes Back*, London, Routledge, 1989.
2) Donn V. Hart, *Preliminary Check List of Novels with a Malayan Background*, Typescript, New York, Syracuse University, 1961.
3) Lewis Hill, *A Checklist of English-Language Fiction Relating to Malaysia, Singapore and Brunei*, Centre for SEA Studies, University of Hull, 1986.
4) Muhammad Haji Salleh, 'Imej Orang Melayu dalam Kesusasteraan Eropah' Working Paper for Hari Sastera '80, Ipoh, Perak, 1980.

It is important at this juncture to state that the European literatures that I have been able to look at initially are British, French, Italian, Spanish, Portuguese and Dutch (the last four with the help of friends in the field). I have later on looked at the Japanese and the American. In the British, French, and Italian literatures, Malay elements are present in quite substantial quantities. I have not found any in Dutch literature (if one does not include the Indonesian characters), nor in Portuguese or Spanish literatures. It is interesting that there are no substantial works set in Malaysia by Portuguese or Dutch authors, as these two countries were the colonisers of Malacca in the sixteenth and eighteenth centuries respectively. According to Father Silvario[5], a scholar of the Portuguese period in Malaysia, the Portuguese who came to the archipelago were mostly sailors, traders, and Catholic priests who had little interest in recording their experiences in literary forms. This reason may also be advanced for the Dutch who were in Malacca from 1641 to 1821.

The absence of any major work with central Malaysian characters and setting in Germany, Switzerland and Scandinavia is easily understood. They had almost no lasting or serious contact with Malaysia in the nineteenth or early twentieth centuries.

A study of this nature also presupposes categories and selection of the works themselves into certain groups. I shall try to select the more important ones and group them by country and according to their literary importance.

Britain

According to Donn Hart and Lewis Hill[6], there are more than two hundred writers who have chosen Malaysia as a background or setting for their works. The more important writers include the colonial officer and later administrator, Hugh Clifford, the sea captain, Joseph Conrad, the tourist, W. Somerset Maugham and the teacher, Anthony Burgess. However, there are others like Barbara Baker who has written three children's novels, Hubert S.

---

5) Interview in Lisbon in 1977.
6) See Donn V. Hart, *Preliminary Check List of Novels with a Malayan Background*, and Lewis Hill, *A Checklist of English-language Fiction Relating to Malaysia, Singapore and Brunei*.

Banner, nine novels, Peter Bendell, seven fictional pieces, F.S. Clark, seven and Marion Osmond, five. These books were published during the first three decades of this century and were quite popular.

Many of them are difficult to obtain now; I shall therefore limit my discussion to two important writers: Conrad and Clifford.

Joseph Conrad

Although Conrad had been to the East three times, he had been in the archipelago only twice. The first time he was in the islands for six weeks, from April to May, 1883. The second time was in 1887; during this trip he was to sail to the islands, ports, rivers, and the estuaries of Borneo. It was to last eight months, from July 1, 1887 to March, 1888. On this trip Conrad could allow his emotions to interact more intensely and within a wider time frame with what he saw and heard in Singapore and the islands.

Almayer's Folly, An Outcast of the Islands, Lord Jim and *The Rescue*, together with a few other short stories, were all based on this brief trip up the Beram River in Northeastern Borneo. Thrown into the company or community of the Malays for short periods of time, he met the prototype of the unscrupulous trader Almeijer and the philosopher Stein and also saw or sailed with the Malay characters who were to populate his work.

The luxuriance of the tropical forest, ponderous and timeless, seems to have attracted many authors. Conrad interprets it in his own northern rhythm in his tight prose – as though tracing the thoughts and moods of the author more than the tropical forests. Yet the luxuriance of ornamented prose is legitimate, giving life to the lushness of vegetation and the unending species and variations of trees of the coasts and mountains of the islands. One cannot help but be hypnotised by this passage from the introductory paragraphs of 'The Lagoon', for example,

> At the end of the straight avenue of forests cut by the intense glitter of the river, the sun appeared unclouded and dazzling, poised low over the water that shone smoothly like a band of metal. The forests, sombre and dull, stood motionless and silent on each side of the broad stream. At the foot of big, towering trees, trunkless ripe palms rose from the mud of the bank, in the bunches of leaves enormous and heavy, that

hung unstirring over the brown swirl of eddies. In the stillness of the air every tree, every leaf, every bough, every tendril of creeper and every petal of minute blossoms seems to have been switched into an immobility perfect and final.[7]

This is a prose steeped in the author's person and the passions of the novelist. A Malay will recognise this scene as more of a concept than a description of individual trees, blossoms and eddies. He has to strain himself to imagine the real forests instead of these psychological ones, as Conrad's effect on him would be more the creation of an emotion rather than a recognition of a physical forest. The resultant mood of mystery and the abstractness of its effect are perhaps the result of Conrad's desire not to particularize and name the real. Except for the *nipa* palms, trees are anonymous, standing with the sun as a strong and rich backdrop to the psychological climate of his story. This seems to be the purpose here. Nature is transformed into a landscape of the mind.

The profound descriptions of nature in Conrad's works become Conrad's idioms, images and symbols. Of the river, the vegetation and the seas we have already said much. They seem to overpower and overwhelm. They are there in their wholeness and transported into Conrad's Malaysian novels and stories. They are natural parts of his works.

However, the genius of Conrad is not seen only in the vast canvases of greens and blues that he paints. It is also in the miniatures and their meanings that we find Conrad at his best. The philosophy of Stein, the trader who found a universe (in *Lord Jim*) centred on the fragile butterfly must be seen in contrast to the flooding green of the jungle. For Stein, the butterfly is 'marvellous'. The beautiful itself is 'nothing'. However, the accuracy, 'the Harmony' – these are the very abstract stuff of mystery. 'And so fragile! And so strong. And so exact!' he says. 'That is Nature – the balance of colossal forces. Every star is so – and every blade of grass stands so – and the mighty Kosmos in perfect equilibrium produces – this. This wonder; this masterpiece of Nature – the great artist.

For Stein, and also for Conrad, the butterfly is the idiom of Nature itself, the perfection within the contrast of fragility and

---

7) See Joseph Conrad, 'The Lagoon', *Cornhill Magazine*. 1897, January, pp. 59-71.

strength. In the butterfly too the whole web of opposites of the cosmos is encapsulated. Here is the balance, the meaning of the 'mysterious and the amazing.'.

'These forests are among the wonderful things of the Earth. They are immense in extent, and the trees which form them grow so close together that they tread on one another's toes'. (Sir Hugh Charles Clifford – see p. 208 below.)

In contrast, how small is man. He is no conqueror but the conquered, and in numerous instances, the vanquished, the weakling who cannot fight the might of nature's forces. Conrad's idea of man and his universe comes out fairly clearly in the interwoven drama of nature and man. And nature here humbles man rather than flatters him. To a writer this experience was necessary in order that man can be viewed from a more balanced and meaningful perspective. Nature found in the islands is important not only as a physical setting for his characters but also a psychological one. Man is pitted against its forces, and thereby he is measured.

There is no doubt that one of Conrad's greatest achievements is his insight into the soul of his characters. His Malay characters can claim to be among the sharpest. While the impersonal and mysterious nature, for all its alienness, is always there, out there under the ships, on the horizon, or land or over Conrad's head, the human inhabitants of the islands initially are not so accessible and must be sought out, not only in their communities but also in all their moods, times, crafts and games. As a captain, or a second mate or just a seaman, he had never had that much contact with the native communities which he wrote about. And his novels show that he has just been able to pick up a number of basic Malay words necessary for his survival in the area. Not much more than these words seem to be known by him – of the language, Malay or Buginese, the arts and crafts, the songs or even literature of the people.

His approach to the Malays in his novels is fairly clearly outlined in his letter to A.T. Saunders:

> I need to point out that I had to make material from my own life's incident, arranged, combined, coloured for artistic purposes.
>
> I don't think there's anything reprehensible in that. After all I am a writer of fiction, and it is not what actually happened, but the manner of presenting it that settles the literary and even moral value of my mental and emotional reactions to life, to men, to their affairs and their passions as I have seen them. I have in that sense kept always true to myself.[8]

Conrad makes his characters partly from life. This is a natural enough path in the labyrinth of artistic creation. He could perhaps delve into the mind of the white seaman and trader because in a way he has been both, and seen many on his many journeys. But the Malay – the mysterious islander is fairly different and has a certain ethos which is not easily understood. Yet for all our criticism of him we must also see his works as he tries to see them. Conrad says he has always kept 'true to himself', his style, his created characters rather than the initial sources. His characters are more often than not a blending of different individuals. Jim in *Lord Jim*, for example, is based on the true episode of the sailor who jumped from his ship carrying Muslim pilgrims to Mecca to

---

8) Norman Sherry, *Conrad's Eastern World*, Cambridge, Cambridge University Press, 1966, p. 13.

save his own life, and Raja Brooke of Sarawak, and of course, Conrad himself. Because he was true to himself, and Conrad is a man of strong passions and idiosyncrasies, his novels are heavy with his own attitudes, morals and perspectives. The characters tend to follow the logic of his passion and ideals rather than the ethos of a people. And this is where the fiction is sometimes remote from local reality, and his Malay characters are sometimes remote from the real Malay. If in detail he misses much, in generalisation, however, he amazes us with his insight.

Perhaps Conrad's thoughts about the Malays are very well condensed in the introductory paragraph of *The Rescue* (1920), a later novel set in the area:

> The shallow sea that foams and murmurs on the shores of the thousand islands, big and little, which make up the Malay Archipelago has been for centuries the scene of adventurous undertakings. The vices and the virtues of four nations have been displayed in the conquest of that region that even to his day has not been robbed of all the mystery and romance of its past – and the race of men who had fought against the Portuguese, the Spaniards, the Dutch and the English, has not been changed by the unavoidable defeat. They have kept to this day their love of liberty, their fanatical devotion to their chiefs, their blind fidelity in friendship and hate – all their lawful and unlawful instincts. Their country of land and water – for the sea was as much their country as the earth of their islands – has fallen a prey to the Western race – the reward of superior strength if not of superior virtue. Tomorrow the advancing civilization will obliterate the marks of a long struggle in the accomplishment of its inevitable victory.

On the huge canvas, the strokes generally touch on the central values of the coastal Malays, especially their love of liberty and the inevitable fall to the westerners who, through means that were supposed to belong to unlettered people, had acquired wealth and power to fuel further their arrogance. The Malays, especially the Buginese of the novels, are great sailors, maritime in their instinct for freedom and love of the world. The coastal Malays are a product of intricate intermarriages of islanders from different ethnic groups like the Banjarese of South Borneo, the Buginese of South Celebes, the Javanese of East Java, the Palembangis, Delinese, Bataks, Achinese and Minangkabaus of Sumatra. The

Malay is generally passionate in his causes, relationships, identity and religion. If he loves freedom, he is also bound to the laws of the *adat* and his religion. The seas, the tropical heat, the very rich earth and rivers make of him a fairly relaxed human being. Conrad met Malays in various places. But we do not have records except that some worked on board his ship and there he came to know them only superficially. His quartermaster and crew were Malay. Of the aristocrats, he met perhaps only one raja on the island of Celebes in the town of Donggala.

There are perhaps two kinds of Malay characters in Conrad's work. The first comprises those in power or in the process of achieving power. In this group would thus be included the reigning rajas and sultans, the princes, ministers, junior ministers and feudal dignitaries of similar status.

The other group is made up of sailors and servants who are sketched as they come into the picture and disappear soon after that. Of these two groups the first seems to be more meaningful in their actions, thoughts and pronouncements for the progress of the various novels and stories. Even though they do not play the main roles in the works (except in *Almayer's Folly* and 'The Lagoon') they are supporting or secondary characters whose fates are also involved in the whole design of the works themselves. The second group of characters plays very minor roles and they are accordingly rather peripheral in their importance.

If we look at Conrad's first novel, *Almayer's Folly,* Malay life and characters obviously dominate the scene and even Almayer himself. He is the only white man in the village and while he marks time to grow rich he is dominated by the bigger and more meaningful personalities and issues. The hero here is Dain Maroola, says Conrad, from Bali and a Brahmin, a fictional human being of course, because in ethnic terms this is a mistake, as Dain, or more precisely 'Daeng,' is an aristocratic title among the Buginese of Celebes. However, Balinese titles are a different matter altogether. Further, the Balinese are essentially insular and do not travel as much as the Bugis. Other than this small but revealing discrepancy (of the knowledge Conrad has of the Malays) Dain Maroola is interestingly, but also, ethnocentrically described by Conrad as a

> lithe figure of medium height with a great breadth of shoulder suggesting great power... face full of determination and

expressing a reckless good humour not devoid, however of some dignity. The squareness of lower jaw, the full red lips, the mobile nostrils and the proud carriage of the head gave the impression of being half-savage, untamed, perhaps cruel, and corrected the liquid softness of the almost feminine eye, that general characteristic of the race.[9]

Dain Maroola is an imposing character, sensuous as well as reckless. He has the arrogance of the traditional Malay aristocrat but this is combined with the good humour of his people. Good humour itself is not realised in the novel as he is more obsessed with his love and design. Dain Maroola is recognizably Buginese. Conrad might have met several Buginese who were good sailors and naturally chosen for work on the ships. And in the area that Conrad frequented there were perhaps many Buginese settlers or they were the original inhabitants.

But Dain Maroola, the prince, is also mysterious. Facts about him are not clear and our information about him tends to come from a secondary source – not so much from the author himself. Maroola has come to Sambir 'allured also by the fact that there was no Dutch resident on the river, which should make things easier, no doubt for illegal gunpowder.' There he easily seduces Almayer as well as the raja, with the help of the latter's minister. It is hinted that the gunpowder, the centre of the plan, is to be used by the Malays against the Dutch – so that a theme of heroism vaguely unfolds here. His love affair with Almayer's daughter is positively described and so is his escape, events that reflect Conrad's empathy for the cause.

The other important character is Babalatchi who also appears in the next novel, *An Outcast of the Islands*. First an exile, he has been able to establish himself here as a smooth, cunning and at times wise diplomat who solves problems and mediates between adversaries. He is an old confidential adviser as well as a 'cut-throat' as Conrad describes him. It is in *An Outcast of the Islands* that he develops further. In this novel he

> blundered upon the river while in search of a safe refuge for his disreputable head. He was a vagabond, a true orang laut. Living by rapine and plunder of coasts and ships in his pros-

---

9) Joseph Conrad, *Almayer's Folly*, London, Nash and Grayson, London, 1921, p. 75.

perous days, earning his living among honest and irksome toil when the days of adversity were upon him.[10]

A beginning clearly not too aristocratic, but a life that is lived according to the shape of fate and opportunities. He could plunder as well as toil on land for his living. He was brave as well as bloodthirsty – and he hated the white man who interfered with his manly pursuits of throat-cutting, kidnapping, slave-dealing and fire raising, that were the only possible occupations for a true man of the seas.

Babalatchi comes from a race of Orang Laut – who live and earn their living from the sea, and besides the usual trading are also involved in piracy and other related professions. He is a diplomat but also a man of opinion, who has dealt with the white man and seen how they, too, were blood-thirsty, avaricious and self-indulgent on the seas and lands of the archipelago. His confrontation with the patronising Lingard is fiery as well as courteous in the Malay style. In the wrath of a post-colonial victim of colonialism he tells Lingard:

> This is how you all talk while you load your guns and sharpen your swords; and when you are ready then to those who are weak you say: 'Obey me and be happy or die'.[11]

Conrad allows Babalatchi expression of nationalistic fervour and insight into the bullying ways of the white sailor and trader. The novelist here may be said to be as empathic as he could be to the feelings of the victimised Malays, who had to suffer the operations, the power play and the greed of the Dutch and British during these times.

Many a novel has been written about the Malays. However, it is only in the works of Conrad that such an angry outburst against the Caucasian is allowed to find its harsh words, and also from the mouth of Malay characters. To the British, the Malay was somebody easily bullied or threatened into treaties. Babalatchi's words to Lingard are thus quite rare, against the grain of colonial thinking:

> You are strange, you white men. You think it is only your wisdom and your virtue and your happiness that are true. You

---

10) See Joseph Conrad, *An Outcast of the Islands*, New York, Airmont, 1966, p. 36.
11) Ibid. p. 139.

are stronger than wild beasts, but not so wise... You do not understand the difference between yourselves and us – who are men. You are wise and you shall always be fools.[12]

Conrad goes to the heart of representative identities here, halving the worlds and their characteristics. The victims retaliate and in doing so define their essential character (and their people's) as a contrast to the oppressors'. The metaphor of wild beasts is also central, as it overturns the European concept that the Malay is less a human being and therefore may be conquered, converted, and changed in his ways. To Babalatchi it is the Malays who are men, and by inference, the white men are not, thus in fact the lesser human beings. While the identity of the Malay is defined, so is the white man's, through opposites, through active debunking and the argument of who is right or better.

And Babalatchi is innately cunning in intrigues, working for the downfall of the greedy trader and the thief, Willem. Conrad finds in Babalatchi a spokesman for his Polish nationalism, I think. He was the son of a Polish nationalist couple exiled in Russia, the colonial power. Both of his parents died when he was young, a fact that seems to have affected him deeply and which emerges later in literary characters fighting for their own country, rights and identity. True, Babalatchi himself is no angel but a 'barbarous politician'. He is also a man proud of his land and he appears in both novels to be a positive character and a spokesman for Conrad.

In comparison to Babalatchi, Lakamba, the raja, is more negative. In *Almayer's Folly* he is cornered by the economic strategies of the Dutch and the Arabs who are trying to outdo each other. Without Babalatchi, whom he tolerated for his own good, the raja would not have survived the situation. Conrad sees the old raja as

> discontented, ungrateful and turbulent; a man full of envy and ready for intrigue, with brave words and empty promises for ever on his lips. He was obstinate, but his will was made up of short impulses that never lasted long enough to carry him up the goal of his ambitions.

This old raja does not transcend his shortcomings, but falls prey to them. He has not many views of the Arabs, Dutch or British who

---

12) Ibid.

fight each other for the wealth of his lands. To him obviously only his own survival matters.

The counterpart or complement to Jim of *Lord Jim*, is Dain Waris, who is also a Buginese, not unlike Maroola in many ways, but more serious, quieter and as though consumed by a great and noble passion to protect his land and people. In his campaigns he is burnt by a powerful flame of patriotism and, like many of his real counterparts in Malay history, he is killed by the coloniser, here represented by Brown and his party, through the tragic misjudgement of his own friend, Jim.

Dain Waris' short but meaningful life in a way epitomises also the tragic fate that awaits many of the fighters of his kind. But Conrad seems to choose him as the exemplary hero, with others following him, because he not only fights the intruder but at the same time is able to think like the white man. Here the identity is mixed and ironic. To fight the invader one must be the opposite, or politically 'the other' in ideology, but in mind he must understand the former's, and also transcend his own Malay way of thinking and acting. Here the western and the Malay identities are fictionally mixed, and perhaps difficult to meet on the streets or in the villages in reality, even in our days. We, of course, re-member Conrad's words that he is true to himself, both as the son of Polish exiles and a writer. And all writers cannot help but be in some way autobiographical in their works.

From *The Rescue* (1920) are two Malay characters of note: Hassim and Jaaffir. Hassim is introduced as having the 'well bred air of discreet courtesy, which is natural to the better class of that people.' From the beginning, his sense of country and pride of nation is passionate and he speaks his mind in harsh tones. It is the Dutch 'who steal our land.' While the Caucasian characters fight for their own skins, Hassim and his friends recover their land and commit their lives to this cause – a sacred duty imposed upon them by the political situation.

There is a part of Maroola in him, the aristocratic grace and the quality of being driven by his ideals. However, Hassim, in comparison, seems to be more gentle, more mature and wiser than the romantic hero of *Almayer's Folly*.

Jaffir, his loyal servant and messenger is also a man who lives and dies according to his ideals and duties. He comes to us as a very practical person, forever loyal to his prince and mysteriously appearing wherever and whenever he is needed. Like Dain Waris, he dies because Lingard negligent in playing his part.

The Malay women, Mrs. Almayer and her daughter, are as fascinating as the men, because unlike Aisa of *An Outcast* who is really an Arab, they are practical and not romantic characters. None of them is painted as the gentle maiden, innocent and pure. Mrs. Almayer, a strong woman who could define and retain her identity before her husband whom she understandably dislikes, is a daughter of the vanquished Sulu pirate killed by Lingard. Lingard adopts her and marries her to Almayer, who in fact wants her only for her inherited money. The insensitivities of her husband, a rough and repugnant man, bring the readers over to her side, and also the Malays. She becomes in fact her own woman with a strong sense of Malayness even though brought up by Lingard, a man not too respectful of Malay virtues. Here we notice that her identity is built through a pride of race, the vanquished father, and no doubt pushed further to the other side by the hated husband and the foster father who looks down on her people. In many instances we find her always returning to the glories of the sultan of Sulu, her ancestor, to his power and his prowess, which had 'benumbed the hearts of white men at the sight of his swift pirate praus.'

Perhaps through the influence of Lingard or Almayer himself (among the Malays, the Dutch are known for their tight-fistedness and love of money) she develops 'an appetite for shining dollars' and this image of her is fairly dominant – and money in a community in search of riches is a total virtue and an indisputable source of power in itself. We even read of her being paid by Maroola for her daughter's hand, an instance that describes an extremity of this aspect of her character. However, on a higher plane, like Babalatchi, her views of white people are strong and heavily coloured by the experience of living close to them. Of them she says:

> They speak lies. And they think lies because they despise us that are better than they are, but not as strong.[13]

This is an insider's view, one put into the mouth of a Malay woman adopted by a Dutchman, but embittered because of the

---

13) See Joseph Conrad, *Almayer's Folly*, p. 198.

treatment she has been subjected to. The story turns when she proudly and happily returns to her own people and their ways. Her feelings towards the Dutch even approach hatred, which again comes from a defensive sense or retaliatory pride of territory and race. Listen to her speaking her farewell to Nina, her daughter:

> When I hear of white men driven from the islands, then I shall know that you are alive, and that you remember my words.[14]

The presence of the whites encroaches upon the ways of the natives. Mrs. Almayer's life itself must be adjusted to that of the European. Thus her sharp words, as direct as Babalatchi's words, are not very surprising.

> Let him slay the white men that come to us to trade with prayers on their lips and loaded guns in their heads... And they are on every sea, and on every shore, and they are many.[15]

This is a painful, yet very insightful lament that would strike a chord of recognition for the Malays of those times as well as ours. And it is a truth observed by Joseph Conrad, a European who travelled their lands and seas as it was not possible for the ruled to write in such a strain except clandestinely as in the poems of Tuan Simi.[16] During these early years the literature of Malay confrontation with the white man was still very young and without any examples to follow.

Mrs. Almayer's ostentatious return to the culture and ways of the Malays is foregrounded as a choice of life styles and confirmation of identity in the face of all the possible choices. This is her statement and also Conrad's, no doubt. For a woman who has known at least two cultures her preference is for the Malay, and it is here that she finds herself. This profound choice is followed, and therefore strengthened by Nina, her Eurasian daughter with Almayer.

Sent to Singapore to be 'civilised' by a white school, Nina was mistreated by the whites, her fate a clear echo of her mother's. She

---

14) Ibid., p. 200.
15) Ibid.
16) Muhammad Haji Salleh, 'Puisi Tantangan Singapura' Mss., 1993.

returns to Sambir, again in an act of choice of culture and identity, away from the white school which 'civilises' her, but does not reflect the 'culture' she was to obtain there. Thus her return to Sambir is also her return to being Malay. In Conrad's own words:

> To her resolute nature, however, after all these years, the savage and uncompromising sincerity of purpose shown by her Malay kinsmen seemed at least preferable to the sleek hypocrisy, to the polite disguises, to the virtuous pretences of such white people as she had had the misfortune to come in contact with.[17]

This return to being Malay is further helped by her falling in love with Dain Maroola who takes her away to Bali, where 'she became a Malay girl.' The Malay hero is also the agent of her total return. His political achievement is completed by finally and physically bringing home the half-breed daughter of Almayer and his Malay wife.

Conrad has not chosen to find the middle ground in cultural alternatives. In a situation where the land was being colonised by harsh and less than civilised agents of colonial powers, there was only one rightful choice, and one rightful identity for his Malays. Genuineness was superior to grace, sincerity was preferable to 'sleek hypocrisy.'

The choice of Mrs. Almayer and her daughter is a rare one indeed in English literature, which according to Ashcroft, Griffith and Tiffin[18] subverts British colonialism. As an agent of that colonialism English literature provides reasons for invasion or intervention in the lives of the natives. That Conrad allowed his Malay characters to choose their own 'savage' culture, and thereby rejected what he calls virtuous pretences and sleek hypocrisy, is a brave act on the part of the novelist, especially in an age when invasion of foreign lands was a governmental and even racial policy of the British.

Hugh Clifford

In comparison with Conrad, Hugh Clifford was a man of much lesser literary achievement. He was better known in the nineteen

---

17) See Joseph Conrad, *Almayer's Folly*, p. 60.
18) Bill Ashcroft, Gareth Griffith and Helen Tiffin, *The Empire writes Back*, p. 48.

twenties and thirties when his books found a popularity both in the United Kingdom and the United States. They are now almost forgotten and referred to more for his colonial involvement in the state of Pahang.

Yet for the student of literature set in the Malay Archipelago, the short stories and novels of Hugh Clifford present a different perspective from Conrad's. While the latter saw the states and people at a distance, Hugh Clifford, the initial adventurer, and later the British colonial administrator, lived among the Malays at close quarters. In the introduction of *The Further Side of Silence* Clifford claims this close relationship and also a certain truth of incidence.

> The stories composing this book, with a single exception – 'The Ghoul', which reaches me at second hand – are all relations of incidents in which I have had a part, or in which the principal actors have been familiarly known to me. They faithfully reproduce conditions of life as they existed in the Malayan Peninsula before the white men took a hand in the government of the native states, or immediately after our coming – things as I knew them between 1893 and 1903 – the twenty years that I passed in that most beautiful and at one time little frequented corner of Asia.

We realise that these words come from the pen of a British colonial officer who was instrumental in bringing the colonial power of the British into Pahang, a Malay state in the east coast of the Peninsula. As if in conscious or unconscious qualification, he confesses, 'They (these works) are written with a full appreciation of the native point of view, and of a people for whom I entertain much affection and sympathy.' For us, too, Clifford seems in a lot of his books and lines to present the essential split within himself, between his appreciation and sympathy for the Malays and his loyalty to colonial chiefs.

Who is Clifford? Roff[19], in his introduction to *Stories by Sir Hugh Clifford* helps us by sketching him thus:

> A thorough Anglo-Saxon, clean-bred and a good specimen of his race, strapped from childhood into the conventions of the English upper-class and the Roman Catholic Church, he had

---

19) See Sir Hugh Charles Clifford, *Stories by Sir Hugh Clifford*, Selected and Introduced by William R. Roff, Kuala Lumpur, Oxford University Press, 1966.

found himself drawn to 'herding with natives, and conceiving for them such an affection and sympathy that he was accustomed to contrast his countrymen unfavourably with his Malayan friends'... Though he remained convinced as he wrote in the preface to *In Court and Kampong* that the Malay interest lies in the increase of British influence in the Peninsula, he could not suppress the fear that by reducing the lead `to a dead monotony of order and peace' the British had helped to destroy much that was good and valuable in the Malay.

For him this ideological dilemma is as real as his person, and has clearly become part of his personality, at least as a writer. We notice the pain of a split world in the works and sometimes he seeks out reasons for his occasional defence of the Malays or allowing them to behave in the way that they have always been used to.

Clifford was prolific. He wrote novels, short stories and sketches. His novels are quite clear in their genre as they are fairly conventional and accompanied by elements of adventure, which seemed to be popular in the early decades of this century. However, in contrast, his stories and sketches are often less clear in their genres, and in many cases they tend 'to merge one into the other'. Many of them are mere sketches without a full-blown narrative development to them. Their saving grace is the author's natural narrative talent, insight and language which are quite poetic even in comparison with Conrad.

These works had been written from Clifford's arrival in the Peninsula in 1883, and until he was posted to Trinidad, Sri Lanka and Nigeria in 1903. He spent a full span of twenty years in Malaya, coming at 21 and going away at 41; a very long time indeed compared to Conrad, Burgess or Fauconnier. He returned again when he was much older, then as a governor of the Straits Settlements.The new world of the tropics and of the Malays fascinated his 'devouring curiosity'. His administrative work took him the length and breadth of Pahang and Perak, thus giving him a really varied and rich physical and cultural experience of the country. He was among the palace nobles as well as the farmers, the imams as well as the shamans. In the upper reaches of Pahang she came to meet the different groups of Orang Asli, whom he has also described.

Clifford is quite painstaking in observing and sketching the rivers, forests, valleys and villages. This is the physical environment that has partaken in the development of the Malays, created their values and beliefs. Like the preponderous coastal forests of Conrad, Clifford too was influenced by this overwhelming tropical vegetation and nature. His language, no doubt through talent and practice, seems natural and made a malleable medium for a world so different from the one in which it developed. Narrative or descriptive details are often well chosen and sketched. The sounds, the sense and the visual presence of this amazingly rich world live out in his prose. Take for example this passage celebrating the trees and rivers in Pahang.

> These forests are among the wonderful things of the Earth. They are immense in extent, and the trees which form them grow so close together that they tread on one another's toes. All are lashed, and bound, and relashed, into one huge magnificent tangled net, by the thickest underwood, and the most marvellous parasitic growths that nature has ever devised. No human being can force his way through this maze of trees, and shrubs, and thorns, and plants, and creepers; and even the great beasts which dwell in the jungle find their strength unequal to the task, and have to follow game paths, beaten out by the passage of innumerable animals, through the thickest and deepest parts of the forest. The branches cross and recross, and are bound together by countless parasitic creepers, forming a green canopy overhead, through which the fierce sunlight only forces a partial passage, the struggling rays flecking the trees on which they fall with little splashes of light and colour.[20]

Or take another example from 'In the Valley of the Telom':

> Very far away, in the remote interior of Pahang, there is a river called the Telom – an angry little stream, which fights and tears its way through the vast primeval forest, biting savagely at its banks, wrestling petulantly with the rocks and boulders that obstruct its path, squabbling fiercely over long, sloping beds of shingle, and shaking a glistening mane of broken water, as it rushes downward in its fury. Sometimes, during the prevalence of the northeast monsoon, when the rain

---

20) See Sir Hugh Charles Clifford, *Stories by Sir Hugh Clifford*, p. 16.

has fallen heavily in the mountains, the Telom will rise fourteen or fifteen feet in a couple of hours; and then, for a space, its waters change their temper from wild, impetuous rage to a sullen wrath which is even more formidable and dangerous. But it is when the river is shrunken by drought that it is most of all to be feared; for at such times sharp and jagged rocks, over which, at ordinary seasons, a bamboo raft is able to glide in safety, prick upward from the bed of the stream to within an inch or two of the surface, and rip up everything that chances to come in contact with them as cleanly as though it were cut with a razor. At the feet of the largest rapids in the Telom one of these boulders forms, in dry weather, a very efficient trap for the unwary.[21]

Clifford's brush is comparative lighter, and with a greater sense of detail and therefore closer to the reality of the Malaysian natural environment than Conrad's. It is more dynamic than Maugham's, more physical than Conrad's derived metaphysical universe.

Clifford presents his myriad characters at the end of late nineteenth century in Pahang and Perak, ranging from the young girl seized by an old chieftain, the elemental Kulop Sumbing who knows no fear, a gambling prince, murderers, shamans and the werewolf. And he describes not merely the Peninsular Malays but also the different groups of Aslian people, the immigrant Rawa and Mandailing in Pahang and Perak, the Murut and Dayak of Sabah and Sarawak and the newly-arrived Chinese and Indians. His themes range from an inter-ethnic marriages that fail because of unbridgeable cultural gaps, to struggles for personal dignity by a young man against his chieftain, insensitive British policies, administrative blunders and perhaps, to crown it all, of the struggle to be a Malay by a prince educated in England in *Sally: A Study* and *Prince of Malaya*.

Among his most memorable descriptions are of Kulop Sumbing from Perak, the mysterious and silent young man, who has no community, comrade or family. He only lives for his ambition. Enormous in size, ugly and living by his instincts he loves 'adventure, was absolutely fearless, and was moreover, a good man with his hands... and as he did not share with the majority of his race their instinctive dread of travelling alone in the jungle, he

---

21) See Sir Hugh Charles Clifford, *The Further Side of Silence*, Grade City, Doubleday, Page, 1923, p. 77.

decided in making a lone raid into the Sakai country.' Physically motivated he does not have a conscience. 'He, of course, felt absolutely no twinges of conscience, for you must look for principle in the rank and file of the race to which Kulop Sumbing belong.'[22]

Another tale, 'The Flight of the Jungle Folk,' also goes into the jungle to delineate the difficult relationship between a Malay husband and his Aslian wife, that echoes with cultural misunderstanding. The death of the latter, Te-U, also darkens our belief in human beings, in Malays who could not look at the Aslian people as equals, and therefore want to exploit them. But here the pictures of the races are not painted in black and white terms, partial to one and against the other. He seems to be loyal to the situation and tries to describe the values of the character being judged. Thus in another tale the love between a Malay boy, Kria, and an Aslian girl, Pi-Noi, rises above the prejudice and humiliation. The tender description of the girl's beauty also rises above the usual prejudice against her race:

> Her skin, smooth as velvet and with much the same downy softness of surface, was an ever yellow-brown, without fleck or blemish, and upon it diamond points of water glistened in the sunlight. Her black and glossy hair was twisted carelessly into a magnificent knot at the nape of her neck, her rounded curls straying here and there to soften cheek and forehead. Her face, an oval of great purity, glowed with youth and life. Her lips had something of the pout of childhood. Her chin was firmly modelled; her nose straight, with nostrils rather wide, quivering and sensitive; her little ears nestled in the glory of her hair.[23]

Studies in Brown Humanity presents a further collection of sketches and stories. Among the most fascinating are those about traditional artists from the native theatre, the *wayang* and the *makyong*. From the *makyong* world one meets Saleh of Kelantan. As that form of theatre was not allowed in his state Saleh has brought his cast down to Pahang where they could freely perform. It is here that he found his narrator.[24]

---

22) Sir Hugh Charles Clifford, *In a Corner of Asia*, London, Fisher Unwin, 1926, p. 81.
23) See Sir Hugh Charles Clifford, *The Further Side of Silence*, p. 7.
24) Sir Hugh Charles Clifford, *Stories by Sir Hugh Clifford*, p. 147.

Leh was a man of many accomplishments. He played the fiddle, in most excruciating ways, to the huge delight of all the Malays who heard him, he was genuinely funny, when he had put on his hideous red mask, with its dirty sheepskin top, which stood for the hair of his head, over his handsome, clever face, and roars of laughter greeted him at every turn; he had a keen eye for a topical joke, a form of satire much appreciated by his Malay audience; he had a happy knack of imitating the notes of birds and the cry of any animal; and above all he was a Rhapsodist, and with that melodious voice of his would sing the wonderful story of Awang Lotong.

With his extraordinary talents Leh was the popular artist of his time, sought after by villagers, girls and even married women. Clifford tells of how at his arrival, girls and married women left their bethrothed, their husbands and their children to greet and woo him. Many times he was attacked by these jealous lovers and husbands.

Clifford seems to be a close observer, fascinated with his subject but, no doubt, consciously or unconsciously, aware that he wrote for the English-speaking public, and that they will judge him and his characters from their own viewpoints and values.

If the many fascinating stories culled from the villages and forests are fragments of a description of a people, his novel, *A Prince of Malaya* (1926), is perhaps a bigger and fuller canvas that also strings together Clifford's many experiences among the Malays. In this novel 'Raja Saleh' or, as mocked by the English, 'Sally', with its connotation of femininity and the notion that foreign names are strange and may be pronounced in any way they please), a prince of the Sultan of the state of Pelesu is sent to England for an English education. He stays with the Mesuriers, who also have a son and a daughter. The first part of this work traces the process of a Malay becoming English, how he changes his ways and in fact, even his feelings. A cultural and racial conflict is more than hinted at. Because he is extremely sensitive, like most Malays, he is thus often hurt by the words of the callous young English natives. However, after a period of five years in England he is able to adjust to the new environment and ways. In the meantime his Malayness has become proportionately diluted. Ironically even his looks grew to become more English.

Also he was handsome – nor with the soft, foreign, almost feline beauty that distinguishes so many Orientals, but with good looks of a sturdier cast, bred of clean-cut features, manly independence, and self-respect, which approximate far more nearly to English standards of taste![25]

He is physically developed and is good at games. He rows, plays cricket, football and hockey and swims. But intellectually and in the classroom, on the other hand, he is 'slack'.

His meeting with an Indian princess, daughter to Maharaja Baram Singh, is a new and profound intellectual experience for Saleh, and continues to disturb his life. The princess who had come to know the English colonial tricks in both England and India spoke eloquently to the surprised Malay prince:

> 'You like the English!' she cried. 'You dare say you like them – you an Asiatic, the son of the many whom they have despoiled! Only cowards like them, cowards who fawn, as dogs fawn, upon the hands that beat them.'[26]

These are strong words, words of the suffering victim. And they haunt Saleh equally in his waking and even sleeping life. Soon these words are to become more real when he falls in love with one Alice Fairfax, who is also at the same time being wooed by a Major Dalton. The emotional crisis comes to a bitter climax when the girl, after choosing the English major, tells Saleh that her relationship with him is in fact merely based on pity!

He cannot help but be awakened rudely from his dream of England and the English. He has conscientiously tried to become English, only in the end to be rejected by them, through the girl he has fallen for. The story turns on these hard words. They help to begin a new realisation in the young man. Says Clifford,

> It was the stirring within him of the Malayan soul that had so long being lulled in anaesthesia; a stirring more violent by the truth so abruptly, so mercilessly revealed, that his transformation into a white man – a transformation he had fondly believed to be triumphantly complete – was a mockery, a sham.[27]

Saleh is brought home to Pelesu by the author to nurse his wounds. His English world lies in shambles. He starts to assemble

---

25) Sir Hugh Charles Clifford, *A Prince of Malaya*, New York and London, Harper and Brothers Publishers, 1926, p. 43.
26) Ibid., pp. 55-56.
27) See Sir Charles Hugh Clifford, *A Prince of Malaya*, op. cit.,p. 84

a new Malay one, one he has lost touch with. Yet the two worlds battle within him. In trying to define Saleh's present predicament, Jack Norris, Saleh's friend says, 'We English folks have done a lot of good in Pelesu, beyond a doubt, but it will take a world of it to wipe out the memory of the harm we have done to him.' (Once again the colonial sense of contribution slips into the story, a sense that Clifford very much believes in.) The plot develops around this 'harm,' for the post-colonial reader, a very positive turn of events. He also rejects the old feudal Pelesu of his father that offers no better alternative.

To cut this long and painful story short, Saleh finally chooses the alternative of the Malay rebels who are opposing the British and is appointed as their leader. In a gunfight, he is mistakenly shot and dies, in the end as a Malay struggling to regain his land from the British, a hero to his people. Juxtapose this, for example, to his possible marriage to Alice Fairfax, to become a doting husband and assimilated into the English community, never to gain an identity of his own. However, the ending is also a clear victory for the colonialists – anybody who goes against the mighty empire must die, an ending formed by the pen of Clifford himself.

In this novel, I suspect that Clifford is partly on the side of the gentle Malay prince, Saleh, the victim of the English and English colonialism. Though Saleh meets his death here, it is a positive death, the death of a hero and martyr, and not an empty one, of say a prince wasting away in despair. Yet, as I have tried to show, Clifford is also the 'convinced imperialist' who stood for British colonialism in his stories, even though he has criticised its officers.

From a literary point of view Clifford's descriptions of the Malays or Aslian (first Malaysians), Muruts and Ibans are comparable with Conrad's, but with a difference. While the former are more visually and empirically anchored the latter are more visionary and metaphysical. Both of them were working on their experiences: Conrad, truer to himself, Clifford to his subject.

Clifford often sees his closeness to the Malay peoples as an advantage when writing in comparison to those who were less intimate with the subject. Thus when he was about to leave for Trinidad he wrote, in the preface to *Sally: A Study:* 'The writer appeals to us that we judge them (his works) – not as literature, but as truth – as fragments whose only value is that they are, as it were, the aftermath of a rich harvest of experience in fry.'

If we now turn to Somerset Maugham, we will feel how much we are missing in terms of Conrad's depth of human vision and Clifford's details of the Malay world. For me Maugham's sojourn to Malaysia was more in search of stories and pleasure than to study the people and their culture.

Written in the 1930s, Maugham's stories have now been collected in *Maugham's Malaysian Stories* (1973) and *Maugham's Borneo Stories* (1976). All of these stories seem to be fairly raw descriptions of his experiences in the Archipelago after the First World War. His ocean travel has taken him to the archipelago and its ports. We can discern that most of his stories were based on flitting observations that consequently produced a superficial or generalised impression of the people of the islands and their environment.

Generally Maugham is not interested in the natives. His natives are mere shadows, the main characters are administrators, adventurers or estate managers. Anthony Burgess partly describes Maugham's situation in his introduction to *Maugham's Malaysian Stories*, 'When an European paid a visit to the East Indies, the Malays, Indians and Chinese he would meet in the rubber estates are houseboys and cooks in bungalows, barmen in clubs and hotels, clerks in offices, orderlies in hospitals. He tended if he could not speak their language to regard them as mere colourful "extras", with the opportunity to star in the drama of oriental life. The forefront of the stage was monopolized by the men who ruled these territories whether as Colonial Office civil servants or estate managers.'

This observation is clear in the stories of Maugham. His Malaysian characters are indeed houseboys and barmen; the villagers, the chieftains and perhaps even cruel nobles are totally locked out of his books.

In a way the Malays are silenced, not allowed the power of the word, their voices are edited out.[28] The extras are mute, dominated by the language (and the colonial force) of their white masters. Neither are they given fictional space to act out their lives, beliefs and therefore their identities. If, in some works, they are sketched with warped nibs, in Maugham's stories they do not

---

28) Gayatri Chakravorty Spivak, *The Post-Colonial Critic*, New York, Routledge, 1990, p. 21.

have identities, except as shadowy voiceless servants of the white men and women.

France

In the earlier decades of the twentieth century some Frenchmen became planters or managers in rubber estates in Malaya. One of them, Henri Fauconnier, became very famous with *Malaisie* (translated as 'The Soul of Malaya')[29] that won the 1930 Prix Goncourt, a coveted French literary prize.

Malaisie, in the original French does not claim to describe the soul of Malaya, as the English translation does. Set in a rubber estate, possibly in Selangor, it describes life around the Europeans with Malay and Indian tappers as extras. Here again the Malay characters are taken out of their village and given a thin existence, mostly as economic servants of the white men. They are not mute though, but are allowed to have some form of independent verbal expression. For example Smail, the servant replies to a question by the narrator:

> 'White men,' said Smail, 'ask the sort of question that little children ask.'[30]

Or again when the narrator asks Ngah, 'Why are you afraid of white men?' comes the reply:

> 'Their hearts are drunken,' said Ngah, 'and besides they drink alcohol.'[31]

Though the whites have centre stage, sometimes the Malay characters take over, especially in the second part of the novel, where the crass and swearing Rolain is often pictured a brute in contrast to his polite and refined servant. The author and Rolain with the two Malay servants take off on a long trip to the east coast to see the Malays in their own setting. For according to the author:

---

29) Henri Fauconnier, *The Soul of Malaya* (Translated by Eric Sutton), London, Elkin Mathews & Marrot, 1931.
30) Ibid., p. 73.
31) Ibid., p. 97.

> You can never know a country well except from the people it produces. In Malaya you must surround yourself with Malays.[32]

There he finds them 'placid, but easily excited. They look melancholic, especially the younger ones, and will laugh at a trifle. They understand that they are understood. Malays are polite because they are proud. Never give displeasure if you would never be displeased. Shame is the only emotion that they cannot bear.'

Fauconnier is especially intrigued by the literary and cultural life of the people. Foremost, there is his fascination with the *pantun*, the Malay short poetic form, which he possibly knew even before leaving France. It is perhaps too much for the translator to claim that the author was trying to catch the *semangat* or soul of Malaya, but to his credit the latter has painted a beautiful soul of the *pantun*, not a small feat, as the form is very much culture-bound and specific. The nuances of suggestion and metaphor are not lost on him. In fact his appreciation of the form is perhaps among the most insightful:

> Here, indeed, are metaphors, but metaphors without life, the first expression that came to mind, of origin unknown. In the Malay dialogue, on the other hand, all is allusion. It would be incomprehensible if one did not know the pantun of the leeches that come from the marshes into the fields; the pantun in which the sugar cane of the other bank symbolises illusion or treachery; the pantun of the hook and of the lamp....Such a dialogue implies a literary training that seems amazing in a still primitive people.[33]

Yet his Malays are not political, or to use the contemporary Marxist and/or post-colonial word, ideological. They seem contented and harmonious, and most of all adapt at a fine culture of allusion and indirect poetic form.

This is one of the best books in its attempt to appreciate the Malays, but it is quite sad that Fauconnier too tends to fall into the old framework of definition. And like too many other writers he also has his Malays going into forgetful fits of verbal 'latah' and

---

32) Ibid., p. 106.
33) Ibid., p. 125.

running 'amok.' Still there is a light humour throughout the book that does not frown upon them with a colonial stare.

Another novelist who sets his novels in the Archipelago is Pierre Boulle. At least two of his books, *L'Epreuve des Hommes Blancs*, 1955, (White Men's Test) and *Le Sacrilège Malaise*, 1955, (Sacrilege in Malaya) are set in Malaya. The first novel is of interest as it deals with a theme of cultural confrontation and adjustment. However, in comparison with Fauconnier, Boulle is a much less serious novelist, who tends to choose the sensation and melodrama of life in the tropics over the people's predicament that goes down deep into the culture or centuries. As Jan Mohamed[34] says of writers like him, the natives are looked upon as mere 'resources'. Fauconnier, on the other hand, has attempted to delve into the mode and mind of his Malaysian characters to search out their soul. Even though he has not fully achieved this, there are many thoughtful passages that provide food for retrospective thought. To me, he is among the very few European authors who have looked hard at the Malays and with quite a fair and balanced perspective. Take for example this famous except which compares worldviews.

> My irritation against the Malays was of recent date. Hitherto my feeling for them had been one of indifference. What interests us is what serves our interests – and the Malays are not servile. Obliging, certainly: but that is little. We are too practical to be content with that. We refer to the population of a country as 'labour,' just as we should like to describe the entire animal kingdom as 'cattle'. But the Malays do not at all wish to be considered in this light. Their point of view is contrary to ours. They can easily get their daily rice by working one day a week and they ask for no more. All fatigue is useless and harmful. Life is long, – why hurry? In the morning, perhaps, they visit their nets along the river or their traps at the edge of the jungle, and there they may find some beast of the water or of the forest, which the Tuan Allah has allowed to be caught, so that their bodies may become man, and their soul, in the souls of men, may learn to know Him better. If he has not so willed, it is because he has caused a hand of bananas to ripen in the corner of the Kampong, or there will

---

34) Henry Louis Gates Jr., *"Race", Writing and Difference*, Chicago University Press, 1986, p. 81.

be some young shoots of bamboo, an excellent vegetable, waiting to be cut. They are sure to find something that will serve to season their rice. Tomorrow, perhaps, fate will be kinder, and there will be more to eat...

I did not know what to make of this people. Their carelessness seemed to me a matter for both admiration and contempt. But I always regretted the Malays of my imagination, as depicted in our stories of adventure. The wild pirates that infest the narrows of the Sunda islands... And I had found only these little placid and polite men. They had destroyed my illusions, like these great pythons shown to children in menageries, inert at the bottom of their tanks.[35]

Natives of colonised states have been differently assessed after commercial enterprises have been established, and are subsequently evaluated from an economic viewpoint, from the aspect of market production.[36] In the British rubber estates only the volume of production and profits may take centre stage. Thus the Malays are considered lazy in this economic evaluation, especially if they do not work to the styles and rhythms of European market enterprises. This is the point that Fauconnier is trying to raise in his criticism of the European treatment or their perspective of the Malays. He sees an otherness that must be respected and given the dignity due to men and women with a culture, art and a worldview that grow from their adjustment to a different environment, different climate, and religion. They are not mere shadowy servants as in Maugham's stories, but more full-blown, allowed to have a different perspective on life, art and death. The identity described for them is not one given by Fauconnier alone, but it seems partly also reasoned out from his observations of real people. Here, the author goes back and forth from the Malays to 'us', i.e. the white men, in a continuous act of comparison. The former appears as the 'other' of the latter, a gentle other, left alone without interference.

It is interesting that a Pole and a Frenchman are able to give that dignity to a people that the English authors often consider to be mere 'extras' or worse still savages, or the primitive, aggressive, backward 'other', alien and therefore inferior, and not just merely different.

---

35) See Henry Fauconnier, *The Soul of Malaya*, pp. 59-60.
36) Henry Louis Gates Jr., *"Race", Writing and Difference*, p. 80.

Pierre Boulle is better known for his *The Bridge on the River Kwai* than for his books set among the Malays. *L'Epreuve des Homme Blancs* deals with a Malay community of what we may now call 'noble savages', but with humane values of love and self-integrity. The plot is wound around the notorious Natrah Muslim-Christian riots of the late 1950s in Singapore, but with French characters replacing the Dutch. It describes the predicament of a French girl who was adopted by the Malays, but later reclaimed by her biological parents and brought back to France. In love with a Malay youth who followed her there, they came to an unhappy end. The plot is powerful, based on the very controversial, real incident. However, Boulle's talent is thinner and profound questions tend to take on the sentimental rather than the passionate and the serious. Still, we find an attempt to describe a cultural struggle, one that has similarities with Clifford's Saleh in *A Prince of Malaya*, though very much less developed. The human aspects of his Malay characters are more limited and perhaps idealised, therefore, quite far from the real Malays. The identities are filtered through these idealised concepts of the innocent and weak 'noble savages.'

Though set on an island not far from Singapore, Boulle does not appear to be as interested in the natural or physical environment of the island as were Conrad or Clifford who relished the opportunity to describe a great and mysterious presence of nature.

Italy

If the cultural links between Malaysia and France are minimal, those between Malaysia and Italy are all the more so. There is evidence of an early Malay-Latin wordlist and also Pigafetta's description of the voyage of Magellan, but no other non-archival materials. The Vatican has a few letters and materials related to the Christian religion.

It is in the twentieth century that Malaysia comes into Italian literature, through the works of Emilio Salgari. Salgari was born in 1920. Equipped with a very rich imagination he wrote stories set in North America, the Caribbean, Europe and the Malay Archipelago. Altogether he published 77 books. Of these, ten were about adventure in the Archipelago – among them *Le Tigre di Mompracem, I Pirati della Malesia, La Tigre della Malesia* and *Sandokan Rajah della Jungle Nera*. Most of the stories were written for children. They are packed with adventure, battles and combats against a backdrop of the exotic East. Around the 1970s there was a renewed interest in his works in Italy and elsewhere. One finds comic books based on his works in Spain and Portugal and, of course, a film and a television series on Sandokan, the native captain who defeated the British and white colonisers. The essential Malay identity here is the political 'other' of the white men, as sailors, as defenders of their own land and sea. They seem resolute in their fight, and bestowed with a bravery through their sense of pride and indigenous identity.

However, Salgari himself has never set foot in Malaysia. Living a very modest life he died a poor man. Without the means to travel, Salgari did his research in the libraries. Travelogues, geography books and encyclopaedias were his main sources. The rest was created by his fertile imagination.

The hero of his adventure books is Sandokan, perhaps based on the name of the town of Sandakan in northeast Sabah, in Eastern Malaysia. Almost all the action takes place on the western shores of Borneo, in the imaginary state of Mompracem, beside Labuan and Sarawak.

Japan

In the first few decades of this century a handful of Japanese workers migrated to the fertile and resource-rich Malay Peninsula. Many set up shops, worked on the land and some of the women even provided nightlife for both Japanese and Malaysian men.

With these workers also came a poet-painter Kaneko Mitsuhara. Michiko Nakahara,[37] a historian of Malaysia, traces his life, wanderings and woes in an enlightening paper. His wanderings took him twice to Malaya, the first time for the months of November and December in 1929. Later, in 1932, he set

---

37) Michiko Nakahara, 'Kisah Seorang Penyair Jepun di Semenanjung Tanah Melayu di Awal Abad ke 20' in *Dewan Sastra*, 1988.

up a home in remote Batu Pahat, then a very small town, surrounded by villages associated with rubber and coconut production.

Mitsuhara came to Batu Pahat, Johor, to sell his paintings! His life of wanderings was for the most part also a life of poverty. He managed on less than the cost of his passage to travel in Malaya, Sumatra and Europe.

The Batu Pahat of Mitsuhara was dominated by the river, its flood plains and the overwhelming nipa and sago palms, the *rumbia*. Such was the Malaysian background that also lent its rhythm to his poems.

In the poem 'Nippah Yashio no uta', this background is also the landscape of his mood and emotions. Like the foreshadowers of the pantun, they carry in imagistic or symbolic forms the germs of the poet's emotions.

Living in a world of overwhelming tropical nature, the slow rhythm of rural life of this tiny town and the surrounding villages, Mitsuhara too was naturally absorbed into its dominant ways. He ate, as he says, like the Malays did, mentioning the 'curried rice' as an example or perhaps his favourite.

According to Nakahara, his Japanese poems also absorbed some Malay words, no doubt giving them local colour and exotic quality. The words of everyday life in Batu Pahat became a natural part of his works – perhaps being the first introduction of such words into Japanese poetry.

Mitsuhara returned to Japan when the anti-Japanese campaign intensified in the wake of the Sino-Japanese War. But yet he was a poet of a wider world than that of a Japanese chauvinist. He belonged to one that was beyond race, colour and religion. In Japan he was to retain this viewpoint and became an anti-war poet – a dangerous choice during these years. His ideas were couched in metaphors and symbols – yet for those who know, the meaning was duly delivered.

As far as Malay characters are concerned, there was not much to be discussed, especially when the Japanese haiku form and style were compact, and more often than not only nature and emotions were allowed into the lines. The human is present behind the images of nature or the poet or narrator.

The next Japanese writer under consideration, Jiro Osaragi, shares the environment of war in Malaysia and Japan with Mitsuhara. It is not clear to me whether Osaragi (or to use his real name Kiyohiko Nojiri) did come to Malaya during the Japanese occupation of the country. However, the specific places named in his novel, *Homecoming*, point to a certain knowledge of that state and Singapore. Malaya became a backdrop for an intriguing plot. The protagonist, Moriya Kyogo, was being hidden by a Mr. Yeh, a Malaccan of Chinese ancestry, from the occupation troops of Japan. He was later revealed to have embezzled public money and had left his family in order to escape arrest. On a trip to Singapore he became involved with a shady lady and was betrayed by her to the Japanese troops. Moriya was imprisoned till the end of the war and returned to Japan to face his family and future.

As far as the Malaysian background and people are concerned, *Homecoming* is not important to our study. There is little attempt to delve into the life and ways of Malaysians. So the Malaysians and their environment are used only as a backdrop of the war and the story, with no serious attempt to understand the Malaysians or their situation. They were a mere exotic resource to colour the plot and narration.

The United States of America

I must confess that my search for Malaysia and Malaysians in the literature of the United States is very preliminary. Thus this study will only consider the few that I have been able to find in the works of Agnes Newton Keith *Land Below the Wind*, *Three Came Home*, and *White Man Returns*. They also seem to be comparatively important autobiographical works set in Sarawak and Sabah during the Second World War and after. Paul Theroux's stories The *Consul's File* and *The Great Railway Bazaar* on the other hand, have no real intention of capturing the real Malaysia.

Agnes Keith writes with a warm heart. Finding herself among the various races and tribes of Sabah and Sarawak – the Kadazans, Ibans, Muruts, Malays, Chinese and Indians, besides the Caucasians during and after the war, she has come to 'realize that I love this country, and feel very deeply about the people.' Her wit and sense of humour have buoyed her characters even during the war, giving them the light but intimate tone that characterises her style.

The suffering and misfortune that the war brought her and her family did little to dampen her natural and sincere appreciation of her environment, friends and those she met in her daily life. Let us take an example from her best known book, *Land Below the Wind*. A Murut couple, Kuta and her husband, Arusap, are expecting a baby after the death of two others. Some faithful old beliefs are woven into the warm description:

> Throughout her months of germination Kuta showed neither change nor maturity in her face. With her small body, her tiny wrists, her delicate little throat, and her immature face, she did not look like a pregnant woman, but rather like a beautiful child whose womb and breasts had swollen overnight into unexplainable fecundity. When she went up and down the stairs to the backquarters we all prayed silently that dogs, cats, and apes would stay out from under her feet, as her appearance threatened that the slightest jolt might precipitate the babe. But Kuta was oblivious of any worry. The larger she grew the less she moved about, the less work she did, the more time she had to lie on her mat and smoke. Special morsels of food to which she as a pregnant woman took a fancy were brought faithfully by Arusap. Sometimes it was the sweet-sour pleasantness of a rambutan fruit, sometimes the rich, creamy kernel of a durian, and sometimes the roasted flesh of a jungle pig which Arusap must take the day off to shoot.[38]

This warmth and humour is repeated through her other works, thus adding up to being perhaps among the few substantial literary works in English to touch on the nature and people of Sabah and Sarawak. Her descriptions are further enhanced by vignettes and sketches that come to life on the page. However, unfortunately most of the natives are servants around the house and their identity does not go beyond that. We do not see them in their villages or forests struggling to eke out their lives, but find them in verandahs and servants' quarters. Again they only play the roles of 'extras', to the central lives of their employers. The Caucasians have the habit of taking centre stage and leaving the verandahs and kitchens to the natives.

---

38) See Agnes Keith, *Land Below the Wind*, Boston, Little, Brown, 1940, pp. 100-101.

When we turn to Paul Theroux, we notice in his work the loose unreality of the setting and people in the Peninsula. The fictional environment that does not add up to a real place (even Air Hitam of the *Consul's File* is not the Air Hitam in Johor or Penang, and for a place that small, as he describes it, no consulate has ever been built!). Everything points to the fact that Theroux looks at literature as a work of imagination and unlimited creative freedom. He is not responsible to a locality or a people. As a writer his only responsibility is to his novels and stories. In him one hears echoes of the flippant Burgess and even Maugham, of stock racial characters and stereotypes of Malays, Chinese and Indians picked up from the trains, judged irresponsibly by political adversaries, and rooted to no country.

Endnotes

I have tried to sketch writings in various languages and translations, wherever available, that in some way describe or contain elements of the Malaysian environment, people and ways and consciously or unconsciously bestow upon them some identity. We have found a great variety of viewpoints among the story writers and novelists; from the imperialist, whose moral duty he thought it was to describe the savages, thus giving the European a further reason to 'civilize' them, to the ambivalent, and to the appreciative and the flippant. In some of the works of Conrad, Clifford, Fauconnier and Keith we gain a further insight into the ways and thinking of the Malays and Malaysians, as we may gain insight into human beings themselves through good literary works. Depending on the writer the Malay has emerged as the proud man or woman in the process of retrieving their lands and their identity from the white men who have colonised them economically or politically. In some of the definitions the Malay is definitely the 'other', as in the works of Clifford and Fauconnier. But they are the good other, appreciated, and left to be different. But this 'other' may also be composed of many 'others,' created by the particular ideology and prejudices of the writers. In these cases, they might at best be the 'noble savages' and, at worst the primitive savages, uncultured and not worth giving a voice. Some others might have been included as exotic backdrops for thrillers or love stories, unimportant literary tools or resource, to serve the plot, the story, or, worse still, the white characters.

Interestingly, talent and the seriousness of an artist are a legitimate measurement too in this study. The Malays are given a comparatively fairer description and put into a more realistic predicament politically and socially when the writer is more talented and serious, whereas in thrillers or exotic travelogues they are mere shadowy characters.

Interesting too is the fact that the non-English, such as the Polish (though the adversary of the Malay in his books was the Dutch), French and Italian were more open and appreciative of the situation of their Malay characters. English writers were bound by their colonial context and more often than not, write as agents of the colonial ideology, or must play to the gallery of their readers. However, no single author has emerged completely free of prejudices or predetermined concepts.

The Malay characters in the literatures of the world have been framed, and by reduction, the real Malays, too, for often enough literature is more real than reality. Once published, they are imprisoned by the various authors and readers, forever.

References:

Literary Works with a Malaysian Background: a Selected List

Boulle, Pierre, The *Other Side of the Coin*, Translated from the French by Richard Howard, New York, Vanguard Press, 1958.

Boulle, Pierre, *Sacrilege in Malaya*, Translated from the French by Xan Fielding, London, Secker & Warburg, 1959.

Boulle, Pierre, *White Man's Test*, Translated from the French by Xan Fielding' London, Secker & Warburg, 1957.

Burgess, Anthony, *Beds in the East*, London, Heinemann, 1958.

Burgess, Anthony, *The Enemy in the Blanket*, London, Heinemann, 1958.

Burgess, Anthony, *Malayan Trilogy: Time for a Tiger, The Enemy in the Blanket, Beds in the East*, London, Pan Books, 1964.

Clifford, Sir Hugh Charles, *Bush-Whacking, and other Sketches*, Edinburgh, London, W. Blackwood & Sons, 1901.

Clifford, Sir Hugh Charles, *East Coast Etchings*, Singapore, 'Straits Times Press', 1896.

Clifford, Sir Hugh Charles, *A Free-Lance of To-day*, London, Methuen, 1903.

Clifford, Sir Hugh Charles, *A Freelance of Today*, 2nd revised edition, (with long biographical and explanatory introduction by the author), London: Methuen, 1928.

Clifford, Sir Hugh Charles, *The Further Side of Silence*, Garden City, New York, Doubleday, Page & Company, 1916.

Clifford, Sir Hugh Charles, *Heroes of Exile, Being certain rescued fragments of submerged romance*, London, Smith, Elder & Co, 1906.

Clifford, Sir Hugh Charles, *In a Corner of Asia: Being Tales and Impressions of Men and Things in the Malay Peninsula*, London, T. Fisher Unwin, 1899.

Clifford, Sir Hugh Charles, *In Court and Kampong, Being Tales & Sketches of Native Life in the Malay Peninsula*, London, Grant Richards, 1897.

Clifford, Sir Hugh Charles, *In Days that are Dead*, London, John Murray & Singapore (etc.), Kelly & Walsh, 1926.

Clifford, Sir Hugh Charles, *Malayan Monochromes*, London, John Murray, 1913.

Clifford, Sir Hugh Charles, *A Prince of Malaya*. New York and London, Harper & Brothers Publishers, 1926.

Clifford Sir Hugh Charles, *Saleh: A Sequel*, Edinburgh & London, W. Blackwood & Sons, 1908.

Clifford, Sir Hugh Charles, *Sally: a Study, and Other Tales of the Outskirts*, Edinburgh and London. Wm. Blackwood & Sons, 1904.

Clifford, Sir Hugh Charles, *Since the Beginning, A Tale of an Eastern Land*, London, Grant Richards, 1898.

Clifford, Sir Hugh Charles, *Stories by Sir Hugh Clifford*, Selected and introduced by William R. Roff, Kuala Lumpur, Oxford University Press, 1966.

Clifford, Sir Hugh Charles, *Studies in Brown Humanity, Being Scrawls and Smudges in Sepia, White and Yellow*, London, Grant Richards, 1898.

Conrad, Joseph, *Almayer's Folly*, London, Nash and Grayson, 1921.

Conrad, Joseph, 'The End of the Tether'. In *Blackwood's Magazine* Vol. 172:1-20, 202-218, 395-408, 520-537, Edinburgh and London, William Blackwood & Sons, 1902.

Conrad, Joseph, 'The Lagoon'. In *Cornhill Magazine* 3rd. Series Vol. 2, Jan.:59-71, New York, Charles Scribner's Sons, 1897.

Conrad, Joseph, *Lord Jim, a Tale*, Edinburgh and London, William Blackwood & Sons, 1900.

Conrad, Joseph, *An Outcast of the Islands*, New York, Airmont, 1966.

Conrad, Joseph, *The Rescue, A Romance of the Shallows*, Garden City, New York, Doubleday, Page & Co, 1920.

Fauconnier, Henri, *The Soul of Malaya*. Translated by Eric Sutton. London, Elkin Mathews & Marrot, 1931.

Keith, Agnes Newton, *Land Below the Wind*, Boston, Little, Brown & Co, 1940.

Keith, Agnes Newton, *Three Came Home*, Boston, Little, Brown & Co, 1947.

Keith, Agnes Newton, *The White Man Returns*, Boston, Little, Brown & Co, 1951.

Maugham, William Somerset, *Maugham's Borneo Stories*, Selected and with an Introduction by G.V. de Freitas. Singapore (etc.), Heinemann Educational Books (Asia) Ltd., 1976.

Maugham, William Somerset, *Maugham's Malaysian Stories*, Selected and with an Introduction by Anthony Burgess. Kuala Lumpur (etc.), Heinemann Educational Books (Asia) Ltd., 1969.

Merwin, W.S, *Asian Figures*, New York, Atheneum, 1975.

Osaragi Jiro (pseud. for Kiyohiko Nojiri), *Homecoming*, Translated from the Japanese by Brewster Horwitz. With an introduction by Harold Strauss. New York, Alfred A. Knopf, 1956.

Theroux, Paul, *The Consul's File*, Harmonsdworth, Penguin, 1977.

Theroux, Paul, *The Great Railway Bazaar*, London, Hamilton, 1975.

Selected References

Ashcroft, Bill, Gareth Griffith and Helen Tiffin, *The Empire Writes Back*, London, Routledge, 1989.

Daille, Francois-René, *Alam Pantun Melayu*, Kuala Lumpur, Dewan Bahasa dan Pustaka, 1988.

Gates Jr., Henry Louis.(ed.), *"Race", Writing and Difference*, Chicago, Chicago University Press, 1986.

Hart, Donn V., *Preliminary Check List of Novels with a Malayan Background*, Typescript. New York, Syracuse University, 1966.

Habibah Bt. Dato Mohd Salleh, 'Anthony Burgess: Malayan Trilogy. The Relations of Background Resources to Art.' Unpublished M.A. Thesis. Kuala Lumpur; University of Malaya, 1969.

Hill, Lewis, *A Checklist of English-Language Fiction Relating to Malaysia, Singapore and Brunei*, Hull, Centre for SEA Studies, University of Hull, 1986.

Muhammad Haji Salleh, 'Imej Orang Melayu dalam Kesusasteraan Eropah.' Working Paper for Hari Sastera '80. Ipoh, Perak, 1980.

Muhammad Haji Salleh, *Cermin Diri*, Petaling Jaya, Fajar Bakti, 1986.

Muhammad Haji Salleh, 'Puisi Tantangan Singapura.' Mss., 1993.

Nakahara, Michiko. 'Kisah Seorang Penyair Jepun di Semenanjung Tanah Melayu di Awal Abad ke 20', *Dewan Sastera*, 1988.

Sherry, Norman, *Conrad's Eastern World*, Cambridge, Cambridge University Press, 1966.

Silvario, Father, Interview, Lisbon, 1977.

Spivak, Gayatri Chakravorty, *The Post-Colonial Critic*, New York, Routledge, 1990.

Wilkinson, R.J. and R. O. Winstedt, *Pantun Melayu*, Singapore, Malaya Publishing House, 1960.

Winstedt, Richard, *Classical Malay Literature*, Kuala Lumpur, Oxford University Press, 1969.

10

'The Most Important Thing Is What Happens inside Us'
Personal Identity in Palestinian Autobiography

Tetz Rooke

Autobiography and 'Palestinianism'

It is not uncommon in the history of modern Arabic literature to find that authors in exile produce significant literary works. One might for instance recall the influential poetry of the *mahjar* poets (immigrant poets) written in the Americas during the first half of this century. The *mahjar* poets were Lebanese and Syrians, who had left their countries because of the difficult economic situation there. As emigrants, they retained their bonds with Arab culture and generally expressed their artistic visions in the Arabic language.

To these writers the exile in North and South America meant stimulating impulses from the host cultures, which influenced their art in many ways. Among other things, it triggered a strong sense of attachment to the native soil born out of the strains of separation and, perhaps, feelings of alienation in the new environment. The attachment to the native soil is felt in the many nostalgic descriptions contained in their poetry of the natural beauty of the Levant.[1]

---

1) For a description of the *mahjar* poetic movement, see the chapter 'Arabic Poetry in the Americas' in Salma Khadra Jayyusi, *Trends and Movements in Modern Arabic Poetry*, Vol. I, Leiden 1977, pp. 67-138. For some bilingual (Arabic-English) samples of their poetry, see M.A. Khouri & H. Algar, *An Anthology of Modern Arabic Poetry*, Berkeley/Los Angeles/London, University of California Press, paperback ed. 1975, pp. 9-12, 23-40.

Looking at Arabic literature of today, the eye is caught by the appearance of another group of important exiles and expatriates, namely the Palestinian writers. Their exile, however, is not primarily a consequence of economic necessity, but a result of political conflict. The establishment of the state of Israel in the former British mandate of Palestine and the ensuing wars of 1948 and 1967 turned hundreds of thousands of Palestinians into refugees. Some of them were destined to become professional writers, and today they are living in Europe or America as well as in different Arab countries. In their writings they, in many ways, reflect similar experiences as those of the *mahjar* poets, even if not forming a distinct literary 'school'; living in a foreign environment on the one hand means exposure to new impulses, and on the other, it strengthens the need to look back and stimulates a quest for lost or severed roots.

Even those Palestinians living under Israeli occupation on the West Bank or in Gaza experience a kind of exile, mentally at least, since they are a people without a state of their own and their national identity is therefore called into question. They too are haunted by some sense of loss, some urge to reclaim.

The literary response to the experience of uprootedness has been not only an out-pouring of poetry as well as a steady flow of novels and short stories, but also an abundance of personal account literature, including a number of autobiographies dealing with different aspects of the Palestinian predicament. This paper will deal with three autobiographies by prominent Palestinian personalities. They are Hishām Sharābī (b. 1927), Professor of History and Arab Culture at Georgetown University, USA, and a leading Palestinian intellectual; Fadwā Ṭūqān (b. 1917), a celebrated woman poet from the town of Nablus on the West Bank; and finally, Jabrā Ibrāhīm Jabrā (1919–1994), poet, novelist, painter and critic, who settled down in Iraq after 1948.

Before discussing their works, we may in passing notice, that even if Palestinian personal account literature is in general written in Arabic, we also find Palestinian authors who prefer to write in English or other acquired second languages. To promote the Arab views, they then direct themselves to the western audience, conceived of as being either ignorant as regards the Palestine conflict or pro-Zionist: Said Aburish writes the history of his family, the destiny and fortunes of its members from 1917 onwards, in *The*

Children of Bethany (1988). Hala Sakakini writes her 'personal record' in *Jerusalem and I* (1987), a book of reminiscences describing the childhood and youth of an Arab woman in Jerusalem. The Galilean priest Elias Chacour produces his autobiography *Blood Brothers* (1985) in English with the help of a journalist. Even in Swedish there is at least one example of Palestinian personal account literature in *Arabernas äganderätt till Palestina. En infödd palestinaarab berättar* (1962) (The Arabs' Rights of Ownership to Palestine. A Native Palestinian Relates) by Mufid Abdelhadi.

Shifting our attention back to the majority of Palestinian personal accounts written in Arabic, we encounter the same mixture of literary genres as in the accounts written in foreign languages, but of a richer blend. Whether in the form of diaries, memoirs, family histories or autobiographies, 'Palestinians assert not only their own identity as eyewitnesses to Palestinian life and experience, but the identity of their own country', as Salma Jayyusi puts it in her foreword to the English translation of the autobiography of Fadwā Ṭūqān.[2]

The experiences of exile, uprootedness, exposure to foreign cultures and ideologies have both stamped Palestinian autobiography and inspired it; and, indeed, we see the same set of experiences contributing to the richness of the autobiography of one of the leading *mahjar* personalities, the poet, novelist and critic Mīkhā'īl Nuʿayma (1889–1988). Even if he wrote his autobiography *Sabʿūn* (1959–60) (Seventy), long after his return from Russia and the USA to his native Lebanon, the effects on the personality of once having lived as a stranger in a strange land is a major theme in his life story, too.[3]

Why then is exile, *ghurba*, in a wide sense, of such importance as an impetus to write and as subject-matter in autobiography? It is, I would argue, because national and cultural identities, made problematic by exile, are basic elements in the larger concept of 'personal identity', which is the central theme in autobiography.

---

2) See F. Tuqan, *A Mountainous Journey. An Autobiography*, translated by Olive Kenny, with a foreword by Salma Jayyusi and an introduction by Fedwa Malti-Douglas, Saint Paul, Graywolf Press, 1990, p. vii.
3) The first part of *Seventy* deals with the childhood and education of the author in Lebanon, Palestine and the Ukraine. In 1911, aged 22, the author emigrated to the USA. The second part of his autobiography deals with the two decades he lived there. The third part, lastly, is set after the homecoming of Nuʿayma to Lebanon in 1932.

'Palestinianism' is part and parcel of the Palestinian writer's self, and it is the riddles of this self that are the main concern when life is transformed into text.

Autobiography and the Self

As a genre of literature, autobiography is modern. In European literature the first texts to be perceived as autobiographies by the public emerge at the end of the eighteenth century.[4] In Arabic literature, the genre of autobiography, *sīra dhātiyya/tarjama dhātiyya*, was established in the first half of this century, when the success of the autobiography of the blind Egyptian writer Ṭāhā Ḥusayn (1889–1973), *al-Ayyām* (part one 1929, part two 1939) (The Days), signalled the event of a new way to formulate and interpret personal experience.[5]

What is a literary genre? A genre of literature primarily consists of a body of texts produced and read in accordance with definite conventions. These conventions are not normative commands or rules of how to write or read, but are rather to be understood as paragraphs in an unwritten agreement that secures a

---

4) See Ph. Lejeune, *Le Pacte autobiographique*, Paris, Editions du Seuil, 1975, p. 13f.
5) Fedwa Malti-Douglas, *Blindness & Autobiography*. Princeton, Princeton University Press, 1988, p. 10f. Cf. with the statement by Wellek and Warren: 'For the definitions of modern genres one probably does best to start with a specific highly influential book or author, and look for the reverberations' in R. Wellek and A. Warren, *Theory of Literature*, 3rd ed., New York, 1962, p. 235. Of course, there are many Arab authors from classical times using their own life as subject matter for their writings, whether in poetry or prose. The so-called autobiographies of the theologian Al-Ghazzālī (d. 1111) and the Syrian prince Usāma ibn Munqidh (d. 1188) are some of the more famous examples. However the modern concept of autobiography was unknown in their times, and so reading their texts as autobiographies produces disappointment since they do not live up to our expectations. Instead of drawing the conclusion from this that the Arabs wrote poor autobiography, as Rosenthal (*Die Arabische Autobiographie*, Studia Arabica I, Rome 1937, p. 16), von Grunebaum (*Medieval Islam*, [1953] Chicago 1962, p. 270), and others have done, I feel it more just to say that there is no such thing as an autobiographical *genre* in classical Arabic literature. As a genre of literature autobiography is recent! What we do have from classical times is personal account literature of other (culture specific) kinds, admittedly forming an autobiographical tradition from the modern reader's point of view, but not a *genre*.

certain mode of interpretation. Per Stounbjerg studying the autobiographical works of Strindberg says: 'The genres do not prescribe what a text is or should be, but rather what it should be read as, what we are enticed to believe.... I see autobiography as a rhetoric that corresponds to set expectations'.[6]

The typical 'rhetoric' and those textual elements that correspond to the (preconceived) expectations of the reader, have in the case of the genre of autobiography been described by Philippe Lejeune. He calls the relation 'le pacte autobiographique', and finds that it rests on a number of common traits in all texts that are read as autobiographies:

1) An autobiography is a narrative in prose.

2) The perspective of the narrator is retrospective.

3) It is fundamental that the protagonist is identical with the narrator, and the identity of both must be that of the author.

4) And most important, the subject treated in an autobiography is the life of the individual, with the accent put on the development and history of the personality.[7]

It is the emphasis on personality, or in other words the theme of personal identity, of Self, that is at the heart of modern perceptions of autobiography. Some have even argued that autobiography is personal identity. James Olney declares that autobiography is tantamount to 'a metaphor of self': 'We do not see or touch the self, but we do see and touch its metaphors: and thus we "know" the self'.[8] Contrary to Lejeune, he sees no reason to attach any formal, cultural or temporal requirements or boundaries to the concept of autobiography, which in his definition extends into being equal to any human activity, not necessarily literary, that centres on self-expression.[9]

However, even in the stricter sense of a literary genre, autobiography is founded on an interest in the issue of identity, its

---

6) Per Stounbjerg, 'Själen, livet och formerna. Berättelse, bild och diskurs i *Tjänstekvinnans son*' in J.P. Roos and A. Vikko, (eds), *Självbiografi, Kultur, Liv*, Stockholm/Skåne: Symposion, 1992: 21.
7) See Ph. Lejeune, *Le Pacte autobiographique*, pp. 14-5, 44-6.
8) J. Olney, *Metaphors of Self. The Meaning of Autobiography*, Princeton, Princeton University Press, 1972, p. 34.
9) Ibid., pp. 3-5.

genesis and history. Looking at the three Palestinian autobiographies under consideration, we find that they express this interest clearly. Jabrā Ibrāhīm Jabrā, in a preface to his autobio-graphy *al-Bi'r al-ūlā* (1987) (The First Well), writes thus:

> What I write here is not a history of that period. There are those more knowing, more suited and more gifted than myself in ordering and depicting the events of the 'twenties and early 'thirties in Palestine. Neither do I write a history of my family, because that is something different, and I do not say that I have the ability to do it. Nor do I make a social analysis of a Palestinian town [Bethlehem], which in those days was small;... No, what I write here is purely personal and purely related to childhood. My approach concentrates on the self, when its awareness is growing, its consciousness is rising, its feelings deepening, without its confusion necessarily coming to its end. (12-13.)[10]

The focusing on the Self, in Jabrā's view, seems to be what distinguishes autobiography from memoirs, family history and reminiscences in general. The same attention given to the Self also marks the narrator's voice in Fadwā Ṭūqān's autobiography *Riḥla ṣaʿba riḥla jabaliyya* (1985) (translated as 'A Mountainous Journey'). Remembering the depression she felt after losing her elder brother, she sees the landmarks on her road through life in terms of inner signs:

> I went back even deeper into my profound inner exile, into journeying inside myself. The most important thing is what happens inside us, not to us. (128 / [105])[11]

The purely personal approach never precludes an inquiry into other aspects of the identity, such as culture or nationality and their connections with politics and history. What happens inside us is dependent on what happens to us. To determine the relationship – alternately harmonious and antagonistic – between this dual nature of the personal identity, its inner dimension of

---

10) All quotes in English from Arabic originals occurring in this paper are translations by the author unless otherwise stated.
11) This and following quotes from the autobiography of F. Tūqān are from the English translation *A Mountainous Journey. An Autobiography*. See the bibliography. The initial figure after the quote refers to the Arabic original. The figure within [brackets] refers to the English translation.

conscious and subconscious impulses, feelings and ideas, and its outer dimension of social role, environment and historical conditions, could in fact be described as the subject matter of autobiography.

There is no Self without what 'happens to us', even if the relationship between 'happens to' and 'happens inside' is more complex than pure cause and effect. The relationship is a dialectical one, and personal identity is maybe best understood as the synthesis of 'happens inside' and 'happens to', a kind of balance that the individual has to achieve in order to arrive at a sense of selfhood, as the Swedish psychologist B. Börjesson has argued.[12]

Indeed, such seems to be the way the autobiographers themselves perceive the concept of self. However personal their approach may be, it by no means excludes an interest in society and its workings. This is why the ordeal of the Palestinian people has an important bearing on their texts. J. Gunn says: 'The reading of oneself is always a cultural reading since self-knowledge, far from being transcendent or free-floating, is always grounded in the signs of one's existence that are received from others'.[13] That the personal is political in a sense, gives the personal experience a significance that goes beyond individual interest and makes it of general concern. Hishām Sharābī stresses this fact when he chooses to preface his autobiography *Al-Jamr war-ramād* (1978) (Embers and Ashes) with a quote from Thomas Mann: 'The individual does not live his personal life only, but also the life of his time and his generation.'[14]

The Didactic Function of the Text

Hishām Sharābī, who was born in Jaffa on the Mediterranean coast, is the youngest of the Palestinian trio of autobiographers here reviewed and he was the first of them to publish his account.

---

12) B. Börjesson, *Samtal med K – en bok om identiteten*, Stockholm, AWE/Gebers, 1976, p. 34.
13) J.V. Gunn, *Autobiography. Toward a Poetics of Experience*, Philadelphia, University of Pennsylvania Press, 1982, p. 31.
14) The quote is from the book *The Magic Mountain* (1924) [org. Der Zauberberg] by Thomas Mann. It is here given in my translation from the Arabic version by Sharābī, and thus probably differs somewhat from the wording of the passage in the original.

In 1978 his autobiography *Embers and Ashes* appeared in Beirut. In a preface to the text, he tells why he felt compelled to write down his personal story. Attempting to resettle with his family in Lebanon after more than twenty years of exile in the USA, the outbreak of the civil war in Lebanon in 1975 aborted his plans. Before unwillingly leaving Beirut, however, he completed the autobiography that he originally began to compose as the final summation of a stage in life he had hoped was over, the time of exile. Yet now, he laments in the preface, the exile seems to be eternal:

> And at this moment I am overwhelmed by a feeling that the opportunity was lost, that I never will return to my homeland and instead spend the rest of my days here in this land of exile, and that I will die in it. But no! This will never happen. My people is a part of my life that I haven't abandoned for a moment, and I carry my homeland in my heart and can't give it up. I will return some day! (9)

The narrative structure of Sharābī's book is a little different from the usual chronological setting of the plot in Arabic autobiographies, which copies the pattern of life itself in the structuring of events: birth – childhood – adolescence – maturity – old age... *Embers and Ashes* begins in *medias res*, in December 1947. The protagonist, 20 years old, leaves Palestine, on board a plane heading for the United States, and unknowingly catches what is to be his last glimpse of his native town Jaffa. Bitterness and sorrow, mingled with the bad conscience of a deserter, are the retrospective emotions of the narrator in this prelude, which ends with the arrival of the youth to Chicago, where he is to study at the university (11-16).

It is only after this dramatization of what is recognized as a momentous event in life, that the narrator proceeds to describe his social background – member of a wealthy and influential Muslim bourgeois family – relates some personal negative experiences of British colonial rule, describes his education in Palestine and Lebanon, and nostalgically recalls a few episodes from his childhood in the Palestinian towns of Jaffa and Acre. In terms of bulk this part of the narrative is a major one (pp. 17-103 represent more than a third of a total of 239 pages). But it is also important in terms of psychological significance, since the narrator in it tries to give a comprehensive picture of the factors in upbringing and social environment that helped form the personality of the protagonist, who, sadly enough, did not hesitate to leave his country even though it was facing a crucial moment in history.

At this stage the narrator returns to the opening scene and resumes the story from the point of the arrival of the hero in Chicago. The following part (104-181) deals in the main with the protagonist's experiences of campus life during 1948. These experiences encompass the strains of cultural conflict and homesickness, but also the sensations of love and academic success. When the war flares up in distant Palestine and Jaffa is captured by the Jews, he resolves to go back and participate in the struggle to liberate his homeland as soon as he has completed his Masters degree.

The next section of *Embers and Ashes* (182-235) is a day-by-day, almost hour-by-hour, account of the dramatic events that ensued upon Hishām's arrival in Beirut in spring 1949. Even before he left to study overseas he had been a political activist in the Syrian Socialist Nationalist Party, or 'Partie Populaire Syrien' (PPS), *al-Ḥizbu s-sūrī l-qawmī l-ijtimāʿī*, under the charismatic leadership of Anṭūn Saʿāda. Now he partakes in the party's violent confrontation with the political establishment in Lebanon, which ends in disaster. The party is banned, its members hunted down and thrown in jail, and *az-zaʿīm*, the Leader, after a summary sentence, is executed.

Hishām manages a narrow escape across the border to Syria and then Jordan, where his influential father, through his connections, secures for his son a Jordanian passport, which makes it possible for him to seek refuge in the USA. The narrative comes to its final halt with a scene recalling the prelude, a plane taking off and the hero leaving his homeland:

> The airplane slowly lifts above Amman heading south. The houses become smaller until they look like toys, then they disappear and nothing remains save the empty land and the naked hills. I look at them through tears that I can't prevent from falling.
>
> You have exiled me, my homeland. I will not return to you. I will never return to you. (239)

As demonstrated, the narrative plot of *Embers and Ashes* is set in the time between 1947 and 1949, and records how the protagonist is twice separated from his homeland, firstly by an exile of his own choice and then by one of compulsion. The dramatized events and experiences connecting these two departures form the skeleton of the narrative structure. The muscles and organs of the body of the text are the discursive parts, which are clad in a much wider temporal cloak: the experiences of childhood in Palestine, the memories of university life, colleagues and friends in America in the 'fifties and 'sixties, and of ideas and ideologies, give vitality and perspective to the portrait of the human being Hishām Sharābī.

On a thematic level, the text deals with a more fundamental issue than (the loss of) national identity, and that is the issue of developing a personal identity, of which national identity is but a part, however important. The dialectics of personal identity is most clearly recognized in moments of conflict, of crisis, before the synthesis between inner self and outer role has been achieved. The protagonist of *Embers and Ashes* experiences a protracted identity crisis during the eventful and formative years of late adolescence, due to the impact of foreign culture, loneliness, national defeat and failure of idealistic political ambitions.

At another textual level the narrator, positioned in time almost thirty years later, again experiences an identity crisis, with the realization that his hopes of returning to Palestine might never be fulfilled. He sees the Arab world of the late 'seventies succumbing to tyranny or anarchy. All the dreams of a great Arab nation and the hopes he harboured in youth, the embers of the title, are dead. Only the ashes remain. It is an identity crisis caused by doubt. What shall I believe in now, when the old visions are falsified by reality? he asks himself, while also echoing the eternal human anguish over life's brevity:

> We disobeyed the orders of our fathers and pretended not to hear our imploring mothers. Without being fully aware of it, we aimed at the overthrow of paternal power, the breaking of family shackles and deliverance from domestic values. We wished to exchange the individualistic life in the stagnant family environment that we grew up in, for a life in the midst of society, wide and rich. So we followed the road of party work, and we paid the price for our "meddling in politics" dearly. I speak not only of the Syrian Nationalists, but also of the Communists, the Baathists, and all the others who joined the parties and ideological movements that appeared during that period.

> Where are they now, my comrades and the children of that generation, the avant garde of that new generation? Their parties have been shattered and fragmented, and before all the Syrian Socialist Nationalist Party, who was the first to pay the price of revolution. Now we, the children of that generation, are in our forties and fifties. Our lives lie behind us and our future has become our past. What did we achieve with our struggle?
>
> Sometimes I tell myself that everything was our own fault, that we are the ones responsible for what happened. We had the opportunities to avoid the catastrophes that we experienced. But then I reconsider and say: there was no other way! Our fault was not that we made revolution, but that we didn't prepare ourselves enough, neither with theory nor with arms. (202)

Identity is formed both on the textual level of the remembered experience in the past, and as a remembering of that experience in the present. In *Embers and Ashes* identity is to be discovered 'not merely as the passive, transparent record of an already completed self, but rather as an integral and often decisive phase of the drama of self-definition.'[15] Remembering an identity crisis of the past and re-enacting it in language reassures the author that he is capable of tackling the problems of today and teaches him (and by implication his readers) how to go about it.

The Therapeutic Function of the Text

In the late 'seventies, serialized in the leftist magazine *al-Jadīd*, published in Haifa in Israel, there appeared another Palestinian autobiography, of which a book-version was published a few years later.[16] This was the autobiography of the woman poet Fadwā Ṭūqān.

---

15) P.J. Eakin, *Fictions in Autobiography. Studies in the Art of Self-invention*, Princeton, Princeton University Press, 1985, p. 226.
16) See the preface by Samīh al-Qāsim, editor of *al-Jadīd*, to *Riḥla ṣaʿba riḥla jabaliyya*, pp. 5-6, and the introduction to *A Mountainous Journey* by Fedwa Mati-Douglas p.1. Parts of the autobiography also appeared prior to publication as a book in the *ad-Dawḥa*-magazine published in Qatar. (letter from Fadwā Ṭūqān to the author 04.12.92)

A Mountainous Journey depicts the initial fifty years of her life. The plot is chronologically structured with few leaps ahead or behind beginning with the birth of the protagonist and ending with the Israeli occupation of her native town Nablus on the West Bank in 1967.[17] The setting is predominantly Palestine or other Arab countries, but a fair section (169-214) is also set in England, where Fadwā for a while studied at Oxford.

The national catastrophe of the June war of 1967, the critics agree, changed the poetry of Fadwā Ṭūqān, which formerly had been introvert and intimate in tone. From then on it became a poetry of anger and protest, predominantly nationalistic in spirit.[18] But the seeds of revolt and resistance had been sown in her personality long before, already in childhood, when her own personal identity was threatened by extinction, when she had to fight a fierce fight to gain independence and freedom from the bonds of tradition. The story of this fight is the story she tells in her autobiography.

When she raised her voice in protest against the occupation, it was like a second harvest of those rebellious seeds that had sprouted a first crop years before, when she succeeded in surmounting the insurmountable, as she at one point puts it (10), to become a poet:

> A seed does not see the light without first cleaving a difficult path through the earth. This story of mine is the story of the seed's battle against the hard rocky soil; a story of struggle, deprivation and enormous difficulties.(9 / [11])

Metaphors from travelling (path), from gardening (seed, light) and from war (battle), are here all combined by the narrator to capture the essence of her individual experience, that life is a troublesome quest for self-fulfilment, and it hurts.

Fadwā Ṭūqān, like Hishām Sharābī, grew up in a family belonging to the upper echelons of society. Her family was

---

17) Fadwā Ṭūqān has lately continued her life-story in *al-Riḥla l-aṣʿab* (The Most Difficult Journey, Amman 1993), which describes her experience of living under occupation.
18) On this change in tone, see for instance the foreword by Salma Khadra Jayyusi to *A Mountainous Journey*. Again by S. Kh. Jayyusi on the same point: *Trends and Movements in Modern Arabic Poetry*, Vol. II, Leiden 1977, p. 657n. Also: Kh. Suaiman, *Palestine and Modern Arabic Poetry*, London 1984, p. 194.

landowning, Muslim and conservative, and about twenty family members of different generations lived close together in the ancestral 'palace', one of the oldest houses in Nablus. The female members occupied their own wing in the house and constituted a kind of harem. They lived a secluded life, and were not allowed to leave the house without the prior consent of their husbands, fathers or brothers.

Fadwā Ṭūqān's autobiography is not the first in Arabic letters to report from such an upperclass upbringing of women marked by the paradox of refined culture and total submission. The autobiography of the pioneer Egyptian feminist Hūda Shaʿrāwī (1879-1947), originally dictated to her secretary and posthumously published in 1981 as *Mudhakkirāt Hūda Shaʿrāwī* ('The Memoirs of Hūda Shaʿrāwī', partially translated into English as *Harem Years*, [1986]), also penetrates this world. But not all women seem to have shared the opinions of these two strong personalities in their rejection of it, judging from the sarcasm of the narrator of *A Mountainous Journey*:

> The house was like a large coop filled with domesticated birds, content to peck the feed thrown to them, without argument. That was their be-all and end-all. The vocation of those tame birds was limited to hatching the chicks and wasting the days of their lives moving between the large brass cooking pots and the firewood burning constantly in the stoves, winter and summer. (133 / [110])

The heroine, however, does not want to be dehumanized into a bird. Returning to the metaphors of war for a moment, one might say that the heroine Fadwā of the text is portrayed as waging a war of liberation in her childhood and adolescence against Arab patriarchal society and its suppression of women. The narrator reviews the enemy troops, the guardians of tradition: father, mother, elder brother, uncle, aunt and others. She describes their strategies and assesses the wounds caused by their weapons, loss of self-esteem and self-respect:

> In their eyes, I was the discordant note in the house, the sheep going astray from the fold. From the outset, they dealt with me accordingly, in order to stifle my striving for self-realisation. They tried in various ways to sow the seeds of self-doubt and misgivings about my abilities. The peril in this

method lies in the fact that, by nature, we see ourselves as others see us, and it is other people's ideas about us that we absorb, especially in the formative period of childhood and adolescence. (98 / [79-80])

But the narrator also acknowledges her defenders, a coalition of friends and relatives, foremost among whom stands her beloved brother Ibrāhīm, enlightened, progressive and poet of fame.[19] He is credited with the spiritual survival of the protagonist because it was he who introduced to her, and welcomed her into, the world of literature. His importance is stressed over and over again, and he is hailed as the saviour that turned the fortunes of war her way.

The enemy forces and the coalition of friends take up positions on opposite sides of an invisible frontline that runs through the mind of the protagonist. Arms clash silently and battle takes place in quiet. The issue at stake is not only freedom, but the prerequisite of freedom, personal identity. The nucleus self of the heroine craves independence. She dreams of becoming an author and a poet, an identity which is denied her by the conservative values of the family tradition. On the other hand, she cannot accept the identity of housewife and mother that is offered to her, and so lives in a perpetual state of war, of unresolved conflict, of identity crisis:

> I was conscious of the humiliation of this situation and my inability to break out of the mould I was forced into. Thus a perpetual conflict arose between two parts of my self, a self defeated by repression, and the grim reality of life, giving me a split personality: one appearing submissively obedient, while the other was in such a thunderous state underneath the surface that it was almost destroying itself. I went on suffering the drama of the wild current running under the surface of calm waters, like one of Chekhov's characters. (95-96 / [77-78])

When the crisis reaches its apogee it consumes all the mental powers of Fadwā. She is totally paralysed:

---

19) Ibrāhīm Ṭūqān (1905-1941) 'Known as the foremost poet in Palestine in the 'twenties and the 'thirties Ibrāhīm Ṭūqān was instrumental in modernizing the poetry of his country.' Salma Khadra Jayyusi in *Trends and Movements in Modern Arabic Poetry*, Vol I, Leiden 1977, p. 284.

> As the misery of repression and subjugation increased, my feelings of individuality and identity also increased. My existence inside the harem wing of the house made me shrink and recoil, so that I was bottled up inside myself. I got to the point where I could do nothing but stare into the reflection of that self, all repressed and bottled up. (134-135 / [111])

It is tradition that is the cause of her agony, but the upholders of tradition have names. The one responsible for its enforcement, in the narrator's view, is her father. He is accused of being the creator of the psychological crisis, caused by the impossibility of achieving a synthesis between the inner aspiration of leading a life in the world, and the outer role of gender prescribing seclusion in the home and a cutting-off of contacts with public life (134). So it is, that not until her father dies in 1948, is the protagonist finally able to break out and follow her own way in life. But by then she has already passed her thirtieth birthday.

Again we meet the same central motive, the identity crisis of a young individual in conflict with society. Hishām in *Embers and Ashes* is in conflict with triumphant Zionism and traditional Arab political leadership. He loses his homeland and his party is crushed. He feels helpless and confused. Fadwā in *A Mountainous Journey*, in her turn, is in conflict with traditional Arab patriarchy and old fashioned mores. She is denied the freedom to go out alone and her will is ignored. She suffers mental isolation and at one point even tries to commit suicide (135).

The motive of the young individual in conflict with society, and the basic theme of self-realization and self-fulfilment inherent in it, has a didactic function; it shows the author, and the readers, that (identity) crisis can be resolved and suggests how to do it. But the motive has another side, too. It reconciles the individual with his past; writing about the misery and unhappiness of an experienced hell is an act of exorcism that may rest the soul. This could be called the therapeutical function of the motive.

Whatever function, behind its prominence is a shared notion that the experiences of childhood and youth are of particular importance in life. Personal identity is firmly and inextricably bound to childhood. The narrator of *A Mountainous Journey* expresses this notion thus:

> I often find that the past has gone, not only in its physical sense, but in its psychological sense too... The world of my

childhood is the only one that has not lost its psychological meaning for me. It is the only world to which I return with the old warmth of heart. With that exception, everything, it seems to me, submits to the laws of change. (141 / [117])

The Poetic Vision

To give prime attention to the events of childhood, seems to be a shared tendency in our three texts. It is also notable in other Palestinian personal accounts.[20] The tendency is not as strong in *Embers and Ashes*, which concentrates on the experiences of adolescence, as in *A Mountainous Journey*, where the portrait of the middle aged heroine appears fragmentary and sketchy compared to the vivid portrait of her as a girl and young woman.[21]

Yet the Palestinian autobiography that most clearly embodies the tendency to concentrate narrative interest on the experiences of childhood, is *al-Bi'r al-ūlā*, (The First Well), by Jabrā Ibrāhīm Jabrā, published in London in 1987. The author received his higher education in England. Just like Hishām Sharābī, he is one of those many Arabic artists and intellectuals who stand with one leg in the Arabic culture and the other in the European culture and manage to bridge the gap. Jabrā has in fact also written a novel in English alongside his many works in Arabic.[22]

His autobiography deals exclusively with the events of childhood. It is set in his native town, Bethlehem, and in Jerusalem. It covers only the ages from five to twelve of the central character Jabrā. In a preface to the work, the author explains this limited scope: Writing a 'complete autobiography', as he originally intended, he says, would either have meant having to skip a

---

20) A good example is the autobiography / reminiscences of Yūsuf Haykal, *Ayyām aṣ-ṣibā* (Days of my youth), Amman: Dār al-jalīl lin-nashr, 1988.
21) Since the completion of this article, a sequel to *Embers and Ashes* has appeared, entitled *Ṣuwar al-māḍī* ('Images of the past', Beirut 1993). The new book shifts the emphasis of the autobiographical project of Sharābī markedly further towards childhood experience, which constitutes the main subject matter of his new contribution.
22) The novel in English by Jabrā is *Hunters in a Narrow Street* (1960). For a discussion of Jabrā's work as novelist and critic see R. Allen, *The Arabic Novel*, University of Manchester, 1982, and more recently M.M. Badawi, 'Two Novelists from Iraq: Jabrā and Munīf' in *Journal of Arabic Literature*, XXIII 1992, part 2, pp. 140-154.

lot of essential matter relating to childhood, or never finishing. Instead he decided that he ought to write a separate volume on each separate stage in his life (11f). This is why the subtitle of *The First Well* runs 'Chapters in an Autobiography', *fuṣūl min sīra dhātiyya*, implying that there is more to follow.[23]

Olive groves at Bethlehem, near the author's birthplace

The narrator of *The First Well*, too, voices the opinion that childhood is of everlasting importance in life. He likens his personal past to a series of wells, 'what is our life but a chain of wells?'(20), where life's experiences and impressions are gathered as rainwater in the wells of Bethlehem. To these metaphorical wells the individual can turn in times of drought or thirst: 'And the first well is the well of childhood(...) It is the well that you cannot do without. Every time you come back to it, you will find in it an ever flowing spring at the heart of your humanity' (21).

Jabrā Ibrāhīm Jabrā's well-metaphor once again shows the temporal complexity of the self in autobiography. On the one

---

23) Just a few months before J.I. Jabrā passed away in December 1994, some new 'parts' of his autobiography were published in *Shāriʿ al-Amīrāt. Fuṣūl min sīra dhatiyya* (The Queens' Street, Beirut 1994).

hand, the text refers to the remembered experience, the self of the past, the protagonist-self, corresponding to the well and its water in the metaphor. On the other hand, the text represents the act of remembering, corresponding to the act of drinking, and displays the narrator-self of the present, who asks questions about the future as much as about the past.[24]

It has been suggested, that in western literature the autobiography of childhood and adolescence constitutes a genre of its own, because such texts are so numerous.[25] But they are many unique in restricting himself to childhood. The pattern had already been set by Ṭāhā Ḥusayn with the first part of *The Days*, which covers the same span of time in the life of its central character as does *The First Well*, i.e. from the first awakenings of conscious memory up to the age of twelve. Mīkhā'īl Nuʿayma also limits the temporal scope of the first part of his autobiography *Seventy* to childhood and adolescence.

In general, it is a childhood marked by hardships and deprivation, material or emotional, which is elaborated in Arabic autobiography.[26] *The First Well* fits nicely into this pattern. The book tells the story of the poor boy of simple origins, who thanks to his own great efforts makes it to the top, i.e. successful authorship.

The same story of self-made fortune is recognizable in all three texts discussed. The difference between them lies in the different obstacles to success (self-fulfilment), that they identify. These differ according to the gender of the protagonist, but also according to social class. While material welfare and physical survival never seem to be troubling issues to Fadwā or Hishām, they are urgent matters in the life of Jabrā. The kind of struggle for self-realization we meet with in *The First Well*, therefore, is neither directed against patriarchal society, nor against political es-

---

24) Apart from being a central metaphor in Jabrā's text, the well also functions as a kind of *Leitmotiv* in his story. The protagonist and his family frequently move from one home to another. At each new home there is a well. The description of it and of its surroundings, the house, the neighbours, and so on, acts as a connecting, unifying element in the narrative and gives it an attractive rhythm.
25) R.N. Coe, *When the Grass was Taller. Autobiography and the Experience of Childhood*, New Haven and London, Yale University Press, 1984, p. xi.
26) Y.I. ʿAbd ad-Dāyim, *at-Tarjama dh-dhātiyya fi-l-adab al-ʿarabī l-ḥadīth*, pp.134f.

tablishment and Zionism, but against the workings of poverty. It is the struggle to get shoes for your feet and food for your stomach, to get money to be able to buy the paper and pen needed in school, or to stay clean and healthy when one's home is infested with lice.

The background of Jabrā differs very much from the background of Hishām or Fadwā. He does not come from a rich family, and he is not Muslim but Syrian Orthodox Christian. Religion in a wide sense, and more specifically the Church as an important community factor responsible for education, culture, ideology and beliefs, and the mediator in conflicts with secular authorities, is a subject-matter frequently touched upon in the narrative. However, belonging to a religious minority is not viewed as an obstacle in life, neither by the protagonist, nor in retrospect by the narrator. The relations between the Christian minority and the Muslim majority in Palestine are described as harmonious.

Poverty is conceived as an enemy in the text, but, paradoxically, it is also associated with positive values. Poverty also stands for simplicity and virtues such as contentment, soli-darity and patience. These qualities are the characteristics of the parents, of simple origin and illiterate, but lovingly portrayed by the narrator. This leads us to the conclusion that identity may be formulated not only in relation to obstacles in society, as a struggle. In *The First Well* it is also formulated as a positive belonging, as harmony and balance. The main motive in *The First Well* is not the young individual in opposition to society, but rather the child living in agreement and concord with his environment (family, culture and society). 'Deliberately or inadvertently, I have perhaps made the self and the environment into two interchangeable subjects. The one is a reflection of the other, and sometimes even a symbolic embodiment of it', writes Jabrā in his preface (13).

If personal identity is the synthesis between the 'happens inside' of the individual and the 'happens to', then what we read in *The First Well* is a poetic vision of the happy balancing of the two faces of the self, the one facing inwards and the other facing outwards. The romantic and pleasant part of childhood experience is of no less importance in defining identity than the tragic and painful part.

There is a tint of nostalgia colouring the picture here. In this the land itself plays a major part. The boy Jabrā often seeks solitude and peace of mind in nature, climbing his favourite mulberry tree (132) or lying on his back watching the swallows shooting across the blue sky and the white clouds passing by (58f). The narrator remembers the wild flowers of Spring and the herbs on the hills surrounding Bethlehem (58, 157, 167, 175, 178, 184) and how he used to hunt goldfinch and house sparrow (60) or watch the sun set over the undulating hills of Palestine (92). We also find similar pastoral passages in *Embers Ashes* and in *A Mountainous Journey*, but there they are not as pronounced.

Conclusion

The French sociologist Jacques Berque has said, that 'the quest for self (country as self, people as self, history as self) constitutes one of the most prominent sectors of contemporary Arab production'.[27] The current vitality and diversity of Palestinian autobiography, preoccupied as it is with the issue of self or personal identity, illustrates this statement. Palestinian autobiography shows how the quest for self is addressed directly in literature, through introspection and analysis of individual experience.

'Metaphorised' in autobiography, the Self is displayed in the text as a composite of past and present, of hero and narrator, and, as a result of the dialectics of an inner personal being and an outer communal one. In two of the Palestinian autobiographies discussed, focus is primarily on the *conflict* inherent in the dialectics: *Embers and Ashes* and *A Mountainous Journey* both tell the story of individual struggle against society, embodied in tradition, custom, patriarchy, foreign oppression (British and Zionist) and political conservatism. In the third autobiography, *The First Well*, the dialectics of the self has resulted in a *synthesis*, a poetic vision of harmony. The story is set in childhood and, of the three, *The First Well* is the most outspoken example of the tendency of the genre to accord childhood experience particular importance.

The land of childhood is lost territory for all adults, its loss being part of our common humanity. But, as Salman Rushdie has

---

27) J. Berque, *Cultural Expression in Arab Society Today*, Austin and London, University of Texas Press, 1978, p. 238.

suggested, perhaps the writer who is out-of-country experiences this loss in an intensified form. Being physically 'elsewhere' may enable the emigrant or exile to speak convincingly and particularly well of a subject of universal significance and appeal.[28] Part of the captivating force of Palestinian autobiography, no doubt, is generated by the frictions of exile.

All three texts analysed express strong attachment to the land of Palestine, its nature, culture and people. The authors grew up in the 'twenties and the 'thirties, before the establishment of the state of Israel. Yet on a deeper textual level, the quest for self in these works represents an effort aiming beyond the reclaiming of a homeland lost in time and space. It is more fundamentally a quest for values such as knowledge, equality, freedom and justice, and according to this author's mind, it is read thus that this literature gains its real significance.

References

Primary sources:

Abdelhadi, M., *Arabernas äganderätt till Palestina. En infödd palestinaarab berättar*, Stockholm, eget förlag, 1962.

Aburish, S. K., *Children of Bethany. The Story of a Palestinian Family*, London, I.B. Tauris, 1988.

Chacour, E. with Hazard D., *Blood Brothers: a Palestinian's Struggle for Reconciliation in the Middle East*, Eastbourne, Kingsway, 1985.

——with Jensen, M. E., *We Belong to this Land*, San Francisco, Harper, 1990.

Ḥusayn, Ṭ., *al-Ayyām*, I–III, Dār al-kitāb al-lubnānī, 1982.

Jabrā I. J., *al-Bi'r al-ūlā. Fuṣūl min sīra dhātiyya*, London, Riad El-Rayyes, 1987.

Nuʿayma, M., *Sabʿūn. Ḥikāyat ʿumr*, I–III, Beirut, Dār Ṣādir, 1959-60.

Sakakini, H., *Jerusalem and I. A Personal Record*, Amman, second printing, 1990.

---

28) S. Rushdie, *Imaginary Homelands. Essays and Criticism 1981-1991*, London, Granta Books, 1991, p. 12.

Sharābī, H., *al-Jamr war-ramād. Dhikrayāt muthaqqaf ʿarabī*, Beirut, 2ed. Dār aṭ-ṭalīʿa, 1978.

Shaʿrāwī, H., *Mudhakkirāt Hudā Shaʿrāwī*, ʿA.F. Mursī (ed.), Cairo, Dār al-hilāl, 1981.

Ṭūqān, F., *Riḥla ṣaʿba. Riḥla jabaliyya*, Acre, Dār al-aswār, 1985.

Translations:

Shaarawi, H., *Harem Years. The Memoirs of an Egyptian Feminist (1879-1924)*, translated, edited and introduced by Margot Badran, London, Virago press, 1986.

Tuqan, F., *A Mountainous Journey. An Autobiography*, translated by Olive Kenny, with a foreword by Salma Jayyusi, and an introduction by Fedwa Malti-Douglas, Saint Paul, Graywolf Press, 1990.

Secondary sources:

ʿAbd ad-Dāyim, Y.I., *at-Tarjama dh-dhātiyya fi-l-adab al-ʿarabī l-ḥadīth*, Beirut, Dār an-nahḍa l-ʿarabiyya, 1975.

Berque, J., *Cultural Expression in Arab Society Today*, Austin and London, University of Texas Press, 1978. Originally published as *Langages arabes du présent*, Paris, Éditions Gallimard, 1974.

Börjesson, B., *Samtal med K – en bok om identiteten*, Stockholm, AWE/Gebers, 1976.

Coe, R.N., *When the Grass was Taller. Autobiography and the Experience of Childhood*, New Haven and London, Yale University Press, 1984.

Eakin, P.J., *Fictions in Autobiography. Studies in the Art of Self-invention*, Princeton, Princeton University Press, 1985.

Gunn, J.V., *Autobiography. Toward a Poetics of Experience*, Philadelphia, University of Pennsylvania Press, 1982.

Lejeune, Ph., *Le pacte autobiographique*, Paris, Éditions du Seuil, 1975.

Malti-Douglas, Fedwa, *Blindness & Autobiography. Al-Ayyām of Ṭāhā Ḥusayn*, Princeton, Princeton University Press, 1988.

Olney, J., *Metaphors of Self. The Meaning of Autobiography*, Princeton, Princeton University Press, 1972.

Rushdie, S., *Imaginary Homelands. Essays and Criticism 1981-1991*, London, Granta Books, 1991.

Stounbjerg, P., 'Själen, livet och formerna. Berättelse, bild och diskurs i "Tjänstekvinnans son"' in Roos, J.P. and A.Vikko, (eds), *Självbiografi, Kultur, Liv*, Stockholm/Skåne, Symposion, 1992.

List of Contributors

Chen Maiping

Lecturer, Institute of East Asian Languages, Chinese Department, University of Stockholm. Since 1992 he has been a doctoral candidate. He is also director of the editing office of *Today Literary Magazine*, Stockholm, Sweden.

Chen Maiping has published short stories, film-manuscripts and plays (under the pen-name Wan Zhi) as well as translations and academic works on literature and theatre plays, Western as well as Chinese. The latest works are 'Rope and Straw by Eugen O'Neill, translation', published in *Complete Plays of Eugen O'Neill*, People's Literature Press, Beijing, 1988; *Old Snow* by Bei Dao, translation, together with Bonnie S. McDougall, New Direction, New York, 1991; *Romance in Brocade* by Wang An-yi, translation, together with Bonnie S. McDougall, New Direction, New York, 1991.

Mason C. Hoadley

Associate Professor of Southeast Asian History and Indonesian, Lund University, Sweden. He has done research on Javanese and In-donesian History and Literature.

Earlier publications include 'An Introduction to Javanese Law. A Translation of and Commentary on the Agama' in *Association of Asian Studies Monograph*, Tuscon, Arizona, 1981. With M. B. Hooker; 'Javanese, Peranakan, and Chinese Elites in Cirebon: Changing Ethnic Boundaries' in *Journal of Asian Studies* 47, no. 3 (August) 1988, pp. 503-517; 'Sanskritic Continuity in Southeast Asia, the Sadatatavi and Asta Corah in Javanese Law' in Lokesh Chandra, (ed.) *Javanese Art and Culture*, New Delhi, International Academy of Indian Culture, 1991, pp. 33-51.

Lisbeth Littrup

Teacher of Malay-Indonesian language and literature at the Department of Asian Studies, University of Copenhagen, Denmark.

Earlier publications: 'The Princess in No Man's Land' in Ainon Abu Bakar, (ed.), *Telaah Sastera Melayu, Himpunan Kertas Kerja Minggu Sastera Malaysia di London 1992*, Dewan Bahasa dan Pustaka, Kuala Lumpur 1993, pp. 77-86; 'Conflict in Malay Short Stories: Islam as Literary Frame' in *Tenggara* 32, 1994:93-107.

Hendrik M.J. Maier

Professor of Malay and Indonesian language and literature, Leiden State University.

His main fields of interests are Malay literature, literary theory and (post)colonial literature. He has published widely on these subjects and translated a number of Indonesian texts.

Muhammad Haji Salleh

National Writer of Malaysia. Professor of Malay Studies, Department of Languages and Cultures of Southeast Asia and Oceania, Leiden State University. Several academic posts at Universiti Kebangsaan Malaysia. Main area of research: Malay Ethnopoetics, post-colonial literature, contemporary Malay-Indonesian poetry, *pantuns*, and oral Malay literature.

Publications include books of poems, criticism, theoretical discussion, translations. Latest publication: *Yang Empunya Ceritera: Mind of the Malay Author*, Kuala Lumpur, Dewan Bahasa dan Pustaka, 1991.

Pertti Nikkilä

Junior Research Fellow, Academy of Finland. He is doing research in early Confucianism.

Earlier publications include *Early Confucianism and Inherited Thought in the Light of some Key Terms of the Confucian Analects, I, The Terms in Shu Ching*, Helsinki, 1982; *Early Confucianism and Inherited Thought in the Light of Some Key Terms of the Confucian Analects, I, The Terms in the Confucian Analects*, Helsinki 1992.

Thomas Rieger

Private consultant in Hamburg for development aid projects. Ph.D. in 1992. His main area of research is contemporary history of Southeast Asia, twentieth-century nationalism, political functions of literary discourse and overseas Chinese studies.

Earlier publications include numerous translations and scientific works. The latest publications are 'La guerre sino-japonaise dans les différents courants de la littérature indonésienne avant 1942' in C. Salmon, *Le moment "Sino-Malais" de la littérature indonésienne (Cahier d'Archipel No. 19)*, Paris, 1992; 'Aufschreiben, Beschreiben, Umschreiben: Literatur und Nation in Indonesien' in I. Wessel and W. Lulei, (eds), *Gesellschaftlicher Wandel in Südostasien. Protokollband*, Berlin, 1992.

Tetz Rooke

Ph. D. Candidate, Institute of Oriental Languages, Department of Arabic, Stockholm University, Sweden.

His present area of research is modern Arabic literature, and his forthcoming thesis is a generic study of Arabic autobiography, surveying the development of the theme of childhood and youth in particular and analysing its literary importance.

Sergei D. Serebriany

Research fellow at the Institute for Advanced Studies in the Humanities, Russian State University for the Humanities, Moscow.

His main research area is Indian (South Asian) culture and the comparative study of cultures (civilisations). He holds a Ph.D. in Indian literature and earlier did research at the Gorky Institute of World Literature, Moscow.

Publications include research papers on various aspects of South Asian culture as well as *Vidyapati*, Moscow, 1980; *Leo Tolstoy and Sri Ramakrishna*, Calcutta, 1987.

Noriko Thunman

Associate Professor, Department of Oriental Languages, Stockholm University, Sweden. Main area of research is modern Japanese literature.

Earlier publications include *Nakahara Chuya and French Symbolism*, Stockholm, 1983; *Gathering in Moonlight – Horiguchi Daigaku and a Crossroad in Modern Japanese Poetry*, Stockholm, 1991.

Anne Wedell-Wedellsborg

Associate Professor at the Institute of East Asian Studies, University of Aarhus, Denmark.

Main areas of research are modern Chinese literature and literary criticism, as well as the history of Chinese literature. Also co-author of a book on the Chinese democracy movement. Recent publications include *Inside Out. Modernism and Postmodernism in Chinese Literary Culture* (ed. with Wendy Larson), 1993.

Index

A

Abdelhadi, Mufid 233
Abe Kōbō 174
Aburish, Said 232
Ah Cheng 77, 89
Ah soeda kasep. Tjoe Ka Lam satoe journalist jang... 161
Alisjahbana, St. Takdir 130, 131, 132, 136, 147
Allah jang palsoe 158, 161, 162
Almayer's Folly 195, 200, 203, 204
Anak Semua Bangsa 105, 109
Analects, Confucian 8, 47-67
Ananta Gs. 166
Andersen, H. C. 93
Anderson, Marston 85
Angkatan 45 132
Anwar, Chairil 130, 132
Apa dajakoe karena perempoean 135
Apin, Rivai 130, 132
Arabernas äganderätt till Palestina 233
Asahi 186
Ashcroft, Bill 193
Atheis 10, 129-150
autobiography 11, 36, 143, Palestinian 5, 231-253
al-Ayyām 234

B

Babad Tanah Djawi 112, 114
Baker, Barbara 194
Bakhtin, M. M. 149
Balai Pustaka 4, 112, 129, 134, 135, 136
Banner, Hubert S. 194
Baudelaire, Charles 72, 75

Bei Dao 21, 35, 39
Belenggoe 131, 135, 137
Benjamin, W. 72, 73, 75, 76, 84
Berdjoeang 167
Berman, Marshall 142
Berque, Jacques 11, 250
al-Bi'r al-ūlā 236, 246-250
Blood Brothers 233
Boekoe sair Indie Weerbaar 161
Boekoe sair kabaikannja orang jang hendak melepas... 158
Bose, Buddhadev 95
Boulle, Pierre 191, 219, 221
Börjesson, B. 237
Bridge on the River Kwai 221
Bumi Manusia 105, 108, 109, 114, 117, 124-125
Bungaku-ron 175
Burgess, Anthony 194, 209, 216

C

Camus, A. 84
Can Xue 78
Chacour, Elias 233
Chaves, Jonathan 41
Chen Duxiu 18, 19, 21, 22, 38
Chen Maiping 5, 7, 8
Children of Bethany 233
Ching, Julia 58
Clark, F. S. 195
Clifford, Hugh 190, 191, 193-195, 207-215, 226
Coleridge 75
Confucius 2, 8, 15, 47-67
Conrad, Joseph 11, 81, 190, 191, 193-207-209, 211, 226
Consul's File 224, 226

D
Dante 34
Dawson, Raymond 51
Days 248
De Bary 2
de Man, Paul 76
Descartes 34
Dewey, John 19
Divine Comedy 34
Dostovjevsky 132, 133, 135
Drama di Boven Digoel 167, 168
Du Fu 2, 3, 32
Düsing, Wolfgang 48

E
Eco, Umberto 77
Embers and Ashes 237-241, 246
Enemy of the People 164
Enlightenment 6, 20, 21, 101,173, 183
Erikson, Erik H. 47, 48
Etō Jun 181
émigré literature, Arabic 5
L'Epreuve des Hommes Blancs 219, 221
L'Etranger 84

F
Fan Zhongyan 37
Fauconnier, Henri 190, 191, 193, 209, 217-220, 226
Fiction and Repetition 84
Firdausi 2
First Well 246-250
Freud 20, 83
Fung Yu-lan 49, 60
Further Side of Silence 208

G
Gadamer, Hans Georg 75
Genji Monogatari 3
Ghose, Sisirkumar 97, 99
Gide 135
Giles, Herbert A. 50
Goethe 75, 98

Gora 97
Griffith, Gareth 193
Gubijinsô 182
Gunn, J. 237
Guo Moruo 38, 39
Great Railway Bazaar 224

H
Halbfass, Wilhelm 100
Hamka 129, 134
Han Shaogong 77, 89
Hansen, Chad 25, 26
Hare, R. M. 49
Harem Years 243
Hart, Donn 193, 194
Hattori, U. 61
Hegel, Robert E. 33, 36
Hidding 129
Hill, Lewis 193, 194
Hindia Serikat 112
History of Classical Malay Literature 192
Hoadley, Mason 5, 9
Homecoming 224
Hong Lou Meng 4, 73
Hototogisu 173
Hsien 190
Hu Shi 18, 19, 21, 38
Huang, Martin Weizong 85
Husayn, Tāhā 234, 248
Hwa Kim Pit 158

I
I-Ching 190
Ibsen 19, 21, 164
Idrus 130, 131, 132
Ivanov 135

J
Jabrā, Jabrā Ibrāhīm 232, 236, 246-250
al-Jadid 241
Jajak Langkah 105, 109, 118
Al-Jamr war-ramād 237
Jameson, Fredric 72, 73, 74, 88,

89, 135
Jassin, H.B. 134
Jataka 190
Jayyusi, Salma 233
Jerusalem and I 233
Jin Ping Mei 3-4,
Jiro Osaragi 223, 224
Jusuf Sou'yb 166

K
Kaneko Mitsuhara 222, 223
Karaki Junzō 181
Karena mentoea 135, 137
Kartha Sarit Sagara 190
Keith, Agnes Newton190, 224, 225, 226
Keyserling, H. 98
Kho Tjoen Wan 161
Kokoro 176
Komi-ya Toyotaka 181
Korbannja Kong Ek 164
Korbannja Yi Yung Thoan 166
Kusamakura 179, 180, 182
Kwee Seng Tjoan 156
Kwee Tek Hoay 158, 161, 162, 164 166, 167, 168

L
Lacan 83
Lafayette, Mme de 3
Lajar terkembang 131, 135, 137
Land Below the Wind 224, 225
Lao Zi 30
Lau, D.C. 50, 51, 52
Lejeune, Philippe 235
Leo Ou-fan Lee 40
Li Bai 32, 39
Li Zehou 22
Li Zhi 15, 16
Liem Khing Hoo 167
Liu Suola 77, 78, 89
Liu Zaifu 23
Liu, James J. Y. 32
Lixue 29, 31
Lord Jim 195, 198, 204

Lu Xun 8, 18, 19, 21, 22, 23, 29, 38, 39, 73, 74, 75, 85
Lun Yü, see *Analects* Confucian

M
Mahabharata 1
Maier, Hendrik 5, 10
Malaisie 217
Mann 132
Manusher Dharma 99
Marsman 132
Maugham's Borneo Stories 216
Maugham's Malaysian Stories 216
Maugham, W. Somerset 190, 191, 193, 194, 211, 216, 220
Max Havelaar 139
Meian 182, 186
Mencius 27, 28
Michiko Nakahara 222
Michikusa 176, 180, 185, 186
Mihardja, Achdiat K. 10, 129-150
Miller, Hillis 84
Miyai Ichirō 174, 178
Moeis, Abdul 9, 103, 105, 107, 109, 110, 111, 112, 120, 121, 131
Mohamed, Jan 219
Mori Ogai 173
Mountainous Journey 236, 241-246
Mudhakkirāt Hūda Sha rāwī 243
Muhammad Haji Salleh 5, 11
Multatuli 139
Murasaki Shikibu 3

N
Neko 186
Nikkilä, Pertti 2, 8
Njoo Cheong Seng 158
Nona Kim Lian 160, 166
Nona Lan Im 161
Nowaki 184
Nuʿayma, Mīkhāʾīl 233, 248

Nu Shen 38

O
Olney, James 235
On Cultural Extremes 8
Ong Siauw King 165
Orwell, George 79
Osmond, Marion 195
An Outcast of the Islands 195, 201, 205

P
Palestinian autobiography, see autobiography
Pane, Armijn 130, 131, 132, 136
Pendekar dari Chapei 166
Pengorbanan di medan perang 166
Phoa Tjhoen Hoay 162
Phoa Tjoen Hoat 161
Picasso 132, 133
Pigafetta 190, 221
I Pirati della Jungle Nera 222
Plaks, Andrew H. 73
Plato 30
Pliny 190
Poedjangga Baroe 130, 131, 132
Polemik Kebudajaan 131, 134, 146, 147
A Prince of Malaya 211, 213, 221
La Princesse de Clèves 3
Ptolemy 190

Q
Qingnian zazhi 18

R
Ramayana 1
The Religion of Man 98, 99, 101
Renaissance 6, 101
The Rescue 195, 199, 204
Rieger, Thomas 4, 10
Rihla saʿba rihla jabaliyya 236
Rilke 132, 133
Robert Anak Surapati 105

Rodin 132
Roff, William R. 208
Rooke, Tetz 5, 11
Rumah Kaca 105, 109, 117-118,
Rushdie, Salman 250
Ryūnankai-zasshi 181

S
Le Sacrilège Malaise 219
Sair Tiong Hwa Hwe Kwan koetika boekanja Passar derma 157
Sakakini, Hala 233
Salah Asuhan (Asoehan)105, 107, 114, 121-123, 131, 135
Salgari, Emilio 191, 221
Sally: A Study 211, 215
Salmon, Claudine 154, 157
Sani, Asrul 130, 132
Sanshirō 176, 185
Schwartz, Benjamin 58
Sejarah Melayu 2, 3,
Serebriany, Sergei D. 4, 9
Seventy 248
Shaʿrāwī, Hudā 243
Shah-name 1
Shang Shu 14
Shārābi, Hishām 232, 237-241, 242, 245
Shi Jing 2, 15
Shimizu Ikutarō 176, 177, 179, 180, 185
Sima Qian 15
Siti Noerbaja 135, 137
Sjahrir 134, 147
Soeami jang boeta 158
Soedjatmoko 134
Souw Leng Tat atawa dari Akalan 158
Sōseki Zenshū 175
Sōseki, Natsume 4, 7, 10, 173-189
Steinbeck 133
Stories by Sir Hugh Clifford 208
Stounbjerg, Per 235
Strachey, Sir John 96

Strindberg 235
Studies in Brown Humanity 212
Sulaiman 190
Surapati 9, 105, 112, 114, 119, 121, 123-124
Suryadinata, L. 152

T
Tagore, R. 4, 7, 9, 92-102
Tamai Takayuki 176
Tan Boen Kim 160, 161, 166
Tan Liok Ee 153
Taylor, Charles 36
Terloenta-loenta 165
Theroux, Paul 190, 224, 226
Three Came Home 224
Thunman, Noriko 4, 10, 11
Tiffin, Helen 193
Le Tigre di Mompracem 222
Tiong Hoa Hwe Koan 156
Tjerita Anak Perempoean di bikin sebagai parit mas atawa iboe jang doerhaka 156
Tjhik tjhik Boeng Nona Kampoeng 162
Tjia Ki Siang 157, 158, 159
Tjie Tek Goan 166
Tjong Kuo Kuo Ko 166
Toer, Pramoedya Ananta 9, 103, 105, 110, 121, 129, 134
Tolstoy 135
Tong xin lun 15
Trauerspiel, German 75
Tu Wei-ming 56
Tūqān, Fadwā 232, 233, 236, 241-246

U
Uchida Michio 181
Umehara Takeshi 182
Untung 112
Upanishads 98

V
Vedic Hymns 1

W
Wagahai wa Neko de aru 173
Waley, Arthur 64
Wang Guowei 38, 42
Wang Wei 33, 40
Wang Yangming 31
Wedell-Wedellsborg, A. 7, 8
Wenhua pianzhi lun 18, 38
Wertheim, W. F. 104, 109
White Man Returns 224
Winstedt 192

X
Xi Yang Ji 3
Xi You Ji 3, 73
Xiandai Hanshi 45
Xin Qingnian 18, 19, 22
Xinxue 31
Xun Zi 28

Y
Yibushen zhuyi 19
Yōkyo-shū 181
Yu Hua 9, 72, 73, 77-89

Z
Zen 180, 182
Zeng Zhennan 80, 87, 88
Zhang Longxi 74
Zhang Yiwu 87, 88
Zhao Yiheng 81
Zhu Xi 29
Zhuang Zi 29, 30, 33

The Nordic Institute of Asian Studies (NIAS) is funded by the governments of Denmark, Finland, Iceland, Norway and Sweden via the Nordic Council of Ministers, and works to encourage and support Asian studies in the Nordic countries. In so doing, NIAS has published well in excess of one hundred books in the last twenty-five years, most of them in co-operation with Curzon Press.

Nordic Council of Ministers

For Product Safety Concerns and Information please contact our EU
representative GPSR@taylorandfrancis.com
Taylor & Francis Verlag GmbH, Kaufingerstraße 24, 80331 München, Germany

www.ingramcontent.com/pod-product-compliance
Lightning Source LLC
Chambersburg PA
CBHW032003220426
43664CB00005B/120